Four Seconds until Impact

The skyrocketing attacks by predators on humans

Bruce Buckshot Hemming

Book Cover Design by SelfPubbookcovers.com/island

ISBN-13: 978-1981502837
ISBN-10: 1981502831

Acknowledgements

A special thank you to all who helped in this project.

Steve Langdon for writing the black bear attack stories and spending countless hours trying to track down pictures and people who have been attacked.

Dean Weingarten from Ammoland Shooting Sports News for granting permission to use his pictures and research for this book.

Jake Blackmore for sharing his pictures and story of his grizzly bear attack.

Ronn Hemstock for sharing his pictures and story of his grizzly bear attack.

Dylan Ross for sharing his pictures and story of his cougar attack.

Renee Walters for sharing her pictures and story of her cougar attack.

Steve Verschoor for granting me a telephone interview to tell his story of the bobcat attack.

UDAP Industries for granting me an interview on their pepper spray.

Jeremy Hill for granting me a phone interview regarding his federal case of defending his family from a grizzly bear.

Tim Sundles of Buffalo Bore Ammunition for granting permission to use his pictures and information on stopping grizzly bears.

Brian Lynn from Sportsman's Alliance for granting me an interview and suggesting solutions.

Scott Rockholm from Save Western Wildlife for his help and advice.

Everyone else that has helped with this project.

Contents

Foreword 1

Chapter 1: Deliberate Indifference 6

Chapter 2: Public Trust Doctrine 20

Chapter 3: Mountain Lions 27

Chapter 4: Grizzly Bears 53

Chapter 5: Grizzly Bears: Five Fatal Case Studies 86

Chapter 6: Coyotes 101

Chapter 7: Black Bear Attack Victims 126

Chapter 8: Wolf Attacks 176

Chapter 9: Other Animal Attacks 209

Chapter 10: Unreported Attacks 217

Chapter 11: Animal Rights Activists 225

Chapter 12: Missing Hunters and Hikers 235

Chapter 13: Staring Death in the Face! 243

Chapter 14: Banning Hunting 258

Chapter 15: US Court System 271

Chapter 16: Government Corruption, Cover-ups, and Refusal
        to Release Documents 280

Chapter 17: Safety 292

Chapter 18: Solutions 299

References 307

Foreword

The mission and purpose of this book is to save human lives. It is, however, not written to instill fear and panic in the population. We must come to terms with living with large predators. Most debates seem to be centered around two trains of thought—coexist with large predators and accept some human fatalities or total extinction of a species. Yet there is a third option that is usually ignored and not even talked about.

The third option is controlled, regulated hunting to instill fear in predators. One must understand how hunting works to achieve this goal. For instance, hunters of grizzly bears successfully harvest large boar grizzlies. When other bears come upon the scene and smell what happened—that the large boar was killed by humans—the mother bear realizes her cubs could be in danger from humans and teaches them to avoid contact with humans. It is the same with other bears that come across the scene. Now, of course, a formula must be worked out.

Say within a certain area there is X number of bears; to maintain the bear population, no more than Y amount can be hunted. The end result is the bear population survives for future generations to see and enjoy. Plus, human safety is greatly increased. There is no such thing as natural fear of man.

We must stop this quintessential approach that predators are cute and cuddly and face reality. Large predators kill for a living. Predators eat meat. Humans are meat. If a cougar could talk, could we understand his train of thought? Their thinking is food first, water, shelter, and, in certain times of the year, mating. Their life involves a constant search for food. Mating and food are directly related. The more food, the more mating, and the higher the population of a given species. That holds true for humans as well. The human population did not greatly increase until we changed from hunters and gatherers and became farmers with domestic livestock for our protein needs. Once food increased, the human population increased. The same is true for animals.

For example, in the Yellowstone wolf studies, they found that in the first eight years, the wolf population increased dramatically at 1000%, with some denning sites producing two litters of pups and even one pair that had three litters of pups in a single year. There was plenty of food with abundant elk in the area. Now that the elk population or food supply has been greatly reduced, the wolves are only having a single litter a year and fewer pups per litter.

When dealing with predators, you must understand what "predator pit" means. "A predator pit is created when elk populations have been reduced for various reasons and existing key predators, like wolves, bears, and cougars can drive those numbers even further into an abyss, perhaps prohibiting a regrowth of the herd."

Lack of food or prey species is directly related to the increased human attacks we are seeing around the country.

Within this discussion, you must understand carrying capacity, which is defined as: the maximum population size of the species that the environment can sustain indefinitely, given the food, habitat, water, and other necessities available in the environment.

Again, once carry capacity is met, competition for food increases, resulting in more human attacks.

In the 21st century, a lot of humans think they know more than the last generation and the "experts" have researched it enough to know all the facts, that the "science has been settled." This is especially problematic in today's world where having that college degree makes an individual an expert even though they have very little real-world experience.

One must remember the Pessimistic Meta-Induction, defined and paraphrased as: What we know now as fact may be proven wrong at any given moment.

When it comes to the subject of wildlife, the Pessimistic Meta-Induction has come about on a regular basis, sometimes resulting in catastrophic results including unintended deaths of wildlife and humans.

Many wildlife biologists today do not have the "Life in Outdoors" upbringing. A lot of them come from urban settings where they had little outdoor interactions with wildlife. They have preconceived ideas from an enclosed school system and their outdoors are made up of concrete and steel. The extent of their outdoor learning is documentaries from National Geographic and the Discovery Channel. It creates an illusion of an ecosystem devoid of humans and wildlife coexisting in a natural balance. Many of these people, including me, through no fault of our own, have been programmed by various entertainment venues like TV and movies.

As such, many of today's wildlife "experts" come out of their college education and into a wildlife biologist career with preconceived ideas that have barely been challenged by their professors or their own limited outdoor fieldwork.

These days, the average dedicated hunter or angler has more knowledge about wildlife and their environment than a wildlife biologist has just out of college. The outdoorsmen may not have scientific details of the biologist, but their knowledge of the area they frequent and the wildlife in it would far outweigh the new biologist.

Another common problem in today's high-tech world is with a click of a button you have all the "expert's" findings right there up on your screen. The problem is much of this expert research has been pre-categorized and positioned in a way to make you believe you have the most up-to-date research available.

This has led to many people becoming complacent in the subject matter and attributing to error blindness. Narcissistic tendencies can make you believe you already know the facts because the experts have spoken. Therefore, you do not want to hear opposing views or research as you already have all the facts, so you may even close down and refuse to listen. This has proven to be a defense mechanism with this type of behavior.

Depending on Google means you're not seeing the opposing research. Research done by third parties and non-biased scientists that is twenty pages in on the search results is almost never seen by researchers.

Not to pick on any vegetarians, but a good example of search perversion of top search results is if you type in "vegetarian" or type in "meat." When I typed in vegetarian, I did not find any negative subject matters or research until I got to page fourteen on Google, where CNN had an opinion piece about whether becoming a vegetarian will help the environment.

Most of the articles on the first thirteen pages dealt with the definition of vegetarian, the positives of being a vegetarian, or becoming one and its many benefits.

When I typed in meat, a negative subject matter appeared on the very first page. You might be thinking, "Well meat's just not that good for you so that is why that happened." Sorry, but you would be mistaken. There are hundreds of organizations that promote being a vegetarian as being better for the environment and personal health, even though there are many opposing scientific views on this subject matter. But these groups have deep pockets with worldwide capital to push this lifestyle for reasons that I will not get into in this book. But these deep pockets will get just about anything they want on the first few pages of Google and Microsoft search engines, including propaganda and even full-out printed lies.

On the other hand, even though most people eat meat, the meat producers and distributors do not have the time, capital, or worldwide organization that so-called environmental groups do. Even the Cattlemen's Association, one of the United States' largest beef promoters, pales in comparison to World Wildlife Fund (WWF), making them spend very little on promoting search engine results to the point of not really "advertising"through search engines at all.

So, what does all this have to do with attacks from wildlife predators? More than you think. Most of us, even today with all the "expert" research and opinions, still believe that wildlife attacks are rare and when there is an attack, the noted cause of attack is usually something that the person did to bring on the attack. In reality, you 're just another prey animal to that predator and they want to eat you. Nothing mysterious at all.

This has created another meta-induction with wildlife, specifically predator wildlife; this book will educate you on the fact that predator attacks are not nearly as rare as we are led to believe and the "experts" are wrong or actually putting the public in danger.

This book is not meant to scare you or to make you think it's too much of a risk to go out in the woods for a hike. Just the opposite. We want you to go explore our beautiful nation. This book is to inform you of the dangers out in the wild so you can be prepared and not end up as a tasty meal for a hungry predator.

Until we come to terms with the need to kill and put heavy hunting pressure on large predators, attacks will increase. It's a mathematical certainty. More attacks, more human injuries, more human deaths, and more missing never to be found people.

Supreme Court Justice Louis D. Brandeis said, "Our government ... teaches the whole people by its example. If the government becomes the lawbreaker, it breeds contempt for law; it invites every man to become a law unto himself; it invites anarchy."

Chapter 1
Deliberate Indifference

Government's first duty is to protect the people, not run their lives.
—Ronald Reagan

In George Orwell's classic book, *1984*, the main character is Winston Smith. He works as a clerk in the Records Department of the Ministry of Truth, where his job is to rewrite historical documents so they match the constantly changing current party line. In researching for this book, I have seen this several times—data hidden from public view, documents changed or disappeared. Finding the truth today on the internet should be easy. But at last, we come down to money, power, and corruption.

Who is the Ministry of Truth today? The animal rights groups like Defenders of Wildlife, the Sierra Club, Earth Guardians, and a host of others working hand in hand with state and federal wildlife biologists do everything in their power to hide the truth from the public. Do a simple Google search on bear attacks and you will quickly be overwhelmed with animal rights propaganda.

I am writing this book to help inform the citizens of America of a trend of rising animal attacks on humans. I noticed the trend a few years ago, where reports of found bodies with no explanation or cause of death keep coming up. Or some reports stated the victim was killed by animals but not specifying which animal. I found this odd and wanted to investigate the reason behind it.

Why not tell the public the truth? Whether it's grizzly bears, black bears, mountain lions, or wolves, something is killing people. Why the big secret and coverup on details? I started tracking wolf attacks on people and what I found is very odd. A newspaper would write up the attack and the story would disappear off the internet. For example, there was a case in Canada along the northern shores of Lake Superior where a lone healthy wolf attacked six people. Two of the victims were children; the wolf was trying to drag them in to the brush. The wolf was killed and tested for rabies and was found to be a healthy male wolf. The story quickly disappeared from the internet.

The mainstream trend in the last thirty years is what I call "hug a predator"—a mass propaganda machine to promote predators. Large apex predators are going to kill humans. That is common sense. So why the coverup?

Interesting is all the grizzly bear attacks in Wyoming, Montana, and Idaho. Grizzlies are listed as a threatened species, which is insane. During the research for this book, I found the 1996 Congressional hearing on wolves. Helen Chenoweth stated that grizzly bears had fully recovered by 1990. But the USFWS simply changed the total goal number of grizzly bears to keep them on the endangered species list. In fact, now twenty-seven later, the grizzly bear is still listed as a threatened species. Why?

A legal term comes to mind—deliberate indifference; this is the conscious or reckless disregard of the consequences of one's acts or omissions. It entails something more than negligence but is satisfied by something less than acts or omissions for the very purpose of causing harm or with the knowledge that harm will result.

With the knowledge that harm will result. Yes, overprotecting large predators equals human attacks and deaths; this is a known fact. Harm will result. "We find it difficult to explain why cougars attacked so few people despite almost certainly having many opportunities" (see Halfpenny et al., 1993; Sweanor et al., 2007).

Yes, you read that correctly. Why cougars attack so few humans? They know for a fact that increased cougar population equals human attacks and deaths.

Here is the very reason why any animal that kills a human is tracked down and killed right away, except for bears. If it's a defensive attack, they are given free rein to kill and maim people.

Studies of other large predators show that man-eating is often attributable to individuals, prides, or packs that have learned to consider people prey, with resulting localized outbreaks of attacks (see McDougal, 1987; Daniel, 1996; Rajpurohit, 1999; Yamazaki & Bwalya, 1999; Peterhans & Gnoske, 2001; Kruuk, 2002; Begg et al., 2007).

In the predator world, it's risk versus reward. If the risk is worth the reward of food and nothing happens to the predator, they will keep killing humans as prey. It's a learned behavior. If one animal sees another killing a human, they learn and copy the attacks.

In the same report on firearms for protection: *"Most people who had a weapon used it, and they typically killed the involved cougar, effectively ending an encounter. These results run counter to speculations that people carrying weapons might not have time to use them or, if they did, would not use them effectively."*

Some scientists believe that the average person is too untrained to use a firearm effectively during an animal attack. The truth is firearms save lives. Americans are armed unlike, say, a poor African farmer who only has hand tools to defend himself against killer lions (lions in Tanzania killed 870 people from 1990 to 2005). In India where people are too poor to own weapons, they die by the hundreds from tigers (150 to 1,300 people per year between 1930 and 1960 [Løe, 2002]).

One theme you will begin to understand is the protection of large predators equals human death. The normal yuppie drinking their triple venti soy no-foam latte who typically says to leave nature alone is unaware of the facts. For example, India put their wolves on the endangered species list in 1972. Dirt poor subsistence farmers are living in the area and cannot afford to be arrested for killing wolves. The wolves lost their fear of mankind and the end result was hundreds of children were attacked. "Wolves from roughly five packs in Hazaribagh, India, attacked 122 children during 1980 to 1986 and 80 children during 1993 to 1995" (Rajpurohit, 1999 as cited in Matterson, 2011).

Benjamin Storrow, a staff writer for *Star-Tribune* wrote an article titled, "Are bear attacks on the rise?"

He quoted Brian DeBolt, large carnivore conflict coordinator at the

Wyoming Game and Fish Department, who stated: *"Look at Yellowstone and surrounding ecosystem as a bucket. It's full and spilling over. They've got to find new areas, new home ranges."*

What he is stating is the bears are fully recovered and they are spilling out closer and closer to human settlement. As unpredictable as grizzly bears truly are, more human deaths are expected.

Yes, one cannot help but remember the mayor in the movie *Jaws*, who was more worried about money coming into the area than protecting people.

If you say bear attack or wolf attack, where are the tourists going to go? Not that area. Is this why some deaths are being covered up? Is money more important than human safety? Why keep people in the dark? What is the agenda?

Trust in government is so important, public fiduciaries are charged with protecting and maintaining the public trust. Toward this end, as stewards of the public trust, public fiduciaries have a duty to avoid even the appearance of impropriety. That is to say, even if a particular course of conduct does not meet all of the elements necessary to constitute a violation of law, it nevertheless may be unethical if it creates the perception of wrongdoing that will harm the public trust. (Wechsler, 2013)

This is most definitely a public trust issue.

Join me in this search for the truth. Let us try to uncover what is really going on. I should warn you this book is not for the faint of heart. Graphic details of human attacks will be examined. I will give you a few examples now of what I am talking about.

March 10, 2016, Human remains found near Yellowstone Park.

"A man on snowshoe found some remains late Wednesday. Dog teams located additional remains on Thursday. Bartlett said they likely were scattered by animals. They haven't identified the person or determined a cause of death."

Human remains found in Gates of the Mountains By ALEXANDER DEEDY Independent Record May 29, 2015

Lewis and Clark County Coroner Mickey Nelson said Friday he is "almost 100 percent" sure the remains found by a hiker Sunday are those of Dale Brownlow, a 52-year-old man from Denver who went missing on Nov. 30, 2013. He would not speculate on the cause of death." A .45 caliber handgun was found at the location. A search with a metal detector found no bullets in the area.

I find this very odd. Why were they searching for bullets? That implies the man was firing his .45 caliber handgun in self-defense.

I called my good friend Scott Rockholm about this because in Montana he had something happen to him. He was surrounded by a pack of wolves a quarter mile from his truck. He carries a .45 semi-automatic pistol. He came across an elk kill and the largest wolf of the pack came out in the open and howled, then started bouncing up and down. In a flash, the whole pack surrounded him. Pulling his .45, he started shooting as the wolves flashed through the thick brush. He emptied the first magazine and reloaded; the wolves were still all around him. He kept them back by firing shots. When he reached his truck a quarter of a mile away, he was out of ammunition.

When I asked him about the missing hiker in Yellowstone, he replied, "This sounds like a wolf attack. The man was fighting off the pack of wolves and managed to travel some distance before the pack came in for the final attack." But this is only a theory; it does fit the narrative of why no bullets were found in the area of the body.

What freaks people out the worst about wolf attacks is normally in the wild the sound of gunshots causes animals to run away. I have talked to several hunters who were shocked and confused when wolves did not react this way. A .45 ACP is a good round but a little light for stopping a grizzly. Another theory is it was a grizzly attack. The man, not wanting to kill the bear, may have fired in the air to scare the bear off. It didn't work and the bear killed him. Again, this would explain why no bullets were found in the area.

Why do I say the .45 ACP is a light round? *Bear Hunting Magazine* from July 14, 2017, has a very interesting article:

45 Caliber Found in Bear 's Skull

The bullet hit the bear (presumably from ground level) a couple inches behind the eye and passed behind it, exiting between the eyes – but the bear lived. The bullet didn't penetrate the brain cavity. No one knows the story, but presumably, somebody has a good one. To hit a bear in the head with a handgun you've got to be pretty close, or really lucky.

The wound was old and the bear was doing fine. The real question is whether there are any missing people last seen carrying a .45 pistol?

Let's compare this to a 30-06 rifle shooting a standard Federal 180 grain soft point. A common hunting round. Muzzle velocity in feet per second is 2913 FPS with muzzle energy in foot pounds of 2700. .45 ACP with standard Federal ammunition. 230 grain bullet traveling at 850 fps with a muzzle energy of 369 foot pounds.

As you can clearly see, the 30-06 has over seven times more knock-down power. This is critical for handling a large apex predator like a black bear or grizzly bear.

I am not saying a .45 ACP is not powerful enough to kill a grizzly. What I am saying is I believe it's kind of a light load to put a grizzly down and out of the fight before he kills you.

The USFS (United States Forest Service) refused and ignored all FOIA (Freedom Of Information Act) requests for this file, as if we don't have a right to know. It makes me think it was a wolf attack that they are covering up.

I believe it's reasonable to say that some of the missing hikers never found could have died and been eaten by apex predators. Remember, if the bodies are never found, there is no way to tell the story of the attack. Even when found, the news releases only say it was an animal attack.

A good read is the University of Calgary's 2011 report, *"Beware of predatory male American black bears: Attack rates are rising with human population growth."* A study of fatal black bear attacks in North America, which shows that predatory male bears are responsible for most historical attacks.

The researchers determined that the majority (88%) of fatal attacks involved a bear exhibiting predatory behavior, and 92% of the predatory bears were males.

The paper confirms other current perceptions and bear management practices. It found that bears that have previously killed people are more likely to attack again.

Bear pepper spray is more effective than guns according to the US Fish and Wildlife Service. Based on their investigations of human-bear encounters since 1992, persons encountering grizzlies and defending themselves with firearms suffer injury about 50% of the time, whereas pepper spray was almost 90% effective, or so the US Fish and Wildlife Service wants you to believe. More on this later.

Remember, this is used against bear attacks. I should mention that spraying pepper spray around your camp thinking this will keep the bears out is the wrong thing to do. The pepper smell attracts bears. It works by hitting them in the face to stop a charging bear.

This is a good time to define predatory attacks. Predator is defined as an animal that naturally preys on others. Attack is an aggressive and violent action against a person. When you read the term *predatory attack,* that means a predator is planning on eating you for lunch, unlike a defensive attack when an animal feels threatened and attacks to protect her cubs for instance.

One last tip would be to make sure you read and understand the instructions on how to use the pepper spray before you go in the woods. Later in the book, we will cover this on actual attacks. I always envision Chevy Chase in *Family Vacation.* Russ is being mauled by a bear and Clark is saying, "Hold on, Russ. I must read the instructions first." Ellen is screaming, "For God's sake, Clark, save your son." Audrey is saying, "Better read it twice, Dad, so you don't mess up." Russ, meanwhile, is screaming at the top of his lungs, "Hurry up, Dad!"

I don't mean to downplay the seriousness of bear attacks or the survivors of such attacks, but this is a lesson to remind people that in real life, this could be a deadly mistake. Read and understand the instructions before you go in the woods. Make sure everyone in your family understands how to use it too.

Animals are more in tune with the weather than people simply because they live in the woods all year round. They sense the barometer dropping and know when a storm is coming. Animals will feed more just before and right at the beginning of the storm. Hunters will tell you they had remarkable success right at the beginning of a snowstorm. The animals are trying to grab a last meal before heading for cover. Hence, they are on the move. Predators are doing the same thing, especially in mountain regions where storms can last for days. A large predator thinks it's a valuable time to grab a deer and stash it in a cave or grab a person.

The public can be very ignorant of the facts. It's not their fault they have been bombarded with "hug a predator" nonsense for thirty years. Most people are under the impression that black bears are cute cuddly teddy bears that would never hurt a flea. Or that wolves are safe to be around because they never attack people. Or people like Timothy Treadwell who taught children that brown bears are safe and misunderstood animals. A quick internet search on any animal you pick will find you plenty of amateurs telling you how safe and how rare human attacks are.

Someone who works with caged animals is not qualified to talk about wild animals. They may help you to identify warning postures of the animals, but they do a huge disservice to the public by giving out "don't worry be happy, it's safe" propaganda. When the bear or wolf or mountain lion is chewing on you, the last thing you're thinking is, "I am sure glad this is a rare event."

The purpose of this book is educational. No matter the species attacking humans, this is not meant to say every bear, mountain lion, coyote, or wolf should be shot on sight. Not every predator animal is going to attack you. But there is a small percentage of them that will under the correct circumstances. It is advisable to be aware and be prepared. Keep an educational balance where you know when to fight for your life and when not to.

There are two schools of thought on animal attacks. One is that everything is always mankind's fault and animals should have more rights than people. Attacks are rare and there are plenty of people who care how many are killed. Save the animals. Yes, those are quotes from animal rights people I have talked to.

The other school of thought is protecting people. We must teach large apex predators to fear humans. The only way to do that is with a hunting season on all apex predators. With the new age religion of worshiping the earth, this is a very difficult case to make.

The Native Americans didn't coexist with the large predators; they hunted and killed them. In Geronimo's autobiography, he talks of the young men being required to kill a cougar, a wolf, or a bear before they could become a warrior. So much for the coexisting theory.

Malice intent with forethought

I would say it is reasonable that the average person knows that bears attack people. An increase of the bear population leads to more bear attacks. The experts themselves are aware of this growing trend.

"Land and wildlife managers throughout North America must take all possible steps to help people avoid injury—but should stop short of destroying the grizzly" (Herrero, 27). It's a proven fact that once a predator has killed a human, they are likely to do it again. The public trusts the experts to remove the problem bears by destroying them. Allowing a man-eater loose is deliberate indifference.

"Most black bear-inflicted injuries occurred in national parks, typically happening in campgrounds where the black bears were seeking food or along the roadside where 'Panhandler' black bears begged for food" (Herrero, 81). These were also locations where bears are not hunted and have no fear of man.

"Hunting is in fact a poor way to teach bear anything, since there is little opportunity to learn. Death isn't an instructor; it is an eliminator. Hunting grizzlies in national parks would eliminate any bear that wasn't elusive and secretive. Human safety might increase, but hunting is incompatible with wildlife-protection objectives of national parks" (Herrero, 194).

That is simply not true. A hunter shooting at and missing a bear, followed up by chasing the same bear is instilling fear into the animal. Successful hunters leave behind a gut pile. Other bears come by and smell the story. Man killed bear. This puts fear into the bear population to avoid mankind.

"Hunting is one potential means of changing grizzly bear behavior so that surviving bears avoid people. This may or may not increase overall safety, because

of the obvious danger to hunters and the possible danger from wounded bears—and from hunters themselves" (Herrero, 243).

Yes, hunters have been attacked by wounded bears. But overall what percentage are attacks? A very small amount. Human safety for the rest of the public greatly improves.

North America is not the only place with grizzly bears. In 1915, a grizzly bear gripped a whole town in terror. The Ussuri brown bear (*Ursus arctos lasiotus*), also known as the black grizzly Tomamae brown bear incident happened December 9 and 14, 1915, when a large brown bear woke up from hibernation. It attacked several houses in the area, killing seven people before it ended with the bear's death. Police formed a sniper squad and wounded it on December 13. They tracked the bear the next morning and killed it with two shots, one to the heart and one to the head. The bear weighed 749 pounds and was 8.85 feet tall.

The attacks didn't stop until the bear was killed.

Cougar attack: Case report of a fatality Lily Conrad MD, Ph.D. Journal of Wilderness Medicine 3,387-396 (1992)

Over the past 20 years, 39 cougar (mountain lion) attacks on humans have been reported; only 17 were recorded in the preceding eight decades. In contrast to injuries inflicted by bears, dogs, wolves, sharks, or other wild animals [33-37], cougar bites and lacerations are often described as sharp and clean. They may be similar to knife or stab wounds in appearance - i.e., clean slashes rather than jagged or torn tissue-loss injuries.

In 1992, the trend of skyrocketing attacks was well documented. Mountain lion attacks on humans have continued to rise. With all this evidence that an increasing predator population causes serious safety issues to humans, what are the experts doing? Trying to get more large predators everywhere.

Habitat Capacity for Cougar Recolonization in the Upper Great Lakes Region, Shawn T. O'Neil

In the event that a population becomes established in the UGL, state DNR agencies will need to address concerns of human safety, pet safety, and depredation of livestock, as well as develop long-term monitoring programs. Strategies necessary to manage a cougar population will likely include plans for education and outreach associated with human safety concerns, potential compensation for livestock losses, mitigation strategies for conflicts with farmers/ranchers, and discussion of possible harvest scenarios

With the wolves already decimating the northern deer herds, adding cougars to the mix is a recipe for disaster. In fact, it's a guarantee that children will be maimed and killed as we will see what happened to Vancouver Island, BC, when wolves were protected for ten years. The wolves put a serious dent in the blacktail deer population. Starving cougars equal human attacks. They have skyrocketed out of sight, resulting in human deaths.

This is the equivalent of letting known serial killers loose. After the serial killers start killing people, scratch your head and say why is this happening? We must study this more. Give me a break.

The groups like Defenders of Wildlife, Sierra Club, Earth Guardians, and several others have many followers. They are fed a constant stream of fear mongering, end-of-the-world propaganda. Good news doesn't open up people's wallets. But fear does: we must do something now or the "Trophy hunters" will wipe out the grizzly bear or whatever species is the hot topic. All these groups hire powerful million-dollar ad companies with the single goal of increasing donations.

Did you ever wonder why all their ads show the animals young? The grizzly bear sow with her cubs. The wolf at the den with the cute little puppies. Using words like "family," "love," "endangered," and "imperiled." You must act now or they will be wiped out by the evil hunters. It really comes down to love the animals and hate the hunters. You must have a bad guy to defeat. Humans have been studied; they know that cute cubs or puppies cause an emotional response. Emotions are manipulated with the goal of raking in more money. Truth doesn't matter; the almighty dollar is all they care about.

The target audience is not rural America but the urban areas where people have lost touch with the natural world. Emotions, propaganda, fear, and hate are used to put the followers in a "save Gaia" mindset.

The court states ignorance of the law is no excuse. There is no excuse for promoting apex predators and allowing them to kill, injure, and maim American citizens. Even the experts can't claim ignorance of the fact predators will attack people. Fish and game departments are directly responsible for causing this mess. They must tell the public the truth. Increased predator populations are going to result in human deaths. Plenty of states with bear hunting seasons have very few attacks.

Has Our Manipulation of Nature Gone Too Far? Outside Magazine Jul 10, 2017

A 1962 report commissioned by Congress, which grew from the increasing frequency of bear attacks in national parks. The report, headed by respected UC Berkeley wildlife management professor Starker Leopold, called upon the Park Service to "'restore or recreate' natural processes and life communities to bring about conditions as close as possible to those that had been seen by the first Euro-American explorers."

Leopold provided specific scenarios in the report. If trees obscured a nice vantage point for park guests, then the trees would have to be kept trimmed. Or if a species that once roamed an area but had since been killed off—like the bison or pronghorn—the animal should be reintroduced and managed to survive. Likewise, native plants that had been choked out by an invasive species should be grown in a nursery and transplanted back to where they had once grown naturally. Ultimately, national parks could "achieve a **'reasonable illusion'** *of primitive conditions.*

The common excuses for the increase in animal attacks are found below.

1) We are stealing all the land from the animals.

These simple maps show how little of the United States is populated (Dennis Mersereau, 06/20/14).

By 2003, we had only developed about 108 million acres, or about 4.47% of the total land area of the United States. Well over 95% of the land is still open for the animals. That excuse doesn't work.

2) People getting too close to large predators for pictures.

Only one case of all the attacks in this book was found to be caused by getting too close for a photograph. Richard White, 49, in Denali National Park.

3) People not recognizing the danger of large predators.

That is true. Way too much propaganda and movies show the wonderful animals that rarely attack people. This gives a false sense of security.

4) Global warming eliminating their natural food source.

The only case I can find for that is white pine beetles. But was that truly a main food source for bears? Bears adapt and find new food. Carrying capacity of the land is overrun with bears and food competition increases.

5) Getting too close to their young.

That is certainly true for bears but it's also from lack of fear of man. When bears are overprotected, they lose the fear of man. We cover this throughout the book.

Or it could be that large predators, for thousands of years, preyed on humans as a food source. It was not until we invented guns that humans became the top predator. Is the natural instinct coming back because they lack fear of humans?

Dr. Edgard Camarós, an anthropologist at the Catalan Institute of Human Palaeo-Ecology and Social Evolution in Tarragona, Spain, said: *"The conflict between humans and large carnivores has been present and constant throughout human evolution, enduring even to modern times."*

Are we back on the menu? Each time we allow an aggressive predator to live after attacking humans, that aggressive bold trait is passed down the gene pool. In our effort to protect wildlife, are we unwittingly changing the large carnivores to be more prone to attacking humans? Think about that for a moment. When we make the excuse "it's a female with cubs" and allow them to live, the cubs are now taught that humans can be attacked. Are those cubs later the source of aggressive bears? How many more bears are they breeding to become more aggressive as the years pass on?

Additionally, individuals may become more vigilant and actively avoid contact with humans during times of intense persecution. (Penteriani 2016)

Therefore, lack of persecution would lead to bolder, more aggressive animals. That is common sense.

6) The animals were here first.

Really, what scientific study has proven that as fact? Mankind is part of the ecosystem. We are not an alien species.

What does coexisting mean?

Andrea T. Morehouse defines it as: *The definition of human-wildlife coexistence varies among individuals and is influenced by human values, attitudes, and tolerance, but in a general sense, human-wildlife coexistence occurs when viable populations of wildlife inhabit the same landscape as humans without infringing on the safety, rights, and property of people.*

Coexisting doesn't mean allowing large predators to drive Americans out of business. Nor does it mean we can be sacrificed as food for large predators.

Chapter 2
Public Trust Doctrine

George Orwell said decades ago, *"In a time of universal deceit, telling the truth is a revolutionary act."*

Sit back like you 're a member of the jury and examine the facts. Place your emotions aside and look at this with a clear and open mind. A crime has been committed against the American people. Dangerous predators are even given pardons after they have killed people. Are you willing to allow a member of your family or yourself to be killed in the name of fake endangered species or protected species? When does human safety become a priority?

Polar bears are listed under two categories: First-time killers and serial killers. Now we will show you evidence that not only polar bears but also cougars, black bears, and grizzly bears fall under these same categories. I want you to think about that for a few moments—first-time killers and serial killers. Now let's say our government had a new program that released and protected violent criminals that could be first-time killers or even known killers loose on the public. The government and the people behind these killers told the public it's a rare event, no big deal. We are the professionals; you're just the ignorant public.

Now really think about that. Would you want a known first-time killer released next to your family? That is exactly what is happening across our great land. Would we allow the government to do this if they were releasing known first time killers? But because these are animals, they are supposed to have special rights? Oh, the poor misunderstood criminal only killed the person because they ran away. Why didn't they just stand there so the poor fluffy bear didn't have to chase them before he ripped them to shreds?

Folks, this reminds me of the Roman Colosseum where the crowds cheered as the lions killed and ate the Christians. Do you know the Romans had a special name for this blood sport? *Damnatio ad bestias,* Latin *for "damnation to beasts."* This is our modern-day version of damnation to beast. No Colosseum, no cheering crowds, and most times no one is around to hear you scream for help.

Would you allow a known child killer to live next to your family? Around your grandchildren? But wait, what if you were told that only one of the people out of thousands is going to kill your child? It's no big deal to lose a few children. In fact, there are too many people in the world. The child killer is more important. Would you be outraged? Would you storm city hall and demand the killer be removed from your community?

What if children were coming up missing in certain areas where this child killer is known to live? Years later, only scraps of bones are found to be returned to the family. But when these families scream for justice for their beloved child, some people say, "So what? The killer is a special animal and is more valuable than your child!" Is that true? Is a child's life not important today?

Some of these experts are going to testify to you, ladies and gentlemen. They will appear professional, polished, charming, and even likable. But you're here to judge them on their actions to see if they are indeed liable for the deaths and multiple injuries on your fellow Americans.

We have the killer's modus operandi. How these killers operate is through a series of steps leading up to the final phase when human blood is spilled.

These steps are outlined as follows:
- Testing the humans.
- Tasting the humans.
- Killing and eating the victim.

Some evidence will show not all killers go through these phases. This is to give you an idea of the warning signs. Some may go right through all the stages at once.

When do we as a society say enough? Are we just like the Romans cheering the animals on to kill people? The hardest part of this book was trying to find out what the true numbers of attacks are. The government doesn't keep a list of attacks. Supposedly, states track all attacks but the records are not open to the public. If it were not for the mainstream press I would not have been able to find most of the attacks listed here.

State and federal governments are no help. Phone calls requesting information were ignored and never returned. How do you count all the attacks? The answer is simple; you can't. There are missing hikers and hunters, never to be found. Or if the body is found the cause of death is never revealed. Newspapers are pressured by the tourism boards not to tell too many animal attack stories; it's bad for business. Fish and wildlife so-called experts spin the tale that this is a "rare event." No records are kept or they are hidden from the public.

The New York Public Library Digital Collections. "On Came
The Vicious Brute," 1896, by Hermann Simon.

An interesting side note on this painting. Note the cross-type spear. This is how you can tell it's real; they made those spears to save human lives. You see they learned that speared bears can fight down the shaft and kill the person. This cross spear prevents that from happening.

But we must ask ourselves, if mankind is destroying the planet and there is no room left for the animals, how did the California black bear population double in the last twenty-five years? Ah, you have been fed propaganda. The truth is, even counting ten-acre plots of land with one house, we are only occupying 6.1% of the land in America. The animals still have 93.9% of the land to use.

But people say we are destroying the whole planet. Let us focus on America. Instead of looking for all the negative things in the world, how about we focus on what we have done right.

For example, look at the great success regulated hunting has done for wildlife in America.

By the late 1800s to early 1900s, extinction of the wood duck seemed imminent. Today, estimates of wood ducks in North America are over 3.5 million.

In 1907, only 41,000 elk remained in North America. Modern hunters helped to restore and conserve habitat. Today there are more than 1 million.

In 1900, only 500,000 whitetails remained. Modern hunters setting up regulated hunting and spending their own money to save wildlife led to there being more than 32 million today.

In 1900, only 100,000 wild turkeys remained. Hunters stepped up to the plate once again, closed hunting, and allowed the turkey population to grow. Once the population was increasing regulated hunting was allowed, and today there are over 7 million.

Most non-hunters have never seen these numbers. If we are stealing all the land, how is this even possible?

Non-hunters just don't understand the simple reality of regulated hunting. Here is another fact. Regulated hunting in the history of the United States has never driven any animal to extinction. As you have just read, the opposite is true; hunting has saved species from extinction.

However, increasing numbers of predators have caused game numbers in some areas to dramatically drop. What happens when the predators run out of food? Human attacks. Until predator populations are heavily controlled, it is guaranteed that more human deaths are the result. Each year, there will be more and more attacks on humans with a certain percentage of these attacks being fatal.

In 1900, black bear numbers dwindled in many areas of the country, nearing the point of extinction. In 2016, the estimated black bear population in North America was one million. Clearly nowhere near extinction level. I can say with all confidence that black bear of North America is a species of least concern for going extinct.

3,200–3,400 bears by 2010, with densities in some areas exceeding 1.3 bears/km²

Since 2001, the New Jersey Division of Fish and Wildlife (NJDFW) has spent over US$9 million on black bear management, responding to over 26,500 human-bear interactions, including >1,400 incidents of verified property damage, >400 livestock kills, >250 pet attacks and/or kills, and seven human attacks, including one fatality (Slide #7). In their comprehensive black bear management report, NJDFW concluded that this level of human-bear conflict is both culturally and fiscally unsustainable. (Raithel et al., 2017)

NJDFW received 26,582 incident reports from the general public between 2001 and 2013 and categorized those as 2,277 Threats, 12,013 Nuisances, and 12,292 Normal interactions.

In North America, coyotes (31.0% of the total number of attacks) and cougars (25.7%) were responsible for the majority of attacks, followed by brown bears (13.2%), black bears (12.2%) and wolves (6.7%). From highest to lowest, the five most common human behaviours occurring at the time of an attack were (a) parents leaving children unattended, (b) walking an unleashed dog, (c) searching for a wounded large carnivore during hunting, (d) engaging in outdoor activities at twilight/night and (e) approaching a female with young. These are clearly risk-enhancing behaviours when sharing the landscape with large carnivores. For example, the most frequently recorded human behaviour was children left unattended (47.3%), which were most often attacked by cougars

(50.8% of the attacks), coyotes (27.9%) and black bears (13.2%). Risk-enhancing human behaviour is not the sole reason behind large carnivore attacks on humans. (Penteriani, 2016)

This paper is taking the always human fault approach. Increased predator population equals increased human attacks. Protection of species equals no fear of mankind. No fear increases damage to humans, especially children. I can't stress this enough to parents. You're not alone in the wilderness; there are large predators and your children are targets.

...some species have rebounded from scarcity to become socially overabundant in particular contexts. While it may not be possible to have a financial trust with 'too much money,' it is possible to have too many individuals of a wildlife trust species within certain contexts, such as those wherein the wildlife have extensive negative impacts on ecosystems and humans. This can result in their status becoming a liability rather than an asset. Controlling the negative impacts of overabundant populations and restoring and expanding the range of other wildlife species necessitates active stewardship of the trust... (Organ, 2014)

Nowhere in case law or in the Endangered Species Act does it claim we must have predator population so high we have to accept a certain amount of animal attacks and human deaths. The Public Trust Doctrine says to take care of wildlife for future generation. I can imagine no children yet to be born who wants to be five years old and be killed by a large predator. This is clearly a violation of the public trust. Only someone in some weird cult that believes in human sacrifice would find this acceptable.

The ESA allows the proactive killing of wild animals before human injury occurs. Looks like the government is way behind on this one.

Chapter 3
Mountain Lions

There is no greater warrior than a mother protecting her child. —N.K. Jemison

(Source: K Fink - NPS, Public Domain)

The most dangerous month for cougar attacks is August, followed by May as the second most dangerous month.

Talking to the enlightened ones, when you tell them we must kill large predators for human safety reasons, you will be given a look akin to the people that told the flat earthers that the world was round.

To understand cougar attacks, we should also look at Tiger attacks. Factors associated with human-killing tigers in Chitwan National Park, Nepal Bhim Gurung (2008) found some interesting facts. Department of National Parks and Wildlife Conservation classified human killing tigers in two categories: one-time killers or SERIAL KILLERS.

One of the serial killer cats quickly killed five people and sat under a tree where the sixth person climbed for hours. The cat was a sub adult living in an intact habitat with no disabilities. In other words, no weak excuses why this tiger was killing people. Other than the obvious he was kicked out of the mother home range and was looking for fresh territory. Lack of prey in the area due to high tiger population equals starving tiger. Come on, it's not rocket science.

The **Champawat Tiger** was a female Bengal tiger responsible for an estimated 436 deaths in Nepal, India. The tiger was killed in 1907 by Jim Corbett. You can read the account in *Man-Eaters of Kumaon* by Jim Corbett (1944). Jim talks about tracking the tiger after it killed a woman. She was totally consumed. All he found were pieces of bloody clothes and a few bone fragments.

The Man-Eaters of Njombe. The most prolific of the man-eaters, this pride of fifteen claimed as many as 1,500 people between 1932 and 1947 in southern Tanzania. George Rushby, the British game warden, was charged with killing the cats. The BBC made a movie of it in 2005. It would be safe to call them a serial killing pride. Unarmed peasants are no match for super predators. Makes you wonder about gun control here in America. For some odd reason, this movie can't be found in America. Wouldn't want the public to see the truth about man-eating lions. Might hurt the Defenders of Wildlife donation drive to save Celia.

Mountain lions—also known as cougars, pumas, catamounts, and panthers—are North America's largest cats. In California in 1909, a woman and a child were attacked by a rabid cougar. Both died from rabies. For seventy-six years, California lived in peace with the cougar with no recorded attacks. From the 1980s until today, however, cougar attacks on people have skyrocketed.

Why? They have lost their fear of man and consider us to be a prey species to be killed and eaten. In 1990, California outlawed cougar hunting; even the fish and game department was not allowed to thin the cougar population. The results were human death. Barbara Schoener on April 23,

1994, was viciously attacked and killed by a cougar with bites to her head and neck.

The *Sacramento Bee*
'WHY WE STILL KILL COUGARS" Nov. 3, 2017
California voters banned mountain lion hunting three decades ago, but the shooting never stopped.

This is a very interesting article. You see the hunting ban doesn't stop the killing. It's about human control, a mindset that the government is all powerful and must cure all our lives. Ridiculous of course.

After losing nine alpacas in one year, Vaughn and her husband installed motion lights, blasted talk radio over loudspeakers, and hung flags and electrified wires to try to keep the cat away at night. But on Thanksgiving weekend, the cougar once again got into her alpaca pen and massacred 10 more animals in a single night. One of the alpacas – a brown-wooled baby named Hope – was left dangling morbidly by its head from the pen's wire fence.

If you're not familiar with these nonlethal methods, they all fail 100% of the time. It's feel-good nonsense. She had to ask the state for a permit to kill the cat. Yes, you read that correctly. She had to beg for permission to kill an animal slaughtering her animals. This is absurd. But biologists didn't want this cat killed because he brought in genetic diversity to the other cougars in the area. He was known as P-45. Of course, in the predator worshipping LA, he was known as a celebrity. His job was to mate with the females in the area and save this tiny population of cats from inbreeding and going extinct. Yes, twelve other cats were in the area. But I guess twelve cats are more important than people.

The biologist claimed there were only 4,000-6,000 cougars in all of California. But I have read others claim there are 8,000-10,000 in the state. With no hunting of cats, I find it extremely hard to believe the low number. Animal welfare activists want the law changed so that small hobby ranchers can't get a kill permit. What? Even after their nonlethal methods fail, they still don't want people to have the God-given right to protect their animals from cougar attacks.

How many cats were hunters taking a year in California before the ban? One hundred and ninety cats a year. Clearly, that tiny number was in no way hurting or endangering the cougar population in the state. Oregon is claiming 6,400 cougars in the state, while hunters and depredation permits combined are taking 419 cats a year (268 from hunters and 151 for livestock depredation). Are their cats at risk for going extinct? Not in anyone's wildest imagination.

Vicky Vaughan had a cougar killing her goats. She received help from a government trapper who placed a live trap on her property. When the cat was trapped her husband shot it. She made the mistake of posting a picture on Facebook. The lunatic fringe lost their mind and started stalking this woman like psychopaths. I am sure she received hundreds of death threats over the dead cat.

One survivor of a mountain lion attack stated it felt like "I was knocked over by a freight train." This was a full-grown man. He fought off the mountain lion with a pocket knife and survived. When it comes to cougars, think of them as highly adaptable heat-seeking missiles that lock on target. A biological, thinking, powerful missile that commits to one target. Normally they attack from the side or behind. A percentage of victims say they never heard a thing until the attack. The cat was stalking them like prey.

Horizontal leaps of 45 ft. have been observed; a 15-20 ft. leap to reach prey is not uncommon. The cougar's 1 to 2 in. sharp teeth, 1 to 1 1/2-inch retractable, needle-sharp claws, and powerful forelegs provide means for a rapid, efficient, and lethal attack. (Conrad, 1992)

Cougar attacks are described as sharp and clean like a knife. This must make you wonder if some bodies that have been found are listed as murder cases instead of animal attacks.

Attacks happen lightning fast. If your child is out of your sight, he or she can quickly be dragged off. I highlight this case as an example.

Picchetti Winery along Montebello Rd. in Cupertino, California, on Monday, Sept. 8, 2014. *"A six-year-old boy was attacked by a mountain lion. State wildlife agency said the attack happened about 1 p.m. Sunday when the boy was walking on the trail only 10 feet ahead of a group of hikers who included four adults and another five children." (Mercury News, 2014).*

The mountain lion attacked, gripping the boy 's head and neck. Once the child was under control the cat started dragging him into a bush. Lucky for the boy, two men in the group saw what happened and charged the mountain lion, shouting at it. The cat let go of the boy and ran off.

Per wildlife experts, a mountain lion can kill another animal four to five times its weight. A human doesn't stand a chance. The mountain lion was treed by dogs and shot; it only weighed sixty-five pounds. Imagine what a full-size 150 lb. cat could do.

I bring this case up as a reminder to parents. If your child is out of sight, you would have no clue if he or she was taken. The child never screamed for help once. People tend to underestimate the strength of wild animals. You must remember a large predator, like a mountain lion, is all muscle. Think about it; they make their living by killing other animals. Humans, especially small children, are easy to grab and run off with.

"A child, however, with a small stature may appear as a small animal to a lion. During the last 20 years, 70 percent of the cat attacks were perpetrated on children and in recent years, that figure has climbed to 90 percent. Uninformed people may find themselves examining the digestive system of these cats from the inside." (Sheley, 1998)

Wikipedia lists the following attacks in North America:

Fatal attacks

1. Robert Nawojski, fifty-five years, June 24, 2008. Searchers found his body on this date near his mobile home in Pinos Altos, New Mexico. Investigators concluded that he had been attacked and killed by a cougar several days earlier.

2. Mark Jeffrey Reynolds, thirty-five years, January 8, 2004. Attacked and killed while mountain biking at Whiting Ranch Wilderness Park in southern Orange County, California. It is believed his chain fell off and the cougar attacked when he bent down to repair his bicycle.

3. Frances Frost, thirty years, January 2, 2001. This Canmore, Alberta, resident was killed by a cougar while skiing on Cascade Fire Road just north of Banff National Park in Alberta.

4. Jaryd Atadero, missing three-year-old since 1999. His remains were found by two hikers in June of 2003. "Duggins Wroe, a wildlife biologist from Wyoming, examined the clothing on Friday. Wroe said, 'The damage to the shirt's shoulders and upper arms is consistent with a lion grabbing its prey.'" Associated Press June 10, 2003

5. Mark Miedema, ten, July 17, 1998. Killed by an adult female cougar in Colorado 's Rocky Mountain National Park while hiking when he got ahead of his family.

6. Cindy Parolin, thirty-six, August 19, 1996. Mother killed while defending her six-year-old son on a horseback riding trip in Tulameen, British Columbia.

7. Iris M. Kenna, fifty-six, December 10, 1994. Killed while hiking alone near Cuyamaca Peak in California 's Cuyamaca Rancho State Park.

8. Barbara Barsalou Schoener, forty years, April 23, 1994. Long-distance runner and Placerville resident was attacked and killed while jogging on the American River Canyon Trail in California 's Auburn State Recreation Area.

9. Jeremy Williams, seven years, May 5, 1992. Attacked and killed in Kyuquot, British Columbia, by a young female cougar while playing in the schoolyard.

10. Scott Lancaster, 18, January 14, 1991. Killed while jogging a familiar route on a hill above Clear Creek High School in Idaho Springs, Colorado.

Non-Fatal Attacks

1. October 17, 2017, Fontana, California. Police responded to a call that a cougar was killing pets. A police officer was charged by the cat and shot and killed it in self-defense. CBS Los Angeles

2. May 29, 2017, Libby, Montana. Unnamed man. The man was working on a tree he cut down when he was attacked. He suffered scratches to his face and stomach. He fought back long enough to make it to his truck and leave the area. KPAX News

3. Feb 23, 2017, six-year-old boy, Dillion, Montana. The lion took a swipe at one of the kid's legs. It didn't break the skin or anything like that. No bite. The mountain lion didn't follow up and chase them. KTVQ News

4. Feb 15, 2017. A West Kootenay conservation officer suffered minor scratches after he was attacked by an emaciated cougar which tried to climb into a West Kootenay home through the window Tuesday night. Deputy Chief Chris Doyle with the BC Conservation Officer Service says the call came in from a home in Salmo, east of Castlegar, around 9:15 p.m. The responding officer had just euthanized an adult cougar which had been hit by a pickup truck about ten kilometers away. When the officer arrived at the home, the juvenile cougar jumped him without provocation, and he was forced to kill it to stop the attack. The Canadian Press

5. Aug. 15, 2016, Green Canyon Hot Springs, Idaho. Kelsi Butt, four years old. Kelsi and one of her cousins were outside her tent when the young cat attacked. Kelsi's cousin screamed. The cat was trying to drag the young child into the brush where it could kill and eat the girl. The screaming brought the adults who drove the cat off. Teton Valley News

6. August 12, 2016, Vancouver Island, BC, Canada. The unnamed jogger was attacked by a cougar. He fought the cat off using a rock. He was treated for bites and claw wounds. The Canadian Press

7. June 18, 2016, Aspen, Colorado, five-year-old boy. The boy was attacked in the backyard. His mother fought the cougar and literally pried his jaws off her son. No list of injuries but he was airlifted to Denver hospital from Aspen medical center. Hours later, the cat was shot, still in the yard. Associated Press

8. September 22, 2015, two-year-old girl, Bree Nielsen Tahsis, British Columbia. Her father saw the cat on her back, biting her ear. The father punched the cat until it let the child go. He shielded his daughter while yelling at the cat and it fled. Digital Journal

9. August 28, 2015, Antelope Valley, California. A mechanic walking up to open his shop was knocked over by a cougar. He ran off. Fish and game was able to tranquilize the cat and relocated it into the wilds. KTLA 5

10. July 2015, north of Dotsero, Colorado. Man attacked while fishing. Two-year-old male cougar. Fox 31 Denver

11. Feb 2, 2015, Dan Laville, Grande Prairie, Alberta. A pipeline worker and a friend were attacked and both received injuries from the cat. Global News

12. October 19, 2014, Alyssa Caldwell, New Mexico. While elk hunting, she first saw the cat low-stalking her. She saw the large cat crouch, ready to leap when she fired at the cat a car length from her. Lucky for her, she was a good shot and the cat died instantly. Gun Watch

13. September 12, 2014. Kayaker attacked on the beach by a mountain lion. Rugged Point Marine Park, BC. CTV News, Vancouver Island, BC, Canada

14. September 7, 2014, Silicon Valley, California. A six-year-old boy was attacked with a family member present who drove off the animal. The Mercury News

15. August 27, 2014, Mykaela Belter, sixteen years, Waterton Lakes National Park, Alberta. While hiking in a group, a cougar grabbed the girl and she had minor injuries. Her older sister ran up, grabbing her and screaming at the cat so loudly it scared the cat off. Calgary Herald

16. August 11, 2014, Kyra Kopenstonsky, Placerville, Colorado. For twenty minutes, the big cat stalked her. She armed herself with a stick. As a last resort, she started singing opera. This confused the cat and she was able to retreat to the trailhead. Outdoor Life

17. August 6, 2014, an unnamed female in Grande Prairie, Alberta. CTV Edmonton

18. Feb 2, 2014, Homeless man, fifty years, Perris, California. The man was attacked by a mountain lion, sustaining lacerations, puncture wounds, and bites. NBC Los Angeles

19. Oct 16, 2013, Port McNeill, BC. An RCMP corporal and his wife were attacked by a cougar while walking their small dogs. No reported injuries. A large cat, 120 to 140 pounds, was shot the next day. North Island Gazette

20. September 10, 2013, sixty-year-old woman, Flores Island, BC. A cougar crushed the woman's skull in a vicious attack. Half her scalp was missing. Her common-law partner drove the animal off with a spear. CTV BC Canada

21. May 26, 2013, Unnamed male in Banff, Alberta, was attacked from behind. He fought the cougar off with his skateboard. No injuries reported besides being knocked to the ground. The Canadian Press

22. May 9, 2013, Crescent Beach, CA. An off-duty park ranger was fishing with his dog. The cat attacked the dog and when the man yelled at the cat, he was attacked. He drove the cat off by hitting it with his fishing pole and kicking it. The cat was shot by fish and game and was listed as a younger cat. The Times-Standard

23. November 23, 2012, Andrea Pinero-Cebrian, Big Bend National Park, Texas. The woman was attacked by a cougar while hiking with friends. No list of injuries but a medic treated her for non-life-threating injuries. Big Bend Sentinel

24. Nov 12, 2012, John Frank Jr., thirty-eight years, Vancouver Island, BC. You have to love the headline. "Cougar Attacks Vancouver Island Man, Pants Torn Off." Except this was a mountain lion trying to kill him. It shredded his pants and took off one shoe as he ran for his life. He climbed a construction boom and called on his radio for help. Friends arrived in trucks, scaring the cat off. CTV News Vancouver

25. October 17, 2012, Kaylum Doherty, seven-year-old boy, Vancouver Island, BC. Kaylum was rushed to the hospital for surgery to repair his scalp and puncture wounds on his shoulder and back. His father drove the cat off the child. CBC News BC

26. Aug 28, 2012, Angie Prime's West Kootenay region, BC. A cougar entered the house from an open door and attacked a woman in her house. She and her dogs fought the animal off and forced it to leave. She was treated for claws slashing her upper leg. CBC News

27. Aug 16, 2012, Vancouver Island, BC. A seven-year-old boy with wounds to his head and shoulders. CTV British Columbia

28. July 2, 2012, sixty-three-year-old male, Yuba River, California. Attacked in his sleeping bag, he fought back. The attack lasted for almost two minutes before the cat ran off. He drove himself to the hospital. CBS SF Bay Area

29. Mar 27, 2012, Robert Biggs, sixty-nine years old, Bean Soup Flat, California. He was watching a black bear sow with cubs. He turned to leave and was slammed from behind by a cougar. He fought back, hitting the cat in the head with a rock hammer. He raised his hammer again when the mommy bear attacked the cat. The battle was over quickly with the cougar hightailing it out of there. The cat may have been stalking the bear cubs. Paradise Post News

30. February 8, 2012, six-year-old boy, Big Bend National Park, Texas. The boy was attacked walking with his family. The father drove the cat off his son by stabbing the cat with a pocket knife. The boy was treated for puncture wounds to the face. Lone Star 98.7

31. Aug 30, 2011, eighteen-month-old baby, Vancouver Island's Pacific Rim National Park Reserve, BC. The family was at the beach when the attack occurred. Parents drove the cat off. The child was taken to the hospital. No list of injuries. CBC News

32. Aug 03, 2011, six-year-old girl, Bow Valley Provincial Park, Alberta. The girl's father drove the cat off. She suffered only minor cuts and puncture wounds. CBC News Calgary

33. Oct 18, 2010, County Road 51 in Divide, Colorado. Kendra Rutter stopped to repair a flat tire at night when the cougar attacked from behind, knocking her into the road. She fought back, kicking the cat in the head. The cat ran off and she drove to the hospital for treatment. KKTV 11 News

34. June 11, 2010, Andy Bell, thirty years, Walker, Arizona. He was attacked at night. The cat hit him from behind and knocked him into his truck. He rolled under the truck and the cat fled. Realtree AZ Man Attacked By Mountain Lion

35. January 4, 2010, David Metzler Jr., Burns Lake, BC. The young boy was tobogganing. Lucky for him his mother was watching when a cougar attacked him. The cougar had the boy down, biting his head. The fearless mother, armed with a dish towel, raced to save her son. She fought the cougar until it ran off. It took twenty-two stitches to close the wounds. CTV News Vancouver

36. September 03, 2009, Coleville National Forest, Washington State, Simon Impey, five-year-old boy. The cat attacked the child and the mother beat the cat with a water bottle until it ran off. Fox News

37. July 18, 2009, Dustin Britton, thirty-two years, Shoshone National Forest, Wyoming. He fought the cat off with a running chainsaw. ABC News

38. Jun 17, 2009, three-year-old girl, Maya Espinosa, Squamish, BC. The mother fought the cat off the child and both had to go to the hospital for injuries. CBC News, British Columbia

39. December 18, 2008, Virginia City, Nevada. An unnamed woman was attacked when she tried to save her dog. She was treated and released the same day from the hospital. The Associated Press

40. October 7, 2008, Kellen Lancaster, Water Canyon, Wyoming. The cat pounced at a father and was snarling at his boots when he tripped. His son shot the cougar, saving his father from a mauling. Fish and game called it an encounter because no contact was made with the person. Star Valley Independent

41. September 30, 2008, Adam Wheat, twenty-nine years, Taos Ski Valley, NM. The Taos News reported "I heard a hissing sound behind me and turned around. All I can remember was this yellow flash going toward me." He picked up a rock and fought back. The cat ran off; he was treated and stitched up.

42. May 19, 2008, Mountain lion attacks five-year-old boy. Bernalillo County NM. Fox News

43. Mar 10, 2008, ten-year-old boy, PJ Schalow, North of Phoenix, Arizona. The boy was riding an ATV at his birthday party. A rabid mountain lion attacked him and his uncle shot the cat. East Valley Tribune

44. March 3, 2008, Ryan Hughes, Sheridan Lake, South Dakota. A man was attacked by the cat while walking off the ice from fishing. He received wounds to his hands and right side of his face. No details on how he drove the cat off. Black Hills Pioneer

45. Nov 12, 2007, Unnamed male near Kalispell, Montana. The man was elk hunting. He spotted the cat and dropped his rifle and tried to climb a tree. The cougar pounced on his back. He pulled his pistol and fired a shot and the cat ran off. He was stitched up at the local hospital. His daypack was shredded and it saved him from more serious wounds. The Daily Inter Lake

46. August 3, 2007, Twelve-year-old Colton Reeb, Clinton, BC. Walking to the outhouse, he was attacked. The cougar bit him on the head, face, and neck. Marc Patterson, a nearby camper, ran to save the boy, grabbing the cougar by his neck and tried to strangle it. The cougar let go of the boy and pulled himself out of the man's grip. They had a stare-down before the cougar ran off. Canadian Press

47. January 28, 2007, Jim Hamm, seventy years, Prairie Creek, Redwoods State Park, California. A horrific attack. His face and head were covered with puncture wounds and scratches. His brave wife Nell drove the cat off with a four-inch diameter log, hitting it repeatedly before the cat finally left. The Associated Press

48. August 22, 2006, four-year-old boy, Vancouver Island, BC. A father was fishing and the son was sitting on a log. The cougar attacked the boy. The father raced into the fight as the cougar tried to kill the boy. Hitting the cougar with his fist, he drove the animal off. The boy had puncture wounds and lacerations to the back of his head and scalp area and he had some lacerations on his shoulders and back. He was rushed to the hospital. CBC News

49. April 15, 2006, seven-year-old boy, Flagstaff Mountain near Boulder, Colorado. A mountain lion seized the boy and tried to drag him in the bush. The family fought back. Without the family fighting back, the young child would have been killed and eaten. The Denver Post

50. July 30, 2005, four-year-old Hayley Bazille from Coquitlam, BC. The cougar attacked the child and the mother fought the cougar off with a cooler. It all started with a simple short walk to the swimming hole. The child was in front and the mother heard a cry for help. Next, she saw her daughter fighting the cougar. It growled and snarled at her, trying to protect its kill but the mother would not give up. Finally, the cougar left. The little four-year-old was in the hospital with bite marks on her head. The Globe and Mail

51. June 24, 2005. A fifty-four-year-old female tourist from Berlin, Germany, was attacked by a cougar at the Spruce Bay campground on Victoria Lake near Port Alice on Victoria Island, BC, Canada. She was drinking coffee with a friend when the friend saw a cougar inside the trailer. Before she could say a word, the cougar attacked her, knocking

her to the ground, holding her head in its powerful claws. But it didn't bite. Her husband defended her, driving the cat off. The Denver Post

52. Feb 2006, "BOULDER - Wildlife officers captured and killed a mountain lion that attacked a seven-year-old boy over the weekend. The boy is recovering at Children 's Hospital in Denver." The Denver Post

53. May 3, 2000, Ken Jones, Siletz, Oregon. The cat came into his garage and attacked his dogs. Defending his dogs with the shovel, the cat scratched his leg before fleeing. Koin 6 News

54. Fall of 1995, photographer Moses Street was jogging on a popular trail in Rocky Mountain National Park near Estes Park, CO. Spotting a cat over his shoulder, he stopped, yelling and waving his hands. The cat backed off. He picked up a large tree branch and used it to keep the cat off him for the second and third attack. Park rangers rescued him after Street 's girlfriend alerted them. Washington Post

55. August 20, 1994, five-year-old Andrew Braun, Olympic National Forest, Washington. A man was walking with his son along the river when he heard something and looked down to see a cougar on top of his son. He picked up a stick from the river and hit the cat so hard the stick shattered. But the cat backed off. A backpacker tended to the wounds as the father and two older brothers kept the cat back by throwing rocks at it. They carried the child back to the camp and finally to the vehicles when he was rushed to the hospital. (Etling, 2001)

56. September 19, 1993, ten-year-old Lisa Kowalski, Cuyamaca Rancho State Park, California. A cat bit the girl and ran off when she screamed. Editor note: "This is the part of the job I hate," Itogawa, the park 's supervising ranger, said while she still had her weapon aimed at the mountain lion. Tears fell on her cheeks. As reported in the LA Times.

57. August 13, 1992, Nathaniel Moore, twelve, Glacier National Park, Montana. A cougar leaped on the child. The father drove it off by kicking the cat. His chest, arms, and wrist had puncture wounds from the cat and facial cuts. (Etling, 2001)

58. March 1992, Darron Arroyo, age nine, Santa Barbara County, CA. He had fifty stitches to sew the child back up. San Diego Union Tribune Associated Press, 04/15/95

59. July 1991, British Columbia. Larrane Leach, age forty-four, saved her two-year-old child that the cat had pinned to the ground. Larrane received scratches on the arms while prying the vicious predator off the victim. The family dog treed the cat. Rocky Mountain News, 07/16/91

60. March 28, 1991, Nevada Test Site, Nevada. Mary Saether was attacked by a cat and was lucky her two male companions were able to drive the cat off. A Wildlife Services Specialist who arrived to investigate the scene was attacked by the same cat. He only had enough time to draw and shoot at point blank range, killing the cat. US Department of Agriculture, Wildlife Services, Reno, Nevada

61. July 24, 1990. A nine-year-old boy, Glacier National Park, Montana. This was a predatory attack. The boy suffered bites and scratches to his head, face, neck, and right arm. Emergency surgery was performed at Kalispell Regional Hospital. (Etling, 2001)

The following are all cited from the list of confirmed cougar attacks In the United States and Canada 2001 – 2010 by Linda Lewis:

62. June 15, 1992, Jessica Vanney, age five, Lake Wenatchee State Park, Washington. The girl suffered cuts, scrapes, and puncture wounds.

63. April 9, 2005, Peter Bysterveld, twenty-three years old, Sheep River Wildlife Sanctuary, Alberta, Canada. Hiking with his friend Sarah McKay when they spotted two cougars. Peter yelled at the cats and one

ran off. The second cat charged him. Thinking of Sarah's safety, he took off running to lure the cat away. He slipped on some mud and fell. The cat pounced on him. The cat bit him on the calf and he threw it off. Peter was a big guy, 6'3" 210 pounds. He grabbed the cat and threw it like a hay bale. Standing up, he picked up a stick and yelled and swung at the cat to drive it off. The cat left.

64. August 14, 2004, just east of Jasper National Park near Hinton, Alberta, five-year-old Chance Stepanick. His parents were setting up camp when Chance was riding his bike. Chance raced back to camp and told his parents a "tiger" was chasing Bryce. The cougar closed in on him and leaped right in front of the parents, knocking Chance to the ground. The two men in the group attacked the cougar with their boots, kicking it off.

65. June 26, 2004, twenty-seven-year-old Shannon Parker Johnsondale, California. Shannon lost her right eye and suffered injuries to her other eye and deep lacerations to her right thigh. This was a very brutal attack. Five people finally drove the cat off her. The cat weighed only fifty-eight pounds, severely underweight for a two-year-old.

66. January 8, 2004, thirty-five-year-old Anne Hjelle, Orange County, California. Earlier that same day, Mark Jeffrey Reynolds was killed by the cat. On the same trail, Anne was bike riding. The cat hit her from behind, working its jaw around her neck toward the front to finish her off. Forty-seven-year-old Deborah Nicholls was her riding companion. The cougar tore at her face, ripping her cheek and her left ear off. Debi screamed at the cat. It grabbed her left leg. But the cat dragged them both off the trail. Five men heard the life and death battle and raced in to help. Picking up softball size rocks they threw at the cat. One of the men hit the cat square in the face. He let go and ran off. Sheriff's deputies shot and killed a healthy two-year-old, 110-pound male lion later that night. Testing proved that the lion was the mankiller and the one that attacked Anne.

67. January 8, 2004, thirty-five-year-old Mark Jeffrey Reynolds, Orange County California. Mark was riding on the trail and his bike was found with a broken chain. That is when they believe the first attack happened. He was dragged off the trail down a ravine. His body was partially consumed and caught a few hours before the same cat attacked Anne Hjelle. If the cat had a full stomach, why did it attack Anne?

68. May 13, 2003, thirty-year-old Chris Kerzman, Big Bend National Park, Texas. Hiking on a trail, he saw the cougar. It charged him several times. He picked up a large rock and when the cat knocked him to the ground, he beat the cat in the head with the rock. This drove the cat off and he watched her lick his blood off her lips. The cat followed for a short distance and disappeared. The park service tracked the cat down and killed it.

69. May 3, 2003, forty-one-year-old Leigh Ann Cox was killed by a large cat near Leslie, Arkansas. Leigh Ann's scalp had been ripped off, apparently from the front to the back, almost in one piece from her forehead to the nape of her neck. She had slash marks that Morton and expert dog witness Darren Huff both identified as typical of a large cat but impossible for a dog to make. Her neck was broken and her trachea probably crushed, but her throat was not torn. Blaming the dogs of the family, they shot two before they even checked to see if blood was on the dogs. No blood was ever found on any of the five dogs, even the two that were shot. Arkansas Game and Fish biologist Eddie Linebarger told Leigh Ann Cox's sister, "Even if you prove that a big cat was present at the scene, at the time that your sister was killed, it is irrelevant. The report is going to say that it was a dog attack."

70. September 18, 2002, Karina Jackson, thirty-five years, of Newkirk, Oklahoma. At her home, she noticed one of her puppies had escaped the pen and she entered the field to retrieve him. She heard some rustling in the tall grass but continued toward the puppy. Suddenly, she was knocked to the ground. The cat ran off. She needed twenty-nine stitches to close up her wounds.

71. September 11, 2002, thirty-one-year-old Gwyn Stacey, Summit Lake, just west of Olympia, Washington. Jogging along a trail, she spotted the cougar. She yelled and waved her arms. The cat stayed back but as she jogged back down the trail, the cougar ran beside her, getting in front of her, setting up an ambush. She saw the cat in time and was able to pull back, receiving a single scratch from the claw. The cat then ran off. This sounds like prey testing.

72. August 01, 2002, sixty-one-year-old David Parker, Port Alice, BC. Out for his nightly walk on the road, it started raining so he sought shelter under a rock outcrop. The cat dropped down under the outcrop. He reached for his pocket knife. The cat pounced on his neck. He tilted his head down to save his neck from being ripped out. During the deathmatch, he was hurled into a ditch, shattering his jaw and breaking his cheekbone. The cat was now clawing away at his face and neck. He managed to open his knife, stabbing the animal and finally slitting its throat. The cat was a healthy three- to four-year-old that had eaten in the last ten to twelve hours. He underwent reconstructive facial surgery and was in intensive care until he made a full recovery.

73. June 23, 2002, eight-year-old Rita Hilsabeck, Vancouver Island, British Columbia. She was walking with her family when the cougar attacked. Quickly knocking the child to the ground, he began dragging the child into the brush so it could finish off his prey. Her father rushed the cat. Seeing the cougar with its jaw locked firmly on the child's head and neck, everyone else in the party charged the cat. The cat dropped the child and ran off. The most serious wounds were on her neck where the cat had grabbed her. She was predicted to make a full recovery.

74. February 8, 2001, Jon Nostdal, fifty-two years, Port Alice, BC. He was riding his bike when he heard a clicking noise. He later figured it was the cougar's claws on the pavement. It hit him from behind, biting his neck and knocking him to the ground. A man driving by saw the battle and stopped to help, hitting the cat with a bag. The cat refused to let go of

Jon 's neck. The man picked up the bike and was able to pin the cat to the ground. Breaking the grip of the cat, he told Jon to run inside his truck. He punched the cat in the head so hard the cat's head bounced off the pavement. He ran to the truck. The cat refused to leave until the man drove off to the hospital.

75. April 29, 2000, Victoria Martinez, a four-year-old girl, Bartlett Lake, Arizona. Victoria was seriously injured. The lion crushed the back of her skull, nicked her carotid artery, and put several deep puncture wounds in her torso. Camping with her family, she was just outside the tent flaps when the cat attacked her from behind, dragging her into the brush. Her parents drove the cat off.

76. 24stopAugust 1999, Jacob Walsh of Kettle Falls, Washington, was dragged off by a lion that released him after being chased off by a screaming adult. Jacob had over thirty puncture wounds and needed 200 stitches. The attack happened at the grandparents' home in rural Washington State. Now the nine grandchildren no longer feel safe out in the yard.

77. August 1998, five-year-old Carmen Schrock, Metaline Falls, Washington. A cougar tore a piece of her skull out. She was walking to the restroom at the campground when the cougar attacked. The mother was able to scare the cat off the child. But the cat hung around the area and was shot by the game warden.

78. August 1, 1998, six-year-old Joey Wing, Swift Dam Campground, Montana. Joey received bites to the back of his skull and on his back, with lacerations from his throat to his ear, requiring 200 stitches. His mother drove the cougar away.

79. July 31, 1998, Dante Swallow, a six-year-old boy, Marshall Mountain near Missoula, Montana, was jumped by a cougar while hiking with about three dozen other campers. The cat attacked, pinning the boy to

the ground and biting his neck. A sixteen-year-old camp counselor, Aaron Hall, pulled the child away from the cat, saving his life.

80. May 25, 1998, Mary Jane Coder, Pine Canyon Trail in Big Bend National Park, Texas. Mary was hiking with her three daughters when a cougar tried to get her children. Armed with a knife, she fought the cat. The determined cat scratched her hand but they were able to reach their car two miles away. Great job, Mary, for protecting your children.

81. April 28, 1998, Andy Peterson, twenty-four years, Roxborough State Park, Colorado. An experienced hiker from Littleton was attacked. He used his knife and fought back. It was an extremely brutal attack from a determined cat. Hiking a trail, the cat attacked, knocking Andy down. But he got back up. He kept the cat back by swinging his shirt at it. When the cat gave him time, he took off his pack and used that as a weapon. But the lightning-fast cat easily avoided being hit. He kept backing down the trail. Reaching a series of boulder steps, he leaped down. The cat followed, knocking him to the ground for the second time. This time the cat latched onto his skull and face. He started slashing the cat with his little Swiss Army knife, with no effect. He raised the knife high over his head and buried it into the back of the cat's neck, with no effect on the cat. He could see the blade was partially closed. Using his other hand, he was able to open the knife. With his right thumb, he forced it into the cat's eye and with his left hand, plunged the knife into the cat's neck. He heard a shriek and the animal jumped backward. Next, he threw a large volleyball-sized rock at the cat. He raced for the trailhead three miles away; he was losing blood fast. But the cat was no longer following him. He was able to locate other hikers who called a rescue helicopter.

82. October 20, 1997, a twenty-year-old mountain bike rider Todd Dunbar near Boulder, Colorado. The cat took a swipe at him. Using his bike as a shield, he kept the cat back. It followed him for a distance and finally left.

83. In 1997, Don Massey, sixty-four years old, Price, Utah. A rancher riding his horse was attacked by a half-starved cat. The cat lunged at him when

he was on horseback, scratching the horse. The horse bucked Don off. The cat chased the horse but soon came back. Don was now armed with a stick. The cat attacked his dog, Blackie. He beat the cat unconscious with the stick and finished it off with a rock.

84. July 14, 1997. A four-year-old French boy was attacked by a lion at Mesa Verde National Park, Colorado. A known problem cat was in the area. Park rangers had tried to frighten it away. The park was reopened. A new report came in on the cat. Park Ranger Bob Erner was helping to escort people out of the park. When Rafael DeGrave saw the cat, he took off running. The cat pounced on him but the parents drove the cat off. It took fifty-two stitches to sew the child up, including surgically reattaching one ear. The family filed suit for failing to protect them from a known risk. The park service needs to train their people to kill problem animals not hug them.

85. May 24, 1996, twenty-eight-year-old Phil Anderson, Olympic National Park, Washington. Phil was a wrestler who was attacked by a cat as he hiked the trail. The cat leaped on his chest. He got his legs around its body, putting the cat down. Using his arms, he tried to choke the cat, pinning the front paws down with his forearms. The cat managed to bite his thumb. He lost his grip and the cat shredded his jacket, causing puncture wounds to his chest. The cat ran off. The park service, unconcerned with public safety, claimed there were too many cats in the park and hunted one down, though they couldn't be sure the right one was killed. This is a lie. Hound hunting dogs are trained to stay on one scent. Dogs brought to the attack site would have quickly tracked down the right cat. Once again, the park service failed to protect the public.

86. March 24, 1995, Scott Fike, twenty-seven years, Angeles National Forest, California. He was riding his mountain bike when he saw the cougar. Using the bike as a shield, the cat tried going around the bike and he ran. He slipped and fell. The cat attacked, clawing and biting his head. He picked up a rock and beat the cat until it ran off.

87. December 13,1994, twenty-five-year-old Susanne Groves, Ute Indian Reservation, Colorado. Taking water samples from the Mancos River, she saw movement above her. She looked up and made eye contact with the cat. Knowing she was in trouble, she started across the river, keeping her eyes on the cat. They crossed the river back and forth several times when she slipped on a rock. As she was falling, the cat pounced. The cat bit down on the back of her head and held her underwater for ten seconds. She broke free and ran for her car. She slipped on the bank and put her arm up to protect her neck. The lion bit down on her arm and she wrestled her way on top of the cat. She shoved her arm down the cat's throat. Pinning it to the ground with her free hand, she grabbed her forceps, planning on driving it through the eye into the brain. The cat bit down harder. She started stabbing the cat repeatedly. For five minutes, the battle raged on until finally, the cat broke free. It stood its ground but didn't continue the attack. She walked out to her truck and drove to the hospital. Later, a federal trapper using dogs killed the cat, an old half-starved female.

88. July 17, 1994, two-year-old boy at Apache Lake in Arizona. A couple camping was awakened by their son's cries. A cougar had been pawing at the sleeping bag and tried to drag their son off. The parents wrestled their son back and flew to a boat until the cat left. The boy needed ten stitches to close a wound on the boy's ear.

One hundred total attacks from cougars on humans.

Man Uses Spear to Kill Mountain Lion Attacking Woman
By Ben Romans September 18, 2013, *Field and Stream*

On September 8, a Vancouver Island woman working behind her cabin was attacked from behind by a mountain lion, which began crushing her skull and tore off half her scalp. Her common-law partner heard her screams and came to her aid, repeatedly stabbing the cat with a spear until it retreated.

Attacking cougar killed with pocket knife
THE ASSOCIATED PRESS
Published Friday, August 2, 2002

VICTORIA, B.C. — A 61-year-old man won a life-and-death struggle with a cougar outside a small northern Vancouver Island village, killing the animal with his three-inch pocket knife.

This is the case I was talking about at the beginning of the book where the man said it felt like being hit by a freight train.

How do you put into words the sheer terror of being attacked? Cougars are commonly referred to as ghost cats because you rarely see them. Your adrenaline is pumping as the 100 pounds of pure muscle, teeth, and claws makes contact. You listen to your bones being crunched as the blood flows into your eyes. You have no choice at that very second but to fight for your life. The cat grabs you by the shoulders and starts to drag you into the brush so he can kill you in private. As this 61-year-old proved, even a small pocket knife can save your life.

Cougar Attacks Family on Horses
The myths and realities of cougar attacks in the great outdoors
By Don Zaidle September 18, 2007

Cindy Parolin, her children Steven 6, Melissa 11, and David 13. A family was riding horses. The horses became alarmed. Soon the reason why became crystal clear as a full-grown cougar launched his attack. The cougar picked 6-year-old Steven as the target. He missed his mark landing on the horse. The cat tried to grab the horse by the neck but fell to the ground.

As mentioned earlier, cougars are heat-seeking missiles locked on target. The target was the smallest human, Steven. It attacked for the second time, trying to pull Steven out of the saddle. This time he ripped off the child's sock and shoe.

The horse, now in full panic mode, bucked wildly, causing the child to fall to the ground. In a flash, the cat was on him, wrapping his powerful claws and teeth into the victim. The cat bared his fangs and buried them into the boy's skull.

His mother, Cindy Parolin, was an avid hunter but didn't have her rifle with her due to Canada's ridiculous gun laws. Hunting season would not open for a few weeks and it's illegal to carry a gun for human protection.

She knew if she didn't act fast, the powerful cat would kill her son in mere seconds. Jumping from her mount, she grabbed a stout limb and started beating the cat. The cat turned on her with the viciousness of a starving animal protecting his kill. A single swipe with razor sharp claws ripped open her arm with a long gash.

She yelled for the other two children to grab their wounded brother and go for help. Half dragging their sibling, they ran off making it the mile on the trail back to where the car was parked. His sister Melissa and the wounded Steven were put in the safety of the car. David ran off to find help. He found Jim Manion at a nearby campsite who quickly agreed to help the child. They drove to the site of the attack. It now had been an hour since the attack had started.

Once on scene, Jim heard Cindy scream and ran to her aid. She was still battling the cat. She turned to Jim, a raging defiance in her eyes.

"Are my children alright?"

"Yes," Jim replied.

After hearing that she said, "I'm dying now."

Jim, armed with a 12-gauge shotgun, was afraid to shoot the cat for fear of hitting Cindy. He fired one round into the ground, hoping to scare the cat off.

The enraged cat now turned his attention to Jim and started to stalk him. Jim tried to cycle the shotgun to put a fresh round in, but the gun jammed. He slowly backed up toward the truck in a panic, trying to fix the jam.

He just cleared the weapon when the cat charged. No time to aim, he fired from the hip. Hitting the cat farther back instead of full in the chest, it worked and the cat ran off. Later, wildlife officials would find the dead cat 150 feet off the trail.

He ran over to Cindy, trying to help but it was too late. She had given the ultimate sacrifice to save her children. Steven received seventy stitches and made a full recovery. The Canadian Government awarded Cindy Parolin the Star of Courage posthumously.

When you have a weapon, especially on cougars, there must be no warning shot. Run up as close as you can and wait for the time to shoot the animal in the rear. Get down on one knee if you have to. Make sure the shot won't hit the person you're trying to save. Get some lead in them. A rear spine or hip shot will drop the animal or wound them enough that they will retreat.

A jammed gun is now a club. People don't understand in high-stress situations you're not thinking clearly. A short cycle on a pump action can jam the shotgun. I know it's easy to say what you're supposed to do when you're not faced with trying to save someone's life and the growling snarling cat is not a few yards in front of you. Don't waste a shot trying to warn it; put some lead in it.

The rise in attacks is directly related to the anti-hunting crowd, city people who watched *The Lion King* one too many times.

Here is the real danger with cougars. Cougars can become specialist targeting one species. (Knopf)

In Alberta, for example, a lone female cougar was responsible for killing 9 percent of a (bighorn) sheep population, including 26 percent of the lambs, over the course of a few months during winter (Ross et al. 1997). Cougar populations are easily controlled by hunting, and increases in cougar population density have been reversed by liberal hunting regimes (Lambert et al., 2006).

This is very important for you to understand. What happens when a cougar specialist is on children? The only cure for a specialist is hunting and removing them from the population.

Hunting and bounties worked for seventy-six years in California to protect humans from cougar attacks. That is seventy-six years of scientific evidence; it is undisputable. Hunting saves lives. Hunting with dogs teaches the animals to fear dogs, making it safer for our pets.

Chapter 4
Grizzly Bears

He was coming like a freight train, in total chase-mode. —Greg Brush

1845 George Catlin. Attacking the Grizzly bear. New York City
Public Library Digital

The most dangerous month for grizzly bear attacks is September. The second most dangerous month is October.

The scientific name *Ursus arctos horribilis*—brown bear horrible—is a very true statement. Reading about attacks is one thing. Reading the autopsy reports grips your soul. It reminds you of how fragile human life is. I must warn the reader if you have a weak stomach, you may wish to skip reading these actual reports. It tears at your heart and turns your stomach when the full realization hits that we are nothing but a food source or a prey animal to these bears. A grizzly jaw can exert 750 pounds of bite pressure.

The number of attacks is very hard to keep straight. To help the reader, I have composed a list of fatalities and non-fatal attacks. Keep in mind this for the last twenty-seven years.

Grizzly bears have always been dangerous, but they seem to have become much more aggressive since wolf reintroduction. For many decades, grizzly bears south of the Canadian border really had no competition and didn't have to fight for an adequate helping to the available food supply. Bear populations have increased substantially, and so have wolves, so increased competition makes for more movement and more aggressive behaviors. (Read the Lewis and Clark accounts about how aggressive grizzlies were back in their day—impressive!) I have a strong suspicion that for several decades, probably since the '70s at least, NPS/USFWS employees were "secretly" translocating problem bears from heavily visited National Parks up into more remote areas such as the Cabinets in Montana, and/or the Selkirk range on the Idaho/Washington border. When I was younger and still doing a lot of backpacking (the late 80s and early 1990s), I met a female backcountry ranger on a trail up in the Selkirk range. As a former B/C ranger myself, we struck up an amiable conversation. I relayed my encounter with a sub-adult grizzly that I had come face to face with on the trail the day before. She asked me if it had a radio collar… I said no. She wanted as much info as I could give her about the bear and told me, "We have 30 grizzlies with collars up here (in the Selkirk range), so any un-collared bear is something we really want to know about." I started wondering where/when all those bears had been trapped and collared. I knew it wasn't done by any USFS employees; they lack the budget and expertise, but I could find no info on it. Well, bottom line, I've hiked my whole life in grizzly habitats including North BC, most of the length of the Canadian Rockies, Kananaskis country, the Selkirks, Cabinets, Gros Ventres, Tetons, and several traverses of Glacier National Park including one trip when the entire north section of the park, including the Highline Trail, was closed due to "aggressive bear activity." I snuck in by boat from the Canadian side and didn't see another hiker for several days. I've hiked thousands of miles in North America's most magnificent mountain ranges without a sidearm. You might say

I was lucky, or just plain stupid, but I was never threatened by bears (or wolves). Well, I don't get out much anymore, kidney disease and old age have taken a toll, but I would never ever consider going into the backcountry unarmed again.

Steve Busch write-up on expanding the grizzly range.

You can read more of Steve's writing at oldmanoftheski.com.

Human injuries inflicted by bears in Alberta: 1960-98

Stephen Herrero

Between 1960-98, fewer grizzly bears inflicted more than twice as many serious and fatal injuries to people as did black bears.

The total number of injuries and fatalities inflicted by both species of bears combined increased in Alberta each decade since the 1960s.

http://www.panoramio.com/photo/24224272 *Credit to* Jens Cederskjold

Tom Smith, a Professor at BYU, said in a *Sports Afield* article in 2012, *"It would be foolish to drop a rifle to attempt to obtain pepper spray while being charged."* I want you to think about that for a moment. You're hunting rifle in hand, you have four seconds until impact to drop your rifle, unsnap the holster, pull the bear spray out, take the safety off, aim, fire, and hope the wind is not blowing in your face. All in four seconds. Any "so called" experts that recommends something that insane should be fired. Of course, Professor Tom Smith is correct; it would be foolish to drop your rifle.

This is not all the attacks that have happened. This is all I could find. The National Post has thousands of human-wildlife conflicts reported across BC in 2017.

Oct. 6, 2017
Nearly 500 bears have been destroyed after encounters with humans, including 469 black bears and 27 grizzlies, said Mike Badry, wildlife conflict manager with the ministry of environment.

Of that over five hundred bears, how many people were attacked? Seriously makes you wonder how many attacks have never been told to the public.

The following attacks can be found under fatal bear attacks in North America Wikipedia.

Here's a look at recent fatal grizzly bear attacks. There have been thirty-six people from 1992 to present day.

1. June 29, 2016, Brad Treat, 38, of West Glacier, Montana. While mountain bike riding on trail, he surprised a bear and was attacked. East of Glacier National Park.

2. August 7, 2015, Lance Crosby, 48, of Billings, Montana. Another very brutal attack. Lance was attacked and the bear partially consumed his body cache for later meals. The female grizzly was later killed because it was a predatory attack.

3. October 2014, Claudia Huber's grizzly predatory attack. Her husband fired his rifle trying to save her. One bullet deflected off a branch and was the cause of her death.

4. September 17, 2014, Ken Novotny, 53, male near Norman Wells NW Territories. His friend had just shot a moose and was field dressing the moose when the bear came out of nowhere. It struck him so hard he died on the spot.

5. September 7, 2014, Rick Cross, 54, male, Kananaskis Country, Alberta. A sow grizzly attacked because he was in between her cubs. He fired one shot and was found with a knife in each hand. His body was so torn up they identified him by his boots.

6. Sept. 4, 2014, Adam Stewart, 31, of Virgin, Utah. The experts can't decide if a black bear or grizzly killed the man. Both species' DNA were found on the remains in Wyoming's Bridger-Teton National Forest.

7. October 2012, Tomas Puerta, 54, male. People saw an unattended skiff and pulled in to shore. They encountered a sow grizzly bear with two cubs. An Alaskan State Trooper and rescue crew arrived on scene. They found a campsite on the beach seeing evidence of a struggle. They followed the trail and found the body partially eaten and cached.

8. August 24, 2012, Richard White, 49, male, Denali National Park, Alaska. A hiker found a backpack and torn clothing. Reporting to the rangers who investigated, the Alaska State Trooper found a large male grizzly bear sitting on his remains and shot and killed the bear. He had been photographing the bear that killed him.

9. August 2011, John Wallace, 59, of Chassell, Michigan, hiking alone on the Mary Mountain Trail in Yellowstone National Park. This was a full-on predatory attack; the body was partially consumed and cached for later meals. DNA evidence links to the same sow grizzly that killed Brian Matayoshi.

10. July 7, 2011, Brian Matayoshi, 57, of Torrance, California. Later in the book, this attack is covered in detail. Wapiti Lake Trail in Yellowstone National Park.

11. July 28, 2010, Kevin Kammer, 48, of Grand Rapids, Michigan. The Soda Butter night of terror. Kevin is believed to be the third person

attacked that night and the only fatality. Undernourished sow grizzly with three cubs. Most of the upper torso was consumed.

12. June 17, 2010, Erwin Evert, 70, a field botanist from Park Ridge, Illinois. This story is a true tragedy. A research team had left behind a male grizzly who was recovering from the drugs used to stabilize the bear. The bear woke up just as Erwin was walking by. The attack was extremely brutal; death was caused by a crushed skull. Seven miles east of Yellowstone National Park.

13. October 1, 2008, Robert Wagner, 48, male Sundre, Alberta. He was reported missing during a hunting trip. His body was found a little over a half mile from his truck. A sow grizzly was responsible for the attack.

14. November 25, 2007, Don Peters, 51, male Sundre, Alberta. His body was found 660 feet from his truck. He was on a hunting trip. His rifle was found and he managed to fire one shot, but he missed the grizzly. His rifle was used as part of identifying the victim. That means he was severely mauled beyond recognition.

15. April 28, 2006, Jean-Francois Pagé, 28, male, Ross River, Yukon. Believed to be a defensive attack when Jean was prospecting a mining claim and walked by a bear den containing a sow with cubs.

16. Sept 20, 2005, Arthur Louie, 60, male, Bowron River, BC, Canada. He was attacked by a sow grizzly with cubs walking back to camp after his car broke down.

17. June 23, 2005, Rich Huffman, 61, male, Kathy Huffman, 58, female, Arctic National Wildlife Refuge, Alaska. Attacked and killed in their tent. This bear was a full-on predatory attack. Three rafters found the camp two days later. The bear was still at the location and chased the rafters for half a mile as they escaped down the river. A police officer investigating the tragedy shot and killed the bear.

18. June 5, 2005, Isabelle Dube, 35, female, Canmore, Alberta. She was jogging with two friends. After the initial attack, she climbed a tree and her friends ran for help. The grizzly brought her down from the tree and mauled her to death. The bear had been relocated a few days earlier.

19. October 5, 2003, Timothy Treadwell, 46, male, and Amie Huguenard, 37, female, Katmai National Park, Alaska. Audiotape recovered at the scene gave the chilling details of how they died. Treadwell was killed first during the attack. Amie came out of the tent with a frying pan, beating on the bear to stop the attack. It was the wrong move. The bear killed them both.

20. October 30, 2001, Timothy Hilston, 50, male, Blackfoot-Clearwater Wildlife Management Area, Montana. Timothy was field dressing an elk he shot when a sow grizzly with cubs killed him to steal the elk.

21. July 14, 2000, George Tullos, 41, male, Hyder, Alaska. His body was found partially consumed in a predatory attack.

22. November 1, 1999, Ned Rasmussen, 53, male, Uganik Island, Alaska. He disappeared while hunting. His body was found during the search and was determined to have been killed by a grizzly.

23. May 25, 1999, Ken Cates, 53, male, Kenai National Wildlife Refuge, Alaska. Ken was out hiking, carrying a rifle. Several spent rifle casings were found on the scene. He may have shot the bear first, but it is unknown if he was attacked and used the rifle for defense.

24. October 24, 1998, George Evanoff, 65, male, Prince George, BC, Canada. Defensive attack of moose. Died of single bite to the neck.

25. August 22, 1998, Christopher Kress, 40, male, Beaver Mines, Alberta, Canada. Killed while fishing.

26. May 17, 1998, Craig Dahl, 26, male, Glacier National Park, Montana. Attacked by a sow with cubs in what is believed to be a predatory attack.

27. February 8, 1998, Audelio Luis Cortes, 40, male, Kenai, Alaska. Walked by a bear den; killed by a single bite to the head.

28. August 23, 1996, Robert Bell, 33, male, Gates of the Arctic National Park, Alaska. Sow grizzly bear defensive of food believed to be feeding on salmon.

29. July 5, 1996, Christine Courtney, 32, female, Kluane National Park, Yukon. Her husband survived the attack.

30. October 9, 1995, Shane Fumerton, 32, Bill Caspell, 40, Radium Hot springs, BC, Canada. He was field dressing an elk; the grizzly killed both of them to steal the elk.

31. July 1, 1995, Marcie Trent, 77, female, Larry Waldron, 45, male, near Anchorage, Alaska. Grizzly defending moose carcass.

32. October 3, 1992, John Petranyi, 40, Glacier National Park, Montana. Killed by a sow with two cubs.

33. September 15, 1992, Trevor Percy-Lancaster, 40, Jasper National Park, Alberta. The bear attacked the wife first; her husband tried to save her and died.

34. July 10, 1992, Anton Bear, 6, King Cove, Alaska. Bear killed the child and ate him.

Of the fatal attacks, July and October were tied for the most dangerous months. August and September were tied for the second most dangerous months.

Non-Fatal Attacks

1. November 7, 2017, Choteau, Montana, Unnamed 69-year-old. The man was pheasant hunting. His dog was charged by a grizzly sow. The man fired once in the air to scare the bear off. The bear turned and charged the man. He fired twice, hitting the bear in the chest and the face, killing it at ten feet with birdshot. Missoulian News

2. November 6, 2017, Tom Miner, Montana. Joseph Kiedrowski was elk hunting when the grizzly charged, biting his right hand. He pushed the bear off, pulled his bear spray, and blasted the bear in the face. The bear ran off. KRTV News

3. October 31, 2017, Shoshone National Forest, Wyoming. John Sheets, a hunting guide with a female client was gutting an elk. A grizzly bear attacked his client. Armed with only his gutting knife, he charged the bear and stabbed it in the neck. The bear knocked him over and dragged the client down the hill. It chewed on her for a while and came back and chewed on the back of his head and ear. Also, in the fight, the bear had broken his leg. The bear stopped the attack, grabbed one of the hindquarters of the elk, and dragged it over the guide and left the area. They both were able to ride their horses out to another guide camp and called 911. KTVQ News

4. October 27, 2017, Cody, Wyoming. Off-duty game warden Chris Queen elk hunting. He was charged by a grizzly bear sow with three cubs. He shot the bear, killing it. U.S. News

5. October 24, 2017, Hebgen Lake, Montana. The homeowner heard something breaking into his garage where an elk was hanging. He stepped outside to see what was going on. The bear was ten paces from the man on his porch. The bear started approaching the man; he shot her dead with his rifle. Investigators saw bloody footprints within ten feet

of the front door and bloody prints on the living room window. Bozeman Daily Chronicle

6. October 7, 2017, Wyoming. Tev Kelley posted on his Facebook page of his attack story. Hunting elk with his friend, Scott, he was cleaning the elk when a full-grown grizzly charged. Tev shot the bear in self-defense. The bear retreated. They packed up as much meat as they could, hanging the rest of the meat and head high in a tree. Returning the next morning with Wyoming Fish and Game, five heavily armed men. A second grizzly was at the kill site. All five men were yelling, screaming, and firing warning shots, but that barely kept the second bear back. As they retreated with the meat, the bear charged in again. They were able to escape the area.

7. September 30, 2017, Fernie, BC, Jake Blackmore. I was able to interview him on Facebook a month after the attack. He was hunting with his sixteen-year-old son when he heard something behind him. He turned around to look. A massive female grizzly was bearing down on him like a freight train. The bear covered ten yards in one second, knocking him to the ground and grabbing his leg, shaking him like a rag doll. (Jake said he was still having concussion problems a month later.) He was pushing on her head, trying to get her off and yelling at her. She backed off. Suddenly, she grabbed his leg again shaking him more. The bear backed off to chase her cub away. Jake was able to retrieve his rifle. Leaning against a tree, the bear came back roaring to finish him off. "I tried to shoot her in the mouth but only grazed her head." In a blind panic, he over-cycled his gun, unloading his last two rounds. Taking another shot, he heard the gut-wrenching click of an empty chamber. That was enough. The first shot spun her around. She ran off and the battle was over. *"I want to promote the speed and stealth of these powerful animals. Really check out your surroundings in bear country. It's easy to think I will react a certain way but that all goes out the window in the one second you have to react."* CTV News

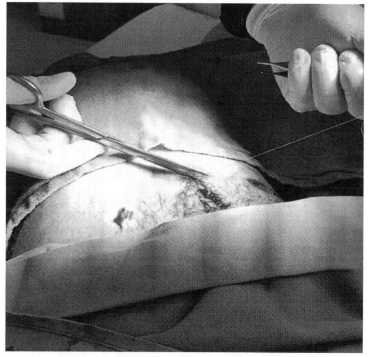

Jake Blackmore getting twenty-eight stitches.

8. Sept. 26, 2017, Teton Wilderness, Wyoming, James Moore, 41 years old. While elk hunting, he heard the brush rustling beside him and the next second the grizzly sow and cubs attacked him. He was able to get free and call his friends to come help him. The bears returned and attacked him again. Moore had severe lacerations on his head, lip, and nose, along with bite marks on his back and rear hip area. He was carrying bear spray and a rifle but said the attack happened so fast he didn't have time to use either. James said these were not cute little cubs but almost full-grown bears. Local News 8 ABC

9. Sep 25, 2017, Hungry Horse Reservoir, Montana. A father in his sixties and adult son in his thirties were hunting in thick brush. A grizzly bear attacked, biting the son on the right arm at the elbow. The father shot the bear three times and it ran off. They drove to the hospital. FWP (Fish Wildlife and Parks) called it a surprise encounter and during their

investigation, found the bear near the attack site. A 250-pound twelve-year-old female bear. It's possible she had a single yearling cub with her; she was not a lactating female. Flathead Beacon

10. Sep. 11, 2017, Dubois, Wyoming. Seth Ziegler, a 39-year-old was bowhunting with his father, sitting on a stump waiting for an elk when he heard something behind him. Turning, he saw a sow grizzly with yearling cubs. Setting his bow down, he retrieved his bear spray and whispered loudly to his father sitting ten yards away, "Grizzly bear, Grizzly bear, grizzly bear." Next thing he saw was all teeth and claws racing at him, knocking him fifteen feet off the stump. The bear spray flew out of his hand when the bear hit him. The bear was on top of him. He used his arms to protect his neck and face. He felt a stinging pain in his back and thought, "Oh my God I'm going to be torn apart now." The bear jumped off him. Opening his eyes, he saw his bear spray laying on the ground within reach. Grabbing the bear spray, he raced to help his father. His father was yelling at the bear with his bow in the air. The bear ran off. *"I can't explain the emotions we had at that point. We never had that feeling of helplessness and fear before. Myself, the helpless feeling of about to be torn apart by a grizzly and there was nothing I could do about it. My dad just experienced the helpless feeling of watching his son possibly being severely mauled or killed in front of him."* As reported County 10 Wisconsin Hunter Survives Grizzly Attack Near Dubois Oct. 11, 2017

11. Sep 11, 2017, Tom Miner Basin, Montana. Unnamed woman attacked by a grizzly bear. The woman played dead, lying on her stomach. The bear bit her legs and back. Two other people used bear spray to drive the bear off her. KULR News

12. Sept. 4, 2017, Southwestern Montana. Tom Sommer was attacked by a grizzly, lashing his head open with a sixteen-inch cut that took ninety stitches to close up. The man said it closed the distance of thirty feet in four seconds. His partner blasted the bear with bear spray, but it didn't stop the attack. Tom reached for his bear spray but couldn't get the safety

off. The bear was chasing him around a tree and he dropped the bear spray. Pulling his pistol, he planned on shooting the bear, but the bear swatted his arm down. His partner blasted the bear spray again at the bear and it ran off. Idaho State Journal

13. August 30, 2017, Sundre, Alberta, Canada. Unnamed man attacked. A wildlife official said it was a non-defensive attack. The man sustained serious but non-life-threatening injuries to his body, head, and face. What? Non-life-threatening injuries but serious injuries? How is that for doublespeak? Man escapes bear attack, is airlifted to hospital in Sundre, Alberta. Global News

14. July 2, 2017, Water Valley, Alberta, Canada. Unnamed man in his fifties was attacked by a grizzly bear while geocaching. He fought the animal off using his walking stick. The man suffered several lacerations to his face and arms. Global News

15. June 30, 2017. Armed 11-year-old boy saves fishing party from charging bear. Kevin Gullufsen was walking in a single line going fishing with two adults in the front. The bear attack was so swift the men in front had no time to take their rifles off their shoulders when the bear plowed through them. Third in line was 11-year-old Elliot Clark carrying a 12-gauge shotgun. He fired his first shot load with birdshot to scare the bear away; it had no effect. The second and third shots were slugs, killing the bear. The bear was so close on the third shot, it left powder burns on the bear's mouth. The bear slid past the young man. A follow-up fourth shot made sure the threat was over.

16. June 26, 2017, Hope, Alaska. Joshua Brekken, 45, Defensive attack from a sow grizzly with a cub. A man was trying to climb a tree and the bear swatted him off the tree. She didn't continue the attack and ran off. Brekken suffered minor injuries. Daily News Miner

17. June 26, 2017, Clunie Lake, Alaska. James Fredrick and Alex Ippoliti were riding bicycles when a bear attacked Fredrick, knocking him off his bike and attacking him. Ippoliti said he was ready after the two fatal black bear attacks and had his bear spray. "

    Alex straight up saved my life," Fredrick said. "I'd be dead right now without Alex." Ippoliti used his shirt "for a tourniquet and asked me to hold it on my neck while he stood there, yelling at the bear," Fredrick said.

    The attack was extremely vicious, grabbing him by the neck. Fredrick received stitches on his eyebrow and nose, lost a portion of his muscle, and sustained major lacerations to his neck. *Alaska Department of Fish and Game spokesman Ken Marsh said the mauling is being investigated as a "defensive attack." "I can't exaggerate how fast this was."* Anchorage Daily News

18. July 24, 2017, Radium Hot Springs, on the BC side. Idaho tourist saves cyclist's life. A young grizzly was chasing the man on a bike. One truck honked its horn and the bear stopped and the Idaho couple was able to put their vehicle in between the grizzly bear and the man on the bike giving him time to escape. Not an attack but a close call. CBC News

19. July 21, 2017, Brown Island on BC. Randal Warnock, 57, heard a snap and saw a grizzly charging out of the brush. In a couple of seconds, it was on him. Attacking his legs, it shredded his pants and grabbed hold of his right knee. He tried to grab his knife but was being shaken so badly he dropped it. With only one choice left, he punched the bear in the nose. The bear dropped him, and backed off a couple of feet. He picked up a log off the beach with plans to beam the bear in the head, but it slipped out of his hand and fell between him and the bear. The bear ran off. CBC News

20. June 17, 2017, Eagle River, Alaska. Three people, including one juvenile, were attacked by a sow grizzly with cubs. The police were called to the

Eagle River campground and safely brought them out of the woods. While they were there, two police officers were charged by the bear. They both fired shotguns and wounded the bear. She left the area. They tracked the bear for three hours and never found her. Editor's note: I could not find the ages or wounds suffered by the three juveniles. Danger City. Craig Medred

21. March 24, 2017, Ryan Arsenault, Vancouver Island in Canada. Tissue and muscle damage to his left arm, a broken right leg, and severe lacerations to his head. Listed as a major attack. He was airlifted to the hospital for emergency surgery. Sounds like a hungry grizzly fresh out of hibernation. CTV

22. October 28, 2016. Ronn Hemstock was walking or jogging with his dog on the airport 's main runway when he was mauled by the brown bear with two cubs accompanying her, said state transportation department spokeswoman Shannon McCarthy. He suffered injuries described as non-life-threatening. "The bear may have attacked the man to protect the cubs, McCarthy said."" The airport has signs warning that trespassing is prohibited but it is not completely fenced in. Notice the official statement. Now here is the truth. I was able to talk to Ronn on Facebook and he filled me in on the truth.

First off, the official report leaves you with the impression that Ron was walking or jogging at the airport and might have been trespassing. It was a sow grizzly with two cubs. Let's see what Ronn had to say. Craig Medred dot news wrote a great article telling the truth about the attack.

Let's deal with the trespassing nonsense. Ronn is an avid pilot and would walk the runway, checking the lights and picking up trash. It was early morning, still pitch-black outside. Ronn never reported seeing or hearing cubs. His dog's hackles rose up. Looking behind him, he could see the bear charging in against the lights that brightened a small part of the airport. In a blind panic, he turned and fled. The bear covered twenty yards in two leaps and was on him.

Ronn in his own words: "In a nutshell, I was walking my dog for his morning outing along one of the runways of our airport and a grizzly came out of the grassy area next to the taxiway and mauled me. The attack took about a minute or so and I believe (I think it was a male bear) he stopped because he thought he had killed me. After the attack ended, he cached me and moved off."

The bear tried to flip him over and "I felt at that point the bear was going to kill me. I thought he was going to eat me. In my mind's eye, I saw my guts being eaten."

Sticking his hand in the bear's face, the bear chomped down, almost ripping his thumb off. But it distracted the bear long enough. He flipped back over to protect his stomach. He played dead and the bear lost interest.

Non-life-threatening injuries? Sounds like it is no big deal. A couple of scratches, right? The pictures tell a different story.

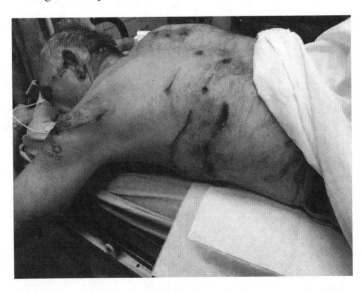

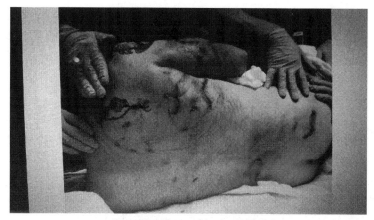

Ronn Hemstock's wounds.

I asked Ronn why the official report said a sow with two cubs. In his words: "I think they went with sow because it is a tourist town and a story that a protective mom (grizzly) attacked is an easier sell to the visitors than a rogue male bear."

23. October 17, 2016, Whitefish, Montana. A father and daughter were walking their two dogs. Thirty-five yards off the road, a sow grizzly with two cubs was feeding on a bear carcass. The bear ran past the daughter and attacked the man. He received some injuries and was able to drive her off using bear spray. KPAX News

24. October 2, 2016, Dubois, Wyoming, a 59-year-old male was attacked by a sow with two cubs while trying to retrieve an elk. He landed in the hospital with severe injuries sustained during the attack. I believe Lee Brooke is the person of this attack. You can read the story of his recovery on Fox 31: Colorado doctors save hunter whose face was ripped off by a grizzly bear. November 16, 2017, by Michael Konopasek

Brooke can no longer control tears. A good portion of his face is gone. He depends on a tracheal tube to tell his story.

25. October 2, 2016, Chichagof Island, Alaska. 30-year-old Josh Dybdahl was out hunting with a friend when the sow grizzly with cubs attacked Josh. His friend was able to shoot and kill the bear, ending the attack. KTUU News

26. October 1, 2016, 50-year-old Todd Orr, Montana. Bear spray failed. He was attacked twice. "Life sucks in bear country"; Man details grizzly attack on Facebook. CBS News

27. Sep 27, 2016, Bozeman, Montana. The unnamed man was attacked by a grizzly while hunting. Bear spray failed. Believed to be a male grizzly. He suffered minor injuries. Not many details on this one. KTVM News

28. Sep 25, 2016, Tom Miner Basin, Montana. Neil Rico was attacked by a bear and sustained bite injuries. His hunting partner said it was a sow with cubs. He was treated and released for bite wounds. Chehalis man who survived grizzly bear attack: 'You could hear every crunch' KOMO News

29. Sep 22, 2016, Chaik Bay, Alaska. Big-game guide LaVern Beier and client Douglas Adkins were returning to their boat after a long day of hunting. In the darkness, they saw a bear charging in their headlamp lights. The bear charged right in, grabbing Douglas Adkins. Suddenly the bear stopped the attack and ran off. They returned to the boat and called the Coast Guard who sent a helicopter to airlift the man to the hospital. Guide in mauling near Angoon was storied Fish & Game researcher LaVern Beier. Alaska Public Media

30. September 15, 2016, Reggie Riebe, Wyoming. He was attacked calling elk. He suffered injuries to his hands, arms, buttocks, and scalp and was reported in great pain. "Elk call triggered a bear attack." Jackson Hole News and Guide

31. Aug 29, 2016, Glacier National Park, Montana. A part-time employee out picking huckleberries was attacked and injured by what is believed to be a defensive grizzly bear. Weekend bear attack injures Glacier Park employee. Missoulian

32. August 2016, Baranof Island, Alaska. Forest service employees had to kill a charging brown bear to save themselves. "Forest Service workers kill charging brownbear near Sitka." Anchorage Daily News September 14, 2016.

33. August 18, 2016, Chichagof Island, Alaska. Anna "Marika" Powers, a 41-year-old guide. She was leading a group of twenty-two hikers. She was carrying bear spray but didn't have time to use it. Behind the hikers was a fellow guide, 26-year-old Michael Justa. Pushing his way through the hikers, he was able to use his bear spray and drive the bear off. Anna was emergency airlifted off the island by the US Coast Guard helicopter. AK bear-attack cluster. Craig Medred

34. August 7, 2016, Baranof Island, Alaska. Don Kluting had to shoot a charging sow grizzly bear to save himself and hiking companion, Denise Turley. While hiking, they ran into a sow grizzly with cubs. The cubs ran off. The sow charged. Don was carrying a .44 magnum and fired a warning shot in front of the bear but she charged on. He luckily was able to fire once more, hitting the bear in the head saving their lives. AK bear-attack cluster. Craig Medred

35. Sep 30, 2015, Glacier National Park, Montana. A 65-year-old man was attacked by a grizzly sow while hiking. The bear bit his leg and the man used bear spray to drive her off. He drove himself to the hospital. Bear injures hiker in Glacier National Park. Billings Gazette

36. August 5, 2015, Gabrielle Markel, Upper Skilak Lake, Alaska. Jogging on a trail with her friend, Kaitlyn Haley, they surprised a grizzly on the trail. Gabrielle used pepper spray, but the bear still attacked. Kaitlyn ran

to the lodge to get help. She returned with several other people and found Gabrielle walking to the lodge. She was airlifted to the hospital. No list of injuries. Alaskan Woman Mauled by Bear While Jogging With Co-Worker. NBC News

37. July 5, 2015, Brian Braconnier and Keith Farkas. The bear knocked Brian down the hill. Keith had a 12-gauge shotgun but it was unloaded and strapped to his pack. Brian said the bear hit him three times and then grabbed his arm and tossed him like a rag doll. He pulled his bear spray and used it on the bear a few feet away. She ran over him. The bear headed up the hill to Keith who was trying to get the strap off the shotgun. Pulling the gun free, he loaded and fired one shot. The bear was on him, knocking him downhill. He yelled at the bear and as quick as it started, she ran off. The bear was not hit. They walked out and survived to tell the story. Two men lucky to be alive after grizzly attack in BC. Cottage Life

38. Not an attack just a home invader. August 9, 2015, Kimberley, BC. Grizzly broke into a house. The wife heard the dog bark. She walked into her kitchen to find a grizzly bear eating the pet food. She ran back to the bedroom, waking her husband at 4:30 in the morning. There was a bear in the kitchen. The man loaded his rifle and entered the kitchen. The bear took one step toward the man and he fired. The bear took another step and he fired again, killing the bear on the spot. Man shoots grizzly bear that broke into his Kimberley home. Global News

39. Oct 12, 2014, 56-year-old man, Wilf Lloyd, Fernie, BC. He was mauled by a bear and his hunting partner shot at the bear, hitting the man with one bullet. They were elk hunting at the time of the attack. Wilf feared for his life as the bear mauled him. He yelled to his hunting partner to shoot the bear. He emptied his rifle into the bear and one bullet hit Wilf in the thigh. The bear ran off and a few seconds later came charging back. His partner's gun was empty. He found Wilf's rifle and shot the bear one

last time, killing it. Large boar grizzly. Man Attacked by Bear Then Shot by Friend. NBC News

40. The CBC report of Dec 24, 2015, wrote about the tragic event that happened in October 2014. "What transpired at that property on that day was an absolute, catastrophic collision of events," said Kirsten Macdonald, Yukon 's chief coroner.

The bear came up to the cabin, pressed on the window that gave way and the bear fell into the house. It chased Claudia and her dog outside. She ran into her parked SUV. The bear jumped on the vehicle several times.

Her husband was in another vehicle honking the horn at the bear. The bear ran off. It's believed she made a break for her husband's vehicle. The bear attacked her, knocking her down and dragging her off in the brush. Matthias Liniger, her husband, ran into the cabin to retrieve his hunting rifle. He fired at the bear until the rifle was empty. He returned to the cabin for more ammunition. Reloading the rifle, he began firing at the bear again. Her injuries from the bear were so horrific they had no clue that she had died from a gunshot wound until the autopsy.

One must keep in mind that bullets travel through the animal and can hit the person. In this case, they believed the bullet deflected off a branch, hitting the woman instead of the bear. When you are firing at a moving target trying to kill an animal, you must be aware of where the bullet might end up. I saw a video of two men that were attacked by grizzlies. Both carried hunting rifles but were afraid to shoot for fear of hitting the other person. Yes, the bear attacked them both. The whole time I was watching I was like, shoot her in the rear, in the hips, break her down. That is an old saying coming from the African hunters that hunted dangerous mankillers. It takes a long time to kill an animal. A heart shot bear might live for ten minutes before he finally dies. But if you spine him, break a shoulder, or shatter a hip, you can get away to a safe distance and finish him off. If the husband would have known this, it might have saved his wife's life.

41. July 12, 2013, Patty Miller, 71 Babb, Montana. On a morning walk with her dogs, she hiked around a lake when she was attacked by a sow grizzly with cubs. *I survived a fractured nose, several deep lacerations on the back of my neck, three bites to my head, and long, deep cuts through my torso. I lay in the hospital for three weeks, half in intensive care, the other half in rehab. The bones in my eyes required more than 24 tiny nails to piece them back together. I only regained sight in one eye; the other is permanently shut—the nerves in my right eyelid are crushed and non-responsive, meaning it will not open on its own.* Backpacker Magazine Aug 14, 2015

42. Sept 22, 2012, 65-year-old male, Houston River, BC. He was attacked by a sow grizzly while fishing. He had severe facial and head injuries, multiple broken bones, and puncture wounds. The worst part is his lower jaw was missing. The man survived the attack and crawled three hundred yards to a road where a woman found him and called emergency services. Nasty Bear Attack on Morice River in British Columbia. Angler Tonic October 1, 2012

43. July 22, 2012, Bob Eder, 50, Eagle River Road, Alaska. The man was walking on a trail and came on a sow grizzly with three large cubs. The sow attacked him; he played dead and she left. He walked out as far as he could. He called 911 and directed the police to find him on the phone. He suffered a long gash along one leg. While waiting for help, he used his shirt as a tourniquet to stop the bleeding. Anchorage Daily News

44. July 14, 2012, Fairbanks, Alaska. A 43-year-old professor hiking with her two nieces was attacked by a grizzly bear. She pepper-sprayed the bear but it kept coming. She was backing up and fell, dropping the pepper spray. She broke her walking stick over its head. The bear backed off but during the mile-long hike out of the area, the bear bluff charged several

more times. Professor, 2 Wash. girls terrorized by grizzly bear in Alaska. KOMO News

45. June 15, 2012, Eagle River campground, Alaska. Tammy Anthony and her husband, Mike, were taking an evening walk on the trail. They saw a sow grizzly with cubs. The sow mock charged. They both tried to run. Tammy was tangled in the brush and fell. Her husband came back, yelling at the bear and it ran off. She suffered a broken bone in her foot and cuts and bruises. Anchorage Daily News

46. July 23, 2011, Talkeetna Mountains, Alaska. *Readers Digest* did a great write up on this attack titled, "The story of seven boys and one grizzly bear." Joshua Berg, 17, was the first to be attacked by a seven-foot-tall 500-pound grizzly. His friends scattered, scared out of their minds. Sam Gottsegen was the next victim of the grizzly's wrath. Sixteen-year-old Noah Allaire and 18-year-old Victor Martin also were hospitalized with injuries. Sam was in serious trouble; one of the grizzly's claws had punctured a lung. Noah Allaire performed first aid, tearing apart a plastic bag to cover the wound, forming an airtight seal. Using an elastic bandage, he wrapped it around his torso. Joshua was in the worst shape; his head was so violently torn up, he was barely recognizable. His legs were numb and his skull was fractured.

47. May 31, 2010, Denali National Park, Alaska. Two unnamed backpackers, one man and one woman. The woman was charged. The man fired nine shots from his .45 caliber pistol. The bear stopped and walked off into the brush. The two reported the attack to the rangers. They found the bear dead one hundred feet from the shooting site. Here is some great doublespeak from The Associated Press. "*It 's legal to carry firearms in that area of the park but illegal to discharge them.*" Wrong; it's perfectly legal to discharge a firearm in defense of your or another person's life. Hiker shoots, kills grizzly bear with handgun in Alaska 's Denali National Park. NY Daily News

48. October 18, 2009, East Kootenay, BC, Canada. Two hunters were attacked in their tent. Ken Scown, 36, and Jeff Herbert awakened to a huge grizzly tearing through the tent. It attacked Ken. He screamed for his friend to shoot the bear. He didn't chamber the round correctly and only heard a click when he pulled the trigger. The bear attacked Jeff too but all the screaming from the two men drove it off. They both got up, built up the fire, packed up what they could, and hiked five kilometers to their truck. They could see in the snow the tracks of two bears that were hunting them straight to the camp. Bear attacks 2 sleeping B.C. men. CBC News

49. Sep 15th, 2009, Gros Ventre Wilderness, Wyoming. Marcello Tejeda, a 46-year-old sheepherder, received a seven-inch gash on top of his head, two punctures to the left side of his chest, three claw wounds to the right side of his abdomen, and a puncture wound to his right wrist. A sow grizzly with one cub was killing sheep. He sent in his dog thinking it was a black bear. The bear killed the dog; he sent in his second dog and the bear attacked it. Running to aid the dog, he was attacked. Jorge Mesa working with Tejeda pepper sprayed the bear twice to drive it off his friend. Grizzly mauls sheepherder, kills dogs and sheep. Wyoming Livestock Roundup

50. Jul 25, 2009, Clark, Wyoming. Jerry Ruth, a retired police officer, was out walking in the sagebrush with his friend looking for elk antler sheds. In a flash, a 275-pound sow grizzly attacked. She grabbed him by the jaw, crushing the jaw, fracturing his rib, puncturing his lung, and leaving deep bite wounds in his calf and scratches. She ran back to her cubs. Jerry pulled his .41 Magnum revolver. The sow turned around facing him ready to charge again. He fired three rounds killing the bear. Retired police officer recounts bear mauling. Billings Gazette

51. Aug. 8, 2008, Clivia Feliz, 51, same trail Davis was attacked, Alaska. Two cubs were spotted. She ran off into the brush out of sight hoping to lose them. The one cub blew right past her, but the sow smelled her. It stared

at her and lunged for her head. Reflexively she brought her arm up and the bear clamped down. The bear held her for a few seconds, pushing her. She bit down, this time breaking four ribs partially collapsing one lung. The bear ran off, leaving her broken and bloodied. She walked back to the road and flagged down a vehicle for help. Mauling victim recounts attack on Anchorage trail. Juneau Empire Aug 11, 2008

52. August 6, 2008, Devon Rees, 18, Eagle River, Alaska. Walking home late at night, the bear attacked and chewed on both inner thighs. His left eye was puffed out from a swat of the massive paw. Eagle River teen fights bear to a draw. Juneau Empire

53. July 23, 2008, Abi Sisk, 21, Kenai Princess Wilderness Lodge, Alaska. She was walking outside at 11 p.m. when a bear charged her. It grabbed her by the head. Another guest saw it and ran yelling at the bear. The bear ran off. The young lady was partially scalped and with a broken jaw. Alaska tourist attacked by grizzly bear near lodge, The Associated Press

54. June 29, 2008, Petra Davis, 15, Eagle River, Alaska. During a bike marathon, he was attacked in what is believed to be a defensive attack. The massive powerful jaws chewed through her bike helmet, crushed her trachea, and cut into her shoulder, torso, buttocks, and thigh. Teen who survived bear attack: "Mostly it was scared." TODAY News

55. September 2006, Montague Island, BC, Canada. John and Shanna (no last name given) were deer hunting when they were charged by a grizzly. Shanna used bear spray and the sow ran right through it. At eight feet John fired a single round from his 30-06, hitting the bear and stopping the attack. https://www.youtube.com/watch?v=4Dry7aDm6ws

56. October 10, 2005, Skilak Lake Loop Road, Alaska. Colleen Sinnott, 50, and her husband, John Poljacik, 56, were out walking their two seven-month-old Newfoundland puppies. The wife was in the lead when the bear came from behind. The husband fumbled trying to get the bear

spray out as the bear held his wife by the head and was shaking her. The bear next leaped at John, knocking him down. That was it; the bear ran off. Collen's injuries included scalp lacerations, broken ribs, and a shoulder injury. One dog was missing. Woman in hospital after bear attack. KTUU News.

57. September 5, 2005, Judy Oliver, Chichagof Island, Alaska. Judy was out berry picking with husband, Carl Oliver. He heard the dog running through the woods and saw the bear attacking his wife and the dog attacking the bear. He was carrying a rifle and shot three times, driving the bear off. No sign of blood and the searchers could not find the bear. Carl carried his wife to the car and rushed her to the hospital. Anchorage Daily News

58. August 25, 2005, Johan Otter and daughter Jenna Otter, Glacier National Park, Montana. A 400-pound grizzly sow with two cubs. One of the most vicious attacks on record. It took nine operations and months to recover for Johan. TV show re-creates 2005 mauling in Glacier. March 12, 2015, Daily Inter Lake

59. April 20, 2005, Scott Mac-Innes, Southcentral Alaska. The unluckiest man in Alaska was attacked by a grizzly bear in his sub-division as he was jogging. The bear inflicted injuries to his abdomen, neck, and face. Scott had already been mauled by a grizzly in 1967. His friend Mike Moerlein was credited with saving his life. He saw the bear shaking Scott like a rag doll. Mike shot the grizzly with his slingshot. The bear dropped Scott and charged Mike, who next picked up a walking stick and hit the bear in the head. That drove the bear off. Anchorage Daily News

60. September 25, 2004, Gary Boyd, Fort Richardson, Alaska. An eight-and-a-half-foot boar estimated at 750 pounds charged Gary, who was walking his dog along the trail. Gary shot and killed the bear before it made contact. Not much information on this one. I would like to know the gun he used and how many shots. Anchorage Dailey News

61. August 22, 2004, Jim Johnson, 52, Fairbanks, Alaska. He was hunting and packing up camp when a sow grizzly with cubs came into view. He tried to get his rifle, but it was too late. The bear mauled him first. Jim suffered a punctured lung, a puncture wound on his neck, and a shattered leg. The attack was over as fast as it started. Jim called 911 and a rescue helicopter flew him to the hospital. Anchorage Dailey News

62. July 13, 2003, Daniel Bigley, Russian River, Alaska. He was walking along the river coming back from fishing. The bear came racing down the trail with no warning and attacked him. Tucking his arms, he used his hands to protect his neck. The bear flipped him over and bit his face. His face was so torn up it was unrecognizable. You can read his incredible story dealing with the physical and emotional devastation and how he recovered in his book, *Beyond the Bear*. Lyons Press; Reprint edition (January 7, 2016)

63. May 14, 2003, Cody Williams, 17, Kenai Peninsula, Alaska. He was hunting when he was attacked by a sow grizzly with two-year-old cubs. One cub charged; he shot and killed it. He started backing away and saw a tall cottonwood tree. He ran towards it but the sow was hot on his trail. As he tried to climb the tree, the bear tore him down. His friend was hunting nearby and shot a single round over the bear's head with his .44 magnum. The bear dropped. Cody yelled, "Kill the bear." His friend emptied the gun at the bear who ran off. But searchers later claimed there was no blood and don't believe the sow was hit. He had a broken hand, several puncture wounds, and claw marks. Teen bear-ly escapes attack. Clarion Peninsula

64. August 21, 2002, Matt Pennington, Russian River, Alaska. He was fishing when he saw a bear pop his head over a bluff. Next thing he knew, the bear was charging full bore at him. Tossing his fishing pole down, he struggled to get his shotgun off his back. He wasn't sure if he had put a round in the chamber. So, when the bear was at three feet, he threw it at the bear's head and dove into the water. His fishing buddies were

brothers Garen and Kalen Brenner. The bear next charged Garen who started shooting at the bear with his handgun. He was carrying a 9mm with full metal jackets. He hit the bear in the front shoulder, breaking it, and the bear went down. Now his brother joined in and they both shot a total of seven rounds, putting the last three in the bear's head. Meanwhile, Matt came up and saw a second bear and yelled, "Shoot! Shoot!" The second bear ran off. Fish and game estimated the weight of the bear as a 450-pound sow grizzly. Biologists wondered if it was the same bear that attacked Justin Dunagan and his mother, Kathy, only eleven hours earlier. Hairy encounter cures trio of fishing bug FULL-BORE FURY: Surprise turns to shock as grizzly charges men on Kenai River. Anchorage Daily News

65. August 20, 2002, Justin Dunagan and his mother, Kathy. Resurrection Pass Trail, Alaska. A sow grizzly with a single large cub. Hiking on a trail with bells on their backs, they rounded a corner on the trail and there, six feet away, was a grizzly sow and cub. The cub ran off. The sow attacked, biting Justin on the arm. Next, it raked a claw across Kathy 's face. Justin kicked the bear four times and it backed off then charged again. Using his camera tripod, he started beating the bear. The bear backed off and wandered off. Anchorage Daily News

66. Sept 4, 2001, Alaska. Johnny McCoy and Cary Corle were moose hunting. The bear first attacked Cary, but his daypack saved him. The bear next attacked Johnny, who stuck his gun in the grizzly's mouth and pulled the trigger and heard the dreaded click, misfire. The bear knocked the gun to the side and viciously attacked. Johnny was severely hurt. His list of injuries is long: bites to his head, both arms torn, hands chewed up, nearly severed right ear, a left eye dislodged from its socket, a rip to his forehead, open enough to show his skull, two compound fractures of his right arm, and a broken left wrist. Anchorage Daily News

67. July 25, 2000, Admiralty Island, Alaska. Steve Byers, 40, was packing up his camping gear. He was heading to his kayak when he spotted the

grizzly bear. In a panic, he ran for his kayak and the bear hit him on the face and took a bite out of his right hip. The bear left. He called for help on the radio. Angoon 's Whaler's Cove Sportfishing Lodge's mechanic heard the call for help and took a boat to his aid. Later, the US Coast Guard airlifted Steve to the hospital. Anchorage Daily News

68. November 1, 1999, Gene Moe, Raspberry Island, Alaska. He was deer hunting on the island and successfully dropped a buck. He had just finished cleaning it, cutting the meat up, and placing it on plastic. In his hands was the liver when he heard a roar. His only choice for a weapon in the few seconds before the attack was his Buck knife. Hitting the sow grizzly in the head, the knife slid off. The bear took a bite out of his arm, removing a large chunk of flesh. *Outdoor Life* did a great writeup on this story. He stabbed the bear's neck four times. Next, he tried closer to the jaw, jamming the knife in. Next, he hit under the jaw and hit something good; blood poured out over both of them. She retreated but came back. Gene now punched her as hard as he could in the head. The bear straightened her head up and fell down nose first into the moss. To be safe he pumped two rounds into the bear to make sure it was over. Last Stand Armed with only a knife, a desperate hunter takes on a grizzly. *Outdoor Life* September 18, 2007

69. October 28, 1997, Eagle River 's Albert Loop Trail, Alaska. Paul Milnar and Al Cannamore were hiking on the trail with their golden retriever. The bear came charging down the trail. The dog jumped in to meet the bear. The two men ran. Milnar ran about fifteen feet then turned to see the bear lunging at him, knocking him down like a linebacker. He curled into the fetal position. He received four puncture wounds on his shoulder and the bear left. The dog survived with scrapes. Anchorage Daily News

70. Joe Huston, Tikchik Narrows Lodge, Alaska, July 2, 1997. He was jogging along the airstrip when the bear attacked, biting him, dislocating Huston 's shoulder, and tearing a hole in his abdominal cavity. He curled

up in a ball and the bear stopped the attack running off. Anchorage Daily News

71. May 17, 1995, Dan Boccia, 26, Eagle River Valley, Alaska. Walking on a trail, he spotted a bear. He played dead and the bear mauled him. He was bitten, scratched, and bruised on his back and legs. The bear was defending a moose carcass it was feeding on. Anchorage Daily News

72. July 30, 1994, seventy miles southeast of Cordova, Alaska. Eleonora Florance, 43. She was dragged from her tent by a three-year-old female grizzly, screaming for help. One of her co-workers shot and killed the bear. No list of injuries. Anchorage Daily News

73. May 19, 1994, 23-year-old Carrie Ward (woman), Kenai National Wildlife Refuge, Alaska. She was jogging near a campground when attacked by a grizzly bear who broke her shoulder bone and clawed her face. Anchorage Daily News

Editor's note: (Carrie Ward [man] was attacked by a black bear in Colorado on July 14, 2017.)

There were many more attacks. Alaska Fish and Game claims five to seven attacks each year. I was unable to find the stories, which is why some years have none.

Consider that in 1967, two different grizzly bears killed two women in Glacier National Park and made national headlines. Human protection and safety were widely talked about. Today, fifty years later, we are told bear spray is the answer. Later in the book, we cover the results of our findings on this topic.

When are we going to make human safety the number one priority? Historically, there were **around 50,000** grizzly bears in North America. Today we have 30,000 in Alaska, 25,000 in British Columbia, Alberta, Yukon, Northwest Territories, and 1,800 in the lower 48. We have 56,800 grizzly bears in North America. This is 6,800 more bears today than the supposed downfall of the grizzly bear. Why are we protecting them when clearly, they are overpopulated?

You know what a bear calls a human in a goose down sleeping bag? A S'more.

When I tell this joke around a campfire, I frequently get nervous laughter. Maybe it's our way as humans of dealing with tragic encounters with bears. After reviewing hundreds of bear attack stories and reading over and over again how "rare" the attacks are, one must ask the simple question: When do rare bear attacks become considered frequent attacks? The animal welfare people always look for the excuse to blame the victim.

The fresh mountain air, the tall green trees of Montana are a sight to behold. Is having a gross overpopulation of grizzly bears making it somehow more special? Allowing bears to kill and maim people is the new green? You can see a pattern from the 1990s until today in the increased HUMAN attacks.

Alaska Fish and Game Overview of Relationships Between Bears, Wolves, and Moose in Alaska

In the boreal forest of northern Canada and Interior Alaska, where bears (either black bears, grizzly bears, or both) and wolves are lightly harvested and are major predators on moose, moose densities typically remain well below levels that their habitat can support. Under these circumstances, moose density fluctuates between about 0.1 and 1.0 moose/mi² over large areas; most commonly densities are 0.4 to 0.6 moose/mi². Biologists refer to this situation as the Low-Density Dynamic Equilibrium or LDDE because moose density fluctuates yet remains low. This occurs primarily because, together, bears and wolves are efficient predators on moose calves, and kill most of the calves born each year. The highest densities reached in these systems (about 1 moose/mi²) tend to occur in very large burns where habitat is excellent and moose apparently are more successful at avoiding predators. Grizzly bears' predation on moose calves from birth to about 2 months old have shown they can seriously deplete the moose population. Some bears have specialized on moose killing both calves and adults. If a grizzly is not common in the area black bears will become the number 1 killer of moose calves, killing about 40% of the calves born each year. Studies have shown most of the predation is from male black bears.

Hunters harvest over 1,000 grizzly bears per year in Alaska from an estimated population of 32,000 bears (Miller 1993). Miller (1990a) estimated the maximum sustainable harvest of Alaskan grizzly bears at 5.7% based on a model. It's fair to say that Alaska could go to 5% or 1,600 bears a year. The BC government relies on results of a modeling exercise performed by Harris (1986b) that estimated maximum sustainable harvest mortality at 6%. This model used reproductive and mortality rates believed typical of "southern interior" grizzly bear populations and included density-dependent effects resulting from the increased survival of young in response to the removal of males. The BC government currently estimates that there are about 14,000 grizzlies occupying a land area of 744,000 km2 (Hamilton and Austin 2001).

According to the National Park Service, "*The estimated Greater Yellowstone Ecosystem grizzly bear population increased from 136 in 1975 to an estimated 717 in 2015, and the bears have gradually expanded their occupied habitat by more than 50%.*"

Now you need to understand what the "Greater Yellowstone Ecosystem" means. A 1994 study listed the size as 76,890 square kilometers (19,000,000 acres). Wait, Yellowstone Park is only 2,219,789 acres. Where did the extra 16,780,211 come from? Scientists are claiming millions of acres, some privately owned, as all part of the Yellowstone ecosystem. The environmentalists love it because it confuses the issue of wildlife management.

In Don Zaidle's book, *American Man-Killers*, he explains maybe vegetarians might be prone to attacks because the bears or other predators recognized the smell as prey species. Like a cow is not a normal animal to be eaten by predators but yet they are targeted. His theory is large predators smell the vegetarian as a prey species.

This fits into what an old timer told me—that if you kill and eat predators, they can smell that on you, causing them to fear you. It would be interesting to study if any of the predator attack victims had ever eaten bear before being attacked. It could be a new trend for the right businessman. Eat your grizzly jerky before hiking; this might save you from being attacked.

Hospital and medical centers should be made aware of the infection problems caused by bear attacks.

Bacteriology of a Bear Bite Wound to a Human: Case Report Dennis Kunimoto.

It has been reported that the risk of infection following bear bite is "considerable," with 4 out of 9 (44%) survivors developing a clinical infection. Consequently, it seems prudent to administer broad-spectrum antimicrobial agents that also possess anaerobic coverage.

Chapter 5
Grizzly Bears: Five Fatal Case Studies

In those adrenaline-charged seconds, I was experiencing one of man's most ancient fears—the prospect of being overpowered and eaten alive. —Guy Grieve

Before going into these studies, let's keep in mind a few points. My theory is wild animals don't know how to attack these upright bipedal animals called humans. I believe they go through three stages.

1. Prey testing. This could be anything from coming into a campground and tearing into a tent to maybe scratching the person but leaving when the person fights back. Testing the water so to speak.

2. Prey tasting. This is when the animal is a little surer and presses the attack, taking a bite out of the victim. Still in the unsure stage, it may kill the victim or be driven off.

3. Prey eating. The final stage when the animal is not only committed to the attack but actually eating the person and caching the body for later meals.

Grizzlies are the Hercules of the bears, a powerful muscled animal that can roll a three hundred pound boulder over to catch a marmot. Think of the strength these animals have.

Brian and Marilyn Matayoshi grizzly bear attack Yellowstone National Park July 6, 2011

Reading the National Park Service report leaves you with one impression, "Professional." The park service employee on this case should be proud of their service. He was on the scene of the attack within minutes. The attack occurred at 10:50 a.m. The first park ranger found the wife quickly and the husband's body by 11:30. Considering how vast Yellowstone park is, having to drive to the trailhead and hike into the location to be on scene within forty minutes is remarkable.

Brian and Marilyn were on their fourth trip to Yellowstone driving in from California. A beautiful day by all accounts; at noon, the temperature was 75 degrees F. Brian and Marilyn were hiking on Ribbon Lake Trail and ran into a man photographing a sow grizzly with two small cubs. The man loaned them his binoculars to see the bears better, which were approximately 450 yards away. Brian took pictures of the bears between 10:12 to 10:15. They hiked about a half mile farther but the mosquitos were bad and they decided to head back at 10:45.

Within four minutes, Brian saw the bear sow with her head down in a meadow. The distance was one hundred yards. He told his wife about the bear. Turning around, they headed for the cover of trees approximately twenty yards behind them, nervously looking back at the bear over their shoulder. At some point, they noticed the bear's head was up staring at them. The bear started toward them and rapidly changed to full bore charge.

Now in full panic mode, they both ran for their lives screaming for help. Looking back over their shoulder Marilyn noticed the cubs behind the sow racing toward them. They ran 173 yards when the bear caught up to them. The bear smashed into Brian knocking him to the ground. Marilyn took cover under some down trees. She heard Brian screaming for help and the bears growling. Suddenly all was quiet. She looked up to see the bear standing over her husband's body and looking directly at her.

She immediately ducked down covering her head with her hands and arms. The sow came over to her and lifted her up by grabbing her daypack and dropping her. She never heard the bear leave.

After a brief time, she looked up and saw the bears were gone. She tried to call 911 on her cell phone but this area of the park was a dead zone. According to her cell phone log, at 11:09 she tried twenty-one times to reach 911.

Other park visitors heard the scream for help and the bears growling. They reported to 911 that a man and woman were screaming for help and they could hear bears growling.

Because of her state of shock of the attack and trying to save her husband, we do not know when she tried to save his life. She tied a jacket as a tourniquet to try to stop the bleeding on his inner thigh. She heard her husband exhale one last time and then silence. She also covered him with two jackets. She was afraid the bears would return but she stayed with her husband, screaming for help.

Other park visitors called 911 again and told the dispatch that now they only heard a woman yelling for help.

She started walking and was at the meadow edge when the rangers found her. One can only try to imagine the shock this poor woman had gone through. From enjoying a vacation to sheer horror in minutes. Listening to your husband breathe one last time, feeling helpless, and alone.

Now this is stranger than fiction. Ranger Derene and Ranger Patti Murphree were heading to the attack location at 11:21, bringing a long gun and medical supplies; they were charged by a large bull bison. Pepper spray was used when the bison was at ten feet. The bison turned ninety degrees and ran off out of sight.

Ranger Patti Murphree was assigned as family liaison. Again, remarkable timing to have a family liaison on the scene so quickly. She was so dedicated. She stayed with Marilyn who refused to leave Brian's side. She accompanied Marilyn in the helicopter flight to Canyons Corral. From there they took a vehicle to Jackson Hole. The communication center arranged for a stay at Antler Inn.

Ranger Patti Murphree stayed with Marilynn until 10:00 p.m. when her family arrived. The park service, going above and beyond, drove a Matayoshi vehicle to the hotel and returned the keys to Marilyn. Every one of these rangers involved have proven what great people they are. Down to earth folks that really care with a dedication to public service.

How did Brian die so fast? His list of injuries did not seem that bad. One wound on the head was visible, an avulsion midline on top of the forehead to the hairline, approximately 6-7 cm long. Chest and abdomen had scratch marks and superficial puncture marks. He had approximately 8 cm long by 1.5 cm wide avulsion on right triceps. Superficial puncture marks on right buttock. The right leg had three visible puncture wounds on the inner thigh. The avulsion closest to the groin was 5 cm long and 5 mm wide. The wound closest to his knee was right over the femoral artery 6.5 cm long and 2.5 cm wide. There were multiple superficial scratches and puncture wounds on the inner thigh. Possible internal bleeding from the liver or spleen caused by blunt force trauma of being hit by the bear. Cause of death was penetrating and blunt force trauma.

This is where I have a problem with the park service. The higher-ups decided that the attack was triggered by the two people running away from the bear. If that was true, why did the bear charge first before they ran? That is an important detail. My opinion is the bear, for whatever reason, decided to prey test and prey taste the victim. We can only speculate at this point. We also don't know if this bear had prey tested humans earlier. It's not like everything is reported to the park service. This bear may have tested humans before and found no negative reaction, emboldening the bear to move to step two, prey tasting.

After the phenomenal service to the public in this case, the ball was dropped and the bear who is a known man-killer was allowed to live.

Final Stage: Prey EATING
August 25, 2011, 59-year-old John Wallace, fatal attack.
John Wallace entered the park on the east entrance to the Yellowstone National Park on August 24, 2011, at 7:53 a.m. The Campground Registration Desk attendant for Xanterra Parks and Resort remembered checking Wallace in. She started to give her "bear speech" and Wallace informed her that he was a grizzly bear expert and did not want to hear the "bear speech" given to all campground registrants concerning bear safety. She gave the speech anyway. He was checked in as normal.

A female from Utah who believed she observed Wallace on Thursday, August 25, 2011, in the morning near the trailhead of Mary Mountain in Hayden Valley believed she witnessed Mr. Wallace on the morning of August 25, 2011, at approximately 7:30 a.m. while stopped near a pullout at the northern end of Hayden Valley north of Alum Creek. She observed a 4x4

SUV parked in a pullout near the river at the Mary Mountain Trailhead.

She took note of a white male between fifty and sixty years old with light colored hair because he ignored the dozens of bison swimming across the river. Several other cars had stopped to watch the bison. This male did not even look at them. She observed this male put on a lot of sunscreen and then a brightly colored backpack (possibly yellow) before walking west across the road into the Hayden Valley towards the Mary Mountain Trail.

On August 26, 2011, at about 1330 hours, I (David PAGE, Park Ranger LE) received a report from the Canyon Backcountry Office that two hikers were reporting that they had discovered a dead body on the Mary Mountain Trail. Rangers M. Plona, Brian Speeg, and I– at about 1340 hours. The hikers, a father and daughter, reported that they were hiking on the Mary Mountain Trail when they came upon a body. They reported seeing the lower legs of a male lying on the trail and the upper body extending off the trail. They reported that the upper body was covered by dirt. They also described seeing a daypack and a water bottle. They believed the body was a male adult due to the size of the hiking boots. Upon discovery of the body, they did not approach any closer than 5-10 yards. They reported that they left the area quickly being concerned that there might be a bear in the area. They both were aware that bears will "cache" or bury food sources (carcasses).

They returned to the Mary Mountain Trailhead in Hayden Valley arriving at about 1315 hours. From here they traveled to the Canyon Backcountry Office to report what they had observed. Prior to arriving at the trailhead, they had contacted two hikers, believed to be French nationals, and told them that they should turn around because of what they had discovered. Through broken English, the couple said that they were going only a short distance. I questioned them briefly concerning the distance of the body from the trailhead and why they were certain it was deceased. They reported the position of the lower legs were not of someone alive, and that the upper body was buried—-reported the hair stood up on the back of his neck and that it was obvious that the person was deceased. They believed they had hiked about 6- 7 miles before making the discovery at about 1030 hours. I had Ranger Speeg respond to the Mary Mountain Trailhead to close the trailhead, interview any hikers returning from the trail, and to note the vehicles parked at the trailhead.

Occasionally boot tracks and bear tracks could be seen in the trail. The tracks, both human and bear, were intermittent and not conclusive of a consistent direction of travel (M. Vandzura later attributed the boot tracks to be those of the deceased).

What happened to John Wallace? We'll never fully know. He was hiking alone. But what he didn't know was another hiker didn't report what happened to him a few days earlier, that there was a high concentration of grizzly bears in the area that were feeding on dead bison.

The hiker on August 22, 2011, reported after John Wallace's death observing nine grizzly bears in the area. He reported the bears feeding on something in the creek. He tried to hide to take photos. But one of the bears saw him. He quickly left the area. When he looked back after crossing a creek, the female with cubs was standing where he previously was hiding. The sow saw he was farther away now and returned to the carcass to feed. He now was standing on top of the ridge above the creek and could see new bears approaching the carcass to feed. At that time, what is believed to be a large male grizzly was descending the hill as he climbed out and they both spotted each other at the same time at forty yards. Both he and the bear jump back surprised.

The bear roared and charged. The hiker stood his ground and raised a hatchet. The boar stopped at fifteen to twenty yards and turned around running off. In the hiker's own words, *"Any other details have been lost due to trauma and an effort to not piss my pants. Sorry for not reporting the incident earlier; I assumed it was unimportant and trivial."*

Reading the case file again is very impressive how quickly and professional the National Park Service Rangers were in handling the case.

The victim was so torn and eaten by the bears the facial recognition could not be made from the driver's license picture.

YNP Deputy Coroner—Colette Daigle-Berg called and advised Mrs. Wallace that John Wallace had been found dead on the Mary Mountain trail on 08/26/2011, that the cause of his death was unknown at present and that a bear (or bears) was known to have been involved. I advised that his vehicle had been observed unattended at the trailhead on 08/25/2011 and that a key to his vehicle had been found in his pocket and a second key to his vehicle was found in his daypack. Mrs. Wallace advised that she had last talked to her husband by phone on the evening of 08/24/2011. She confirmed that he had uneven teeth on the bottom row; that he owned a green Jeep Cherokee; that he owned an orange daypack; that he wore a simple gold wedding band on his left ring finger; and that he did chew his thumb and fingernails. She advised that he would never hike without his identification on him. She also advised that he was healthy and had no known medical conditions.

Figure 2. Sketch of Wallace fatality site along the Mary Mountain trail displaying the body location and other key evidence.

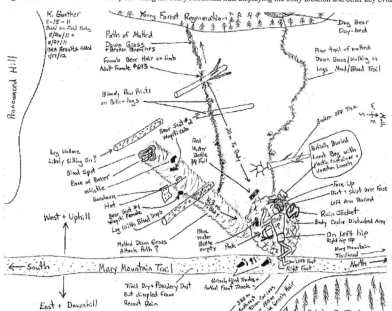

CASE INCIDENT NUMBER
11-4555
DATE OF INCIDENT
08/26/2011
Examination of the body revealed the following injuries:

- left facial and scalp lacerations, right eyebrow laceration

- puncture wounds and lacerations of the right hand and forearm- consistent with defensive type wounds

- extensive anterior torso lacerations, breastplate and rib cartilages fractured with resultant opening of the chest and abdominal walls

- several large puncture wounds across the posterior torso measuring approximately 6 cm on top, 5 cm on bottom. (Per Bear Management Specialist Kerry Gunther, these puncture wounds are consistent with the size and shape of a mid-sized bear's canine teeth and inconsistent with the characteristics of the canine teeth of mountain lions and wolves)

- large and small intestine mostly absent

- kidney and adrenals absent

- extensive musculocutaneous injuries to buttocks and lower extremities

- obvious bruising surrounded the lacerations and puncture wounds consistent with injuries occurring prior to death

Dr. Bennett listed probable cause of death as: exsanguination due to grizzly bear attack. He listed other significant conditions as: postmortem anthropophagia (animal predation). Bruising surrounding some of Wallace's injuries indicated they occurred prior to his death while blood was still circulating. Wounds to his neck and back suggest that the bear came from behind. Defensive wounds on his arms and hands and compacted dirt under his fingernails indicate that he likely attempted to fight the bear's attack. Canine teeth puncture wounds on his back were measured at approximately 6 cm top canine and 5 cm bottom canine—typical size of sub-adult male grizzly bears or adult female grizzly bears (per Bear Management Specialist Kerry Gunther). Dr. Bennett recorded that the majority of Wallace's wounds appear to have been post-mortem. This observation and the fact that Wallace's body was covered with dirt when found suggest that he was killed by a bear, partially consumed, and then cached. Scat, bear tracks, and hair collected at the scene and from the body were inspected by bear management specialists and found to be consistent with those of grizzly rather than black bears.

Bear Trapping Operations

Bear traps were set at the fatality site of Mr. Wallace on Saturday, August 27, 2011, the day after Mr. Wallace 's body was discovered. Initial trapping operations at the fatality site used minimal bait to increase the chances of catching the target bear while minimizing the chances of luring bears that were not involved in the incident to the site. Later, traps were set over a larger perimeter to catch any bears in the area. Some trap sites were used primarily to attract large adult male grizzly bears away from other trap sites to increase the probability of catching females with young and subadults, the sex and age classes of the bears thought to be involved in the incident based on track and bite wound evidence. Bear trapping operations continued through the morning of October 16, 2011.

Traps were set at ten different locations in the Hayden Valley area. In 173 trap-nights of effort, there were twenty-five captures of thirteen individual grizzly bears. Five adult males, four adult females, two yearling males, and two male cubs-of-the-year were captured. Adult male grizzly bear #281 was captured six times, adult male #394 four times, adult male #211 three times, adult female #321 twice, adult female #448 twice, adult male #155 once, adult male #589 once, yearling male #688 once, yearling male #689 once, adult female #693 once.

September 28, 2011,– On Wednesday evening, the unmarked adult female grizzly referred to as the Wapiti sow was captured at the Wapiti trap site. Weight= 113 kg (249.5 lbs); upper canine width= 58.0 mrn; lower canine width= 52.9 mrn; front foot pad width= 12.1 cm; hind footpad width= 11.0

cm. The Wapiti sow was estimated to be 6-7 years old. DNA from the Wapiti sow matched DNA from the female bear scat found near some of Mr. Wallace 's possessions and 4.4 meters (4.8 yds) from his body. DNA evidence indicates that the Wapiti sow was responsible for the death of Mr. Matayoshi on the Wapiti Lake trail in Hayden Valley on July 6, 2011. The Matayoshi fatality site is approximately 13 kilometers (8.1 mi), straight line distance, from the Wallace fatality site. DNA from the Wapiti sow is a DNA match with hair snagged on Mr. Matayoshi 's eyeglasses and from a bear scat collected at the Matayoshi fatality site. Although the Wapiti sow had never been previously captured and was not wearing a radio collar or ear tags, she was the only female with cubs-of-the-year known to be frequenting Hayden Valley during the spring and summer of 2011. The Wapiti sow was also easily recognized by the presence of one of her cubs which had a very distinctive blonde head.

Bear saliva DNA evidence from multiple bite wounds on the victim 's body and clothes were swabbed with swabs moistened with sterile water to collect saliva of the bear that attacked and/or partially consumed the victim. All of these swabs were non-reactive for DNA. Heavy rain and hail on Thursday afternoon which saturated the victim's clothes may have contributed to the deterioration of saliva DNA evidence.

Reading the evidence, we can only speculate at what happened. Looking at the drawing, it appears John Wallace hiked in six miles, decided to have a snack, and sat on a log just off the trail. He made some type of noise to alert the bear he was in the area. It could have been opening the Zone bar or maybe the sloshing from his water bottle. It appears he never heard or saw the bear until she made contact with his body, knocking him forward, then pouncing on him and chewing on his back and neck.

He fought back. With no eyewitness, we have no clue if it was the sow bear only or if one or both cubs helped in the attack. He was still alive when the sow started eating on his stomach. I can think of no more horrible way to die than to watch your flesh being ripped off your body and consumed in front of you. The broken ribs may indicate that he tried to fight and a powerful swat from the sow to the chest broke the ribs. Hopefully, he passed out before they consumed too much of his body.

The sow mankiller now became a man-eater. One or both cubs fed on his body. Stashing the body in a bear cache means the bears fully intended to return to finish eating. The sow received no negative repercussions from killing a person just two months earlier. It may have felt that man is just another animal to feed on. Was the bison carcass they were feeding on completely eaten at this point? She was sleeping nearby. She may have heard John Wallace and decided it was time for a fresh meal. The bears go into hyperphagia before winter. This means simply they're eating up to 20,000 calories a day to put on the needed fat to survive the winter. Maybe the sow was worried about her cubs having enough fat to survive the winter.

Reading the trapping report, it was hard to believe that many grizzly bears were in one area.

Some people, a tiny vocal percentage of Americans, said the sow should have been allowed to live. These people say there are too many humans in the world and the bears are more important. I believe the only way to cure these types of people is to put a known man-eating grizzly in their house with them and see if they change their mind about how important human life is.

Fatality of Mr. Adam Thomas Steward Bear Attack in Cub Creek on the Bridger Teton National Forest, Sep 4, 2014

The bear killed Adam Thomas Steward on September 4, 2014, and his remains were found September 12, 2014.

Timeframe

Adam Steward's GPS Garmin recorded a reading at 9:51 a.m. Sept 4 at the Brooks Lake trailhead.

Early afternoon – Adam Thomas Steward set up his campsite five miles from the trailhead.

2:33 – Mr. Steward takes picture time stamped on camera.

Mid to late afternoon is when he is believed to have been attacked.

Sept 5, 2014 – Mr. Steward is due to leave the area.

Sept 7, 2014 – His employer reports him missing to the Fremont Sheriff's Department at 12:56 p.m.

Sept 7, 2014, at 3:48 p.m. – Fremont Sheriff's Department find his vehicle at the trailhead and leave two notes to contact Fremont Sheriff's Department.

Sept 8, 2014 – No report from Mr. Steward and his vehicle is still at the trailhead. Initiated search and rescue.

Sept 12, 2014 – His remains are found one point eight miles from his campsite.

Sept 13, 2014 – His remains are flown out by helicopter.

Adam Steward was assigned a vegetation plot to survey. He was to camp in the area and had set up his camp. Enroute to his assigned plotline is when it's believed he entered the fatality site. The wind had blown down his tent, but his food was stored properly, still hanging from a tree and neither had been touched by bears.

Report statement from Detective Jason Cox, Fremont County Sheriff's Department.

Case Number C14-06615

Upon arriving at the scene, I observed about 1 inch of snow on the ground where the body believed to be Adam Steward was located. Looking at the main scene I observed a large blue backpack and could see the bottom of a shoe that was neon green west of the backpack. I could then see a skull and what appeared to be a pelvis and femur near the skull. I could see clothing next to a backpack. In the main scene area, I could see a deer hide near the pelvis and femur that was visible.

His remains were almost totally consumed. Remains from two mule deer were also found in the area. Signs of both black bear and grizzly were in the area. Entering an area of thick cover, it's believed he surprised the bear. Hair and DNA samples collected in the area were sent to Wildlife Genetics International for testing. Within a half a mile of the fatality site, there were three grizzly bears, one female and two males, plus one male black bear. Where the remains were found, one male grizzly and one male black bear were identified. With the long time between Adam Steward's death on Sept 4 until the samples were taken on Sept 13, there was no way to positively identify which bear had killed him.

The autopsy report said he "died of blunt force injuries consistent with a bear bite." The pathologist determined that there were canine punctures in Mr. Steward's skull that occurred while he was still alive, as indicated by subdural hemorrhaging, and these contributed to the cause of death.

No bear spray or firearms were found at the fatality site. Five-day trapping efforts in the area caught one male subadult grizzly that didn't match the DNA samples. No other bears were captured. One female grizzly bear hair was found in the trap area but didn't match the DNA found at the fatality site.

The known man-eater was never captured.

Investigation Team Report for Attacks by grizzly bear in Soda Butte on the Gallatin National Forest on July 28, 2010.
The Soda Butte campground is located off Hwy 212 five miles east of the northeast entrance to Yellowstone National Park.

Let's go through the three phases of attack.

1. Prey testing. Mr. Singer was sleeping in a tent with his girlfriend, Maria Fleming. They had a young pup inside the tent with them. Mr. Singer woke around 2:00 a.m. when the tent was moved several feet to one side. Next thing he knew, he felt something bite him on the left leg right through the tent. He was unable to see what it was. He started punching through the tent, hitting the animal in the head several times. Maria woke up and screamed, turning on a light, and the bear ran off. As you can see this was still prey testing; the bear was unsure and easily driven off.

2. Prey tasting. The next victim in the night of terror was Deborah Freele, who was sleeping in a one-man tent with her husband in another tent thirteen yards away. She was awakened approximately five to fifteen minutes after the Mr. Singer attack when she felt a bite on her upper left arm. The bear shook her, let go, and bit her lower on the left arm. She believed there were two bears attacking her because at the same time her

left arm was being torn up, she felt a bite on her left leg. The bear let go of her left leg and arm. She screamed for help and then played dead hoping the bear would leave. Another camper approached her tent in a car and that might be what drove the bears away. Again, the bear was unsure how to kill these two-legged animals. She did say that she thought the bear thought it was biting her neck instead of her arm.

3.   Prey eating. Kevin Kammer was camping in an isolated spot six hundred yards from Deborah's campsite. This part of the campground was near the creek that was reported as very loud. No witness to the attack, so once again we can only speculate based on the evidence. It's believed Kevin was pulled out of the tent by his head or shoulders and dragged about four feet from the tent where he was killed. After he was dead, the bear dragged him another ten yards closer to the creek. His body was not discovered until 4:21 a.m. when law enforcement was clearing the campground. By the time his body was discovered, the bears had consumed a significant portion of his upper torso and his legs.

Fatality of Erwin Evert from a bear attack at Kitty Creek on the Shoshone National Forest, June 17, 2010.

A grizzly research team was trapping and tagging grizzly bears for research. They had captured a large male grizzly using Telazol to knock the bear out for easy handling. The bear was a ten-year-old male weighing 430 pounds. The bear was radio-collared. They left the bear laying on the ground in recovery. As the drug wore off, the bear would wake up and walk off. They pulled the warning signs because this was the end of their trapping in the area. They left the area around 12:30.

They had another grizzly set in a different location. Using the same Telazol to knock out the bear, they put on the radio collar and took samples, packed up their gear, and left. Returning to pass the cabins at 6:00, they saw an elderly lady and stopped to talk. Mrs. Evert was asking if they saw her husband who left the cabin around 1:00 p.m. and said he would be home no later than 4:00 p.m.

Chad Dickinson, a team member of the research team, quickly rode his horse back to the first trap site and found Erwin Evert dead. He rode back and had the heartbreaking job of telling Mrs. Yolando Evert that her husband was deceased by an apparent grizzly bear attack.

The investigation team found the attack site twenty-one yards from where the bear was left on the ground. His head was terribly mauled with no sign of life. The first attack site was found with blood on the trail. Two yards farther east, a pair of prescription glasses was found; one more yard, a hair comb was found. Three more yards to the east was the body. Evert's body was covered in puncture wounds with the exception of his hands.

There were several fatal puncture wounds to the left side of his face. A series of puncture wounds completely fractured the skull and penetrated the brain. Puncture wounds near the left eye had resulted in the separation and loss of the left eye.

I have researched a lot of attacks, but this one must be one of the most brutal I have ever read.

Chapter 6
Coyotes

I had to guess what animal would be responsible for a fatal attack in eastern Canada. I would have guessed black bear, never coyote. — Mike O 'Brien

The most dangerous month for coyote attacks is May. The second most dangerous month is October.

By Marya (emdot) from San Luis Obispo, USA - Flickr, CC BY 2.0

Information on the type of attack site was available for 121 of the attack incidents. Most of these incidents (70%) occurred on or immediately adjacent to the victim's residence. One-quarter of attacks (25%) occurred in parks.

We were able to classify 108 of 142 (76%) reported attack incidents by behavioral category (Figure 3). The greatest number of attacks was classified as predatory (37%), followed by investigative (22%). Attacks were classified as pet-related in 6% of the cases and defensive in 4% of the cases. In 7% of attack incidents, the coyote was verified as rabid.

However, most attacks occurred within the western portion of the United States, with 49% of attacks occurring in California and 13% in Arizona. (White and Gehrt, 2009)

You must ask yourself why those two states have the highest amount of attacks.

California banned steel traps in 1989. In 1996, Massachusetts banned steel traps. The Arizona Public Land Trapping Statute (1994) prohibited the use of leg-hold traps, instant kill body-gripping traps, poisons, or snares to take wildlife on any public land with exceptions made for uses related to health or safety, scientific research, wildlife relocation, or rodent control.

Let us use the three phases of attacks for coyotes. With 130 attacks on humans, we can't call this rare. I disagree with Lynsey White on several points. First, if you can't classify the type of attacks, you need to find a new job. Second, investigative attacks should be called prey testing. This is the animal testing to find out if humans are good to eat. The general narrative from the experts is no matter what, the animals are never at fault. It was the human's fault always.

The following attacks can be found under "Coyote Attacks on Humans" in Wikipedia.

California (1978–2003)

A study published in 2004 documented 35 incidents in which a child escaped likely "serious or fatal injury" if the child had not been rescued in time. These included:

1. In May 1978, a coyote bit the leg of a 5-year-old Pasadena girl in the driveway of her home.

2. In May 1979, a coyote grabbed by the throat and cheek a 2-year-old Pasadena girl who had been eating cookies on her front porch.

3. In July 1979, in Pasadena, coyotes lacerated the leg of a 17-year-old girl who was attempting to save a dog from being attacked.

4. In August 1979, a coyote attacked a 5-year-old La Verne girl. Her father and a neighbor saved the child from being dragged off, but not before she had suffered deep bites on her neck, head, and legs.

5. In July 1980, a coyote grabbed a 13-month-old Agoura Hills baby girl by the midsection and started dragging her off. The baby suffered puncture wounds but was saved by her mother.

6. In August 1988, a coyote nipped and bruised a 4-year-old Oceanside boy who had been playing in his yard.

7. In August 1988, a coyote in Oceanside bit the roller skate of an 8-year-old girl who had just fallen but was chased away by two women throwing rocks.

8. In August 1988, a coyote in Oceanside grabbed a 3-year-old girl by the leg, pulled her down, and then bit her on the head and neck before being chased off by her mother and neighbors.

9. In June 1990, in Reds Meadow, a coyote bit a 5-year-old girl on the head while she was sleeping at a campground.

10. In May 1992, a coyote attacked a 5-year-old San Clemente girl, biting her several times on her back. The girl climbed her swing set to escape, and her mother chased the coyote off.

11. In October 1992, in Fallbrook, a coyote bit a 10-year-old boy on the head while he was asleep on the back porch of a residence.

12. In March 1995, in Griffith Park, a 5-year-old girl was knocked down twice by a coyote before being saved by her mother.

13. In June 1995, a coyote chased three boys on University of California, Riverside property, biting a 7-year-old.

14. In July 1995, a Griffith Park coyote was chased away once, but returned and bit the leg of a 15-month-old girl.

15. In September 1995, a coyote attacked a 3-year-old Fullerton girl in her yard, biting her face, head, and thigh.

16. In November 1995, a coyote at University of California, Riverside chased playing children, biting a 3-year-old boy.

17. In June 1996, a coyote grabbed a 3-year-old Los Altos boy 's head and hand and began dragging him toward some bushes before he was saved by his 15 year old brother.

18. In February 1997, a coyote severely bit a 4-year-old girl in her yard in South Lake Tahoe. The heavy snowsuit she was wearing protected all but her face, and she was rescued by her father. The coyote stayed in the unfenced yard until police arrived and shot it dead. Earlier that morning, the coyote had bitten the hand of a man who was feeding it.

19. In May 2000, in La Mesa, a 3-year-old boy was bitten on his side, resulting in four puncture wounds.

20. In June 2001, in Northridge, a coyote seriously injured a 7-year-old, but was fought off by her mother.

21. In July 2001, a coyote bit a 3-year-old Irvine boy in the leg while he was playing in his yard. The boy was saved by his father.

22. In October 2001, in San Clemente, a coyote attacked three children playing on a playground at Truman Benedict Elementary School, biting and scratching an 8-year-old girl on the back of her neck and a 7-year-old boy on the back and arm. A third student was also attacked, but the coyote only bit his backpack.

23. In November 2001, in San Diego, a coyote that a family had been feeding bit their 8-year-old daughter.

24. In December 2001, in San Gabriel, a coyote bit a 3-year-old girl in the head, grabbed her shoulder, and started to drag her away, but was chased off by her father.

25. In May 2002, in Anza-Borrego State Park, a coyote bit a boy, who was sleeping in a sleeping bag, on the head.

26. In May 2003, in Highland, a coyote came into a neighbor 's garage chasing after a 2-year-old girl, biting her on the arm.

27. In July 2003, in Granada Hills, a boy was walking his family 's two dogs when they were attacked by three coyotes. One dog was killed and the other injured before they were rescued by his father.

28. In August 2003, in Apple Valley, a coyote attacked a 4-year-old boy on a golf course, biting him on the face and neck before he was saved by his father.

Other reports of coyote attacks on children in California:

29. On June 28, 2010, a coyote jumped on a 12-year-old girl in Spring Valley. The girl fell backward and injured her elbow, but she was not bitten.

30. On July 18, 2013, at Forest Lawn Cemetery in Cypress, a 2-year-old girl was attacked by a coyote while playing about ten feet away from her mother, who was visiting her grandmother 's grave. The coyote grabbed the playing child and started to drag her off into the bushes, but dropped the child and ran away when "lunged at" by the mother. The child was hospitalized for a 2.5-inch gash to the leg and began precautionary treatment for rabies. Authorities killed three coyotes at the cemetery later that day. On October 9, the mother filed suit alleging that the cemetery, by not warning her of the risk, had liability.

31. On November 16, 2014, a woman claimed that her 4-year-old daughter was knocked down by a coyote outside her Hollywood home. After the attack, the Department of Fish and Wildlife investigated but couldn 't

find any coyote, and a local television news program described the attack as "alleged."

32. On December 25, 2014, a boy was bitten in an attack by an apparently sick coyote. He was saved by his father. Before the attack, about a block away, the coyote had just bitten the leg of a man walking his children to his car outside a home. After the attack, the coyote chased and bit a jogger on a nearby street but ran away when kicked; the police arrived and shot the coyote, which tested negative for rabies.

33. On January 12, 2015, in Ladera Ranch outside a baby girl's residence, a coyote with a limp tried to attack and grab the girl from her mother's arms. The mother fought the animal off enough to get inside to safety. After the attack, the animal killed two dogs and was being pursued by authorities.

34. On May 22, 2015, in Irvine, a 3-year-old girl was picking up after their dog that she, her twin sister, and her mother had been walking, when a coyote ran out of a hedge and bit at the back of her neck. She was saved by her mother and other nearby adults. After the attack, the Department of Fish and Wildlife were trying to track and trap the coyote and planning educational programs to educate residents how to prevent and behave properly during coyote encounters. Before the attack, a coyote had chased another girl in the area.

35. On May 22, 2015, in Irvine at Silverado Park, a 2-year-old girl was in her garage when the door was opened and a coyote in the driveway came in and bit her on the neck and cheek.

36. On October 14, 2015, in Irvine, a 31-year-old man and his 3-year-old son were attacked by a coyote while they were in a garden.

37. On October 9, 2016, a coyote bit a 6-year-old boy who was playing in Irvine's Springbrook Park. The boy's father along with bystanders shouted at it and one woman threw sand.

Coyote attack in California:

38. On July 22, 2016, a coyote bit a 17-year-old girl on her leg at Grant Rea Park in Montebello.

39. On December 17, 1997, coyotes bit two children in Scottsdale, Arizona. Neither child had serious injuries.

40. On July 29, 1998, a 4-year-old boy was bitten by a coyote while playing in the backyard of his home in Cape Cod, Massachusetts. His mother tried to force the coyote to go away, but it kept being around. A police officer responded to her telephone call to shoot and kill it.

41. In April 2006, two coyotes bit two young children in Bellevue, Washington. They were euthanized afterward.

42. On April 6, 2007, in Middletown, New Jersey, a coyote bit a 22-month-old boy who was playing in his family yard with a friend.

43. On May 21, 2007, a coyote jumped out from a small line of bushes and bit a 5-year-old as he and his sister walked home from a neighbor's house in Middletown, New Jersey. He survived due to his sister's scream when she saw the incident, but the boy needed 46 stitches in the back of his head and rabies shots.

44. On December 4, 2008, a 9-year-old boy in Erie, Colorado, was snowboarding with his 6-year-old brother on a golf course behind his house when a coyote attacked him. He used the snowboard to fend off the attack, but he was bitten on the arm. A coyote in the area was then killed, but it wasn't clear if that was the same one that had bitten the boy, so he began a course of treatment for rabies.

45. In June 2010, a 3-year-old girl and a 6-year-old girl were attacked and seriously injured in separate attacks by coyotes in Rye, New York, a suburb of New York City. The 6-year-old was attacked by two coyotes on June 25 and the 3-year-old was attacked by one coyote on June 29. There was no indication the animals were rabid, but the girls were given treatment as a precaution.

46. During a period of two months, from July to September 2011, three children between the ages of two and six were bitten by a coyote, and a fourth was approached by a coyote within two feet in a neighborhood of Broomfield, Colorado. All four encounters are thought to have involved the same adult male coyote, who was lethally removed after the last attack.

47. On August 24, 2011, before noon, a 2-year-old Weymouth, Massachusetts, girl was walking next to her stroller with her grandmother when a coyote lunged out of some hedges along the sidewalk in a suburban residential area. The animal attacked from behind, knocked the child down, and bit her on the back of her head, leaving a large wound. The grandmother was having trouble saving her from the coyote, when a neighbor came out of a nearby house and got the pair into the house, shutting the coyote outside, where it stayed, listening, while the homeowner dialed 911. The girl was taken to the hospital to have her scalp stitched. The authorities hunted the coyote but finding nothing, called off the hunt, but later that night police were called back to the area by calls that the coyote had returned. They shot the animal, and although it escaped, it was presumed to have been fatally wounded, but the body was not found, so the girl began a course of rabies treatments. One week earlier, a coyote in the same area tried to attack a landscaper, who successfully fended the animal off, sustaining no injury, so the area coyotes had not been hunted or trapped.

48. On October 12, 2011, in Saginaw, Texas, the *Star-Telegram's* Deanna Boyd reported that a 3-year-old boy was about to get into the car Wednesday morning for his daily ride to daycare and spilled his Cheerios. His mother dashed back inside the house to refill the bowl, then heard a scream and ran back outside where she found the boy lying on the ground confronted by a coyote. The toddler, Colton, said he had seen it "coming too fast" and that it had "knocked me over." He suffered a scratch or welt on his right hand that did not break the skin. The coyote

turned its attention to the mother and then the father who came out of the house and shot the coyote, which tested negative for rabies.

49. On June 22, 2012, at Nehalem Bay State Park on the coast of Oregon, a coyote attacked a 5-year-old girl who was following her family back from the beach on a sand path through benchgrass. The coyote first grabbed a stick which the girl had been trailing behind her, then "lunged at" the screaming child, nipping at her ribcage and feet and breaking the skin on her back, before cutting off the attack to confront her father, who succeeded in driving the determined coyote off. The coyote was not caught, so the child began precautionary treatments for rabies.

50. In the evening of March 12, 2013, two young boys in Boulder, Colorado, were playing near a creek some distance away from their father, when they were surrounded by two coyotes. The boy who did not run was not bitten, but the 5-year-old who ran toward his father was bitten on the leg before being saved by his father. Before this incident, the city had been having problematic encounters with coyotes for some time in the area, known as Boulder Creek Path, including attacks on adults, so they had instituted and just completed a four-week "hazing program" to instill fear of humans into the animals. After the incident, officials hunted down and killed two coyotes believed to be the same ones that had bitten the boy.

51. On May 16, 2013, between six and seven p.m., a 2-year-old girl in Goose Gossage Park, Colorado Springs, Colorado, was playing on the slide with her mother and her brother. She came down the slide, her mother caught her, and set her aside, and just in the brief moment when her mom turned to catch her brother, a coyote bit the girl by the head and ran away. Doctors used stitches to close a large gash just over her right eye, and staples to close the gashes on the back of her head. The animal was not caught, so she began a course of rabies treatments. In the aftermath of this and the second attack, below, authorities conducted a large-scale hunt for the animal, which resulted in the death of two adult animals. Also, the media printed criticism from area residents that the authorities

had been slow to act on their complaints and warnings that the animals were dangerous. Authorities were quoted as saying that hunting or trapping would not help because other coyotes would take their place and that the state "wasn't interested" in spending the money.

52. On May 16, 2013, within an hour before the above attack and in the same place, a coyote had attacked a 4-year-old girl, knocking her down and biting her on the backside, tearing her clothes. Authorities thought it was probably the same animal and planned to kill it.

53. On October 27, 2013, a 3-year-old boy in Austin, Illinois, within an alley was bitten by an animal badly enough to require plastic surgery. The authorities suspected a coyote and trapped "a handful" in the area.

Coyote attacksin other states:

54. On August 6, 2010 in Port Aransas, Texas, Executive Lt. Darryl Johnson of the Port Aransas Police Department told Phil Reynolds of the *South Jetty News* that the latest coyote confrontation led to two Boy Scouts, 14 and 15 years old, from San Antonio, being bitten while sleeping outside their tent near Pole 3 on the beach. The boys were taken to a Corpus Christi hospital where they were treated. The boys took preventive rabies shots.

55. On April 15, 2011, a coyote bit a 2-year-old girl on the neck at a regional park playground in Cave Creek, Arizona. Her parents took her to a hospital for rabies treatment afterward.

56. On February 22, 2012, a 17-year-old boy in Hopkinton, New Hampshire, was attacked by a "possibly rabid" coyote while walking his dog in the woods near his house. The coyote approached, the dog ran away, and the coyote attacked the boy, who stood his ground and punched until the animal ran off. The boy was scratched by the animal's claws and possibly teeth and so began precautionary rabies treatments.

57. On October 15, 2012, KVUE's Heather Kovar reported a 14-year-old boy in Austin, Texas, was knocked down by a coyote then attacked on a

trail near his home. Neighbors say they have encountered aggressive coyotes. Texas Wildlife Services said they have had lots of sightings and animal attacks reported. The teen has had a series of 11 rabies shots.

58. In November 2013, a 15-year-old-girl in Johns Creek, Georgia, was jogging in her neighborhood with her black Labrador-mix when a coyote chased her. She hit the coyote with her cellular phone but fled while the two dogs fought against each other. The teenage girl knocked on her neighbor's door and called her father when she got inside her neighbor 's home.

59. On July 12, 2015, a 15-year-old boy in Grapevine, Texas, was bitten by a coyote when he and his girlfriend were exiting a movie theater.

Coyote attacks on children in Canada:

60. On June 29, 2009, a coyote bit a 2-year-old girl on a school playground in Port Coquitlam, British Columbia. Adults around the school 's vicinity rescued the girl and chased the coyote away.

61. On May 31, 2010, a 5-year-old girl in Vernon, British Columbia, was bitten by a coyote while walking with her parents and dog near a greenbelt area at about 5 p.m. An official quoted in the story stated that there had been four other attacks on humans in British Columbia in the preceding fifteen years.

62. In January 2012, an 8-year-old girl in Oakville, Ontario, was playing in her backyard with a friend when a coyote jumped the fence and attacked. The coyote chased the children inside the house, then stalked around outside the house, but ran away before the police arrived. The authorities killed a coyote found in the area later that day, and the girl was taken to the hospital, treated for bites to the leg, and given rabies shots because it was not clear whether the rabies-free animal that was killed was the same one that had attacked the child.

63. On September 25, 2013, in St. Catharine's, Ontario, a coyote attacked an 8-year-old girl who was walking on a sidewalk behind her stepfather,

when the coyote leaped up at her, biting her ribcage. He turned around and saw it biting her foot, and then her torso. The girl was treated and released for "coyote bite." The animal was not found, so she underwent a course of rabies treatment as a precaution.

64. On June 26. 2015, two coyotes mauled an 11-year-old girl in Valleyview, Alberta. Her mother sent her to a hospital for stitches.

Coyote attacks on teenagers in Canada:

65. On July 14, 2003, a coyote bit an 18-year-old American girl on one of her arms while she was hiking with her parents on the Skyline Trail at Cape Breton Highlands National Park in Nova Scotia.

66. On August 9, 2010, a coyote bit a 16-year-old girl 's head twice while sleeping in her tent at Broad Cove in Ingonish, Nova Scotia, when she went camping with her parents on the Cabot Trail east of Cape Breton Highlands National Park. She was taken to a hospital for stitches and treatment to prevent any rabies.

67. On May 15, 2012, a 14-year-old boy in Westmount, Nova Scotia, wore body armor, motocross pants, and boots when a coyote attacked him on a trail near his home. All three protective gears helped him survive the predatory incident.

68. On September 21, 2012, a 16-year-old girl was attacked by a coyote in New Waterford, Nova Scotia, while she was walking to school. She heard some growling in the bushes, but, seeing nothing, continued walking and was hit from behind and knocked down. Just at that moment, a car happened along, and the motorist sounded his horn, scaring the coyote away. The Department of Natural Resources hired a professional to trap the animal.

Coyote attacks on adults in other states:

69. On May 22, 2008, 10:00 a.m., in an unpopulated area of Maine, a hunter was hunting with a friend, staying hidden and using a turkey

call, when he was knocked down and bitten by a coyote. His thick hunting clothing prevented more serious injury but he suffered several small puncture wounds and tooth scratches, and one of his teeth was damaged when he was knocked down. The other hunter soon arrived, and the animal fled. After the attack, the victim was treated at the hospital for his wounds and started a course of expensive precautionary rabies treatments.

70. In June 2008, in the Shadow Wood area of the Brooks community of Estero, Florida, a woman was walking her dachshund on a short leash when a coyote suddenly appeared, grabbed the dog, and tried to run away with it. She dropped to the ground, grabbed the severely injured dog, saving it from being carried off, but the coyote bit her on the right calf. She was taken by ambulance to a hospital where she was treated for four puncture wounds and began precautionary treatment for rabies, as the animal could not be found and killed for rabies testing right away. The incident was preceded by coyotes regularly feeding on dogs in the area and followed by authorities hiring a professional trapper to cull area coyotes.

71. In January 2010, in Greenburgh, New York, a woman was taking a daytime walk through a wooded park when she was pounced on by a coyote. She screamed, and although she was aware that experts don't recommend it, she turned and ran as fast as she could and escaped, but not before she received puncture wounds and scrapes to her arms, legs, back, and buttocks. The coyote later attacked a pit bull terrier at its home adjacent to the same park, was spotted and chased by a police helicopter, and plans were being made for policemen with hunting backgrounds to try to track down the animal. The woman 's wounds were treated, and although the coyote did not appear sick, she began a course of treatment for rabies.

72. On May 22, 2010, a 24-year-old man sleeping on his friend 's patio in Port Aransas, Texas, was awakened by a coyote biting him four times in quick succession on the arm and hand. When he stood, it retreated

to the street, but stayed in the area, watching. The man took a series of rabies shots as a precaution.

73. On July 13, 2010, a man sleeping on a beach in Port Aransas, Texas, was bitten by a coyote licking and biting his hand. He completed a precautionary course of rabies treatments.

74. On August 4, 2010, in Port Aransas, Texas, Port Aransas Animal Control Officer Jim Williams stated, "In the 9 and a half years I 've been there, this is the worst I 've ever seen it," when speaking to KRIS TV about a 19-year-old female from San Antonio, Texas, that was bitten in the head by a coyote. The 19-year-old underwent rabies treatment in San Antonio.

75. On December 25, 2010, in Dalton, Minnesota, a 48-year-old man was walking his dog near a trailer court when a coyote attacked his domestic dog. While defending the dog, he was bitten on both hands by the coyote.

76. January 23, 2011, Port Aransas, Texas, *Corpus Christi Caller-Times* writer Mark Collette 's article confirms a sixth person reported a coyote bite in Port Aransas. The man was sleeping on the beach when bitten by a coyote. Police Chief Scott Burroughs said precautionary rabies vaccinations were received.

77. In March 2012, coyote bit two women and a man in Peoria, Arizona.

78. In December 2012, in Kent, Washington, a man spent the night in the hospital after being attacked by coyotes in his own backyard.

79. On Wednesday, December 12, 2012, at about 2:00 a.m., in Waltham, Massachusetts, on the campus of Brandeis University, an animal, thought to be a coyote, attacked a student walking back to her dorm. The animal appeared from dense cover and in a very dark location and quickly disappeared, so the victim did not get a good look. Multiple residents had sighted a pack of coyotes in the area. The woman was treated for a tooth or claw wound.

80. On the evening of October 8, 2012, a security guard was manning a booth at the Bingham Canyon Mine, Salt Lake County, Utah, when a coyote entered through an open door and attacked her. She managed to escape and call for backup, but not before she received defensive wounds to her forearm. The coyote was shot by a policeman and the victim was taken to the hospital for stitches. Results of rabies tests were not available at press time.

81. In October 2012, in Malabar, Florida, a woman armed with a broom rushed to her backyard chicken coop to see what was causing a commotion, when she was attacked by a rabid and extremely mangy coyote. She was being very badly mauled but was saved by her daughter who shot the coyote and, as she was a trained medical professional, performed first aid and called an ambulance.

82. In January 2013, in Boulder, Colorado, officials were trying to decide what to do about coyotes attacking joggers, bicyclists, and dogwalkers on a popular bike path along the Boulder Creek. The jogger who was bitten at first stood her ground and acted aggressively toward the coyote, but then turned and tried to run away, and was then bitten on the ankle.

83. In May 2013, in Wrentham, Massachusetts, a woman was with her dog at night when it was attacked by a coyote. The woman was bitten on the hand by the coyote while trying to save her dog. The coyote was not caught, so the woman began treatment for possible rabies.

84. In late June 2013, residents of the Rocky Creek subdivision of eastern Wichita, Kansas, received an email from the homeowners' association stating that an irrigation worker had been attacked by a coyote near a sidewalk west of a bridge. The email stated that the attack resulted in torn clothing, not skin, but residents were warned to watch the area.

85. On Monday, September 2, 2013, at 5:30 p.m., a man was waxing his car in the driveway of his home northwest of Cumming, Georgia, when he was painfully bitten by a coyote on the back of the left leg just above

the knee. He slapped the coyote with a towel, but the coyote kept attacking, but then the man 's white German Shepherd came running and body-slammed the coyote. Both animals tumbled and ran off chasing each other. The dog, "Charmin," returned without the coyote but with a bite wound to the back-right leg. The man was treated for the bite and started a precautionary course of treatment for rabies, but the dog 's vaccinations for the disease were current.

86. On Monday, October 14, 2013, at about 5:00 a.m., on a dark road just outside Niwot, Colorado, in Boulder County, three coyotes attacked a 22-year-old man who was walking to work. The attack lasted one or two minutes before the pack retreated. The man concentrated on keeping his balance, wielding his flashlight with one arm, and pushing the coyotes with the other, keeping the animals in front of him, protecting his neck and face, and retreating. He landed at least one solid blow with his flashlight to the side of the head of one of the animals. They circled, dodged, and attacked in turn, lunging at his throat, biting, clawing, and landing leaping body-blows. He was treated and released for multiple bleeding cuts and abrasions to the arms, head, face, and neck. Two days later, officials announced the three coyotes had been killed and that none of them were rabid.

87. On Friday, November 1, 2013, about 11 a.m., on a property near a country club on the north end of Mansfield, Ohio, a groundskeeper did not notice a pack of at least three coyotes until one latched onto his arm. The attacking animal was with at least two others. The man knocked the animals off him, escaped on a riding lawnmower, and drove himself to the hospital to have the arm bite wound and claw marks treated and to get precautionary injections. Authorities responded, but the coyotes were not found. Before the attack, the coyotes had been seen "almost every day" on the nearby golf course.

88. On February 10, 2014, in Clement Park, Colorado, a woman was walking her dog in a park when a coyote approached quickly. She picked up her dog, but the coyote lunged at the pair. The woman

kicked the coyote, and it retreated. Before the attack, others had noticed aggressive behavior from coyotes in that park. After the incident, authorities killed five coyotes in the area.

89. On March 14, 2014, a man walking his Yorkshire terrier in an alley behind his house in Yorba Linda, California, was jumped on and knocked down by two coyotes, which took the dog and ran off. The man had not seen the coyote when it suddenly jumped on his back.

90. At about 7:00 a.m. on Tuesday, March 25, 2014, a woman walking her dog on a street in a residential neighborhood of Orangeburg, New York, was attacked by a rabid coyote. She used her jacket as a shield and escaped with the help of neighbors. Police shot the coyote in a nearby backyard, EMTs treated her leg and took her to the hospital, and animal control officers collected the body and sent it to a New York State Troopers laboratory in Albany where it tested positive for rabies.

91. On Monday, March 31, 2014, in a wooded area of Gibson Township, Pennsylvania, a man was bitten by a coyote while breaking up a fight between it and his dog. He then shot the coyote. The dog was unhurt, and the man began rabies treatments.

92. May 14, 2014, in a wooded area on the campus of The University of Colorado, Boulder, a man was walking his dog on a leash when it was attacked by a coyote. While defending the dog, the man was bitten on the arm. He kicked the coyote and swung a stick at it, and it ran away. Before the attack, the coyote had been following them for some time. After the attack, university authorities had warning signs put up and arranged for experts to study the matter.

93. May 14, 2014, in Bourne, Massachusetts, a man was attacked by a pack of three coyotes outside his house while defending his 5-year-old boxer. The pair managed to drive the pack away, but not before sustaining bite wounds. Before the attack, coyotes had killed the man 's cats and attacked his neighbor 's dog. After the attack, the man called animal

control officers, who agreed to visit the man 's home to discuss the matter the following morning.

94. On Thursday, September 25, 2014, in Okatie, South Carolina, a person was bitten by a rabid coyote. It was the fourth coyote to test positive for rabies in Beaufort County in the year.

95. On Saturday, October 4, 2014, about a mile and a half on a bicycle path from the Pleasant Hill Road entrance into Black River Wildlife Management Area, a rabid yet apparently healthy coyote launched itself at a cyclist, causing him to dismount. During the ensuing fight, which lasted about two or three minutes, he used the bicycle to defend himself and to attack the coyote, which launched approximately eight or nine bite attempts, including open-mouthed leaps at his face. At one moment he had to hold the bicycle and coyote off the ground. He finally slammed the bicycle on the paw and the coyote ran off. Before the attack, the man was already tired from riding on the trail. After the attack, he was so tired that he wouldn 't have been able to fight much longer, and had difficulty fleeing due to exhaustion, coyote-mangled bicycle tires, and fear not letting him rest. He was not bitten but began precautionary treatment for rabies because of the coyote 's saliva on his skin. Later that day, another park visitor had been approached by the coyote, and another cyclist was bitten on the leg. The next day, the coyote was killed in a fight with a hunter, who was bitten.

96. On Sunday, October 5, 2014, at 12:55 p.m., in Black River Wildlife Management Area in Chester Township, NJ, a hunter was bitten by a rabid coyote. The hunter killed the animal before police and fish and wildlife officers could arrive. The coyote tested positive for rabies. Two days before the attack, a cyclist had been bitten and another attacked.

97. On Tuesday, October 14, 2014, at about 9 p.m., while walking on a street in a wooded residential area of Clinton, Connecticut, a 35-year-old man was attacked by a canid, probably a coyote, but possibly a coywolf. The animal leaped up and bit him severely on the face. Before the attack, coyotes had been detected in the area. After the attack, the

man was given 14 stitches to the left of his nose, began precautionary rabies treatments, and an appointment to return for evaluation for plastic surgery. The coyote was not found.

98. On the morning of Monday, November 18, 2014, in Greenland, New Hampshire, a woman walking her retriever was attacked by a coyote in a field behind her house. The coyote was not seen until it charged, biting both. Her husband heard the commotion and drove his truck into the field and tried but failed to drive the animal away with it. He had a gun, but the coyote was too close to the pair to aim at it, so he shot into the air, trying but failing to scare it away. The dog was credited with finally driving the animal off, although the dog was bitten many times. After the attack, the woman and dog were given medical treatment for multiple coyote bites, and both she and her husband started precautionary rabies treatments. Before the attack, coyotes had been often heard, but not often seen in the area.

99. On December 25, 2014, just after 6 p.m., in Fremont, California, the leg of a man walking his children to his car outside a home was bitten by an unhealthy-looking coyote. The man and the children escaped into the house. The man was treated at the hospital. After the attack, a boy was bitten by the coyote about a block away, but saved by his father, and then a jogger on a nearby street was chased by the coyote which ran away when kicked. Police arrived, shot the coyote, and sent the body to be tested for rabies.

100. On January 5, 2015, in Groveland, Massachusetts, two men were attacked outside their houses. One of them had his 4-year-old daughter with him.

101. On January 20, 2015, in a residential area of Kensington, San Diego, California, a woman was attacked while jogging. While trying to run away, she was bitten on the leg. She then stopped and shouted and acted threateningly toward the animal, and it eventually ran off. After the attack, the bite wound was treated at the hospital and she began

precautionary rabies treatments. The authorities stated the animal was a threat and were planning to remove it from the neighborhood.

102. On April 6, 2015, a man was bitten on the calf by a coyote on the three-acre property outside his home in Saddle River, New Jersey. Earlier, the coyote had attacked a Labrador Retriever and left seven dead pups in the area. Initially, the man scared off the coyote, but when his back was turned, it bit him from behind. Authorities tracked and killed the animal, which tested positive for rabies.

103. On July 11, 2016, a rabid coyote mauled a visitor at Leita Thompson Memorial Park in Roswell, Georgia.

104. On July 27, 2016, a coyote bit a 53-year-old man in Manchester, New Jersey 's POW-MIA Memorial Park. The man was taken to Ocean Medical Center in Brick, where doctors stitched up his wounds.

105. On August 7, 2016, a woman was bitten by a coyote while walking her dog outside the Cowesett Hills apartment complex in Warwick, Rhode Island.

106. On August 8, 2016, a rabid coyote mauled a man who was walking in the woods with his two daughters in Lincoln, Pennsylvania.

107. On October 2, 2016, coyote bit two women and a domesticated dog in Wolcott, New York.

108. On November 30, 2016, a rabid coyote mauled a trapper. In addition, it mauled two neighborhood residents and a domesticated dog in Ossining, New York.

109. On January 11, 2017, a rabid coyote mauled a 66-year-old man who walked with two other adults and their domestic dogs along the Columbia Trail in Long Valley, New Jersey. The man fended it off with a stick and police officers subsequently euthanized the animal.

Coyote attacks on adults in Canada:

110. On February 10, 2010, in Saint-Charles, New Brunswick, a woman brought her puppy on a leash outside in the middle of the night to relieve himself, when a coyote suddenly appeared and made for the dog. The woman tossed the puppy about ten feet away to save it, and the coyote turned on her. The pair fought for more than ten minutes until the woman managed to land a left hook to the jaw, and the animal finally ran off. The woman was not seriously injured, although she needed a bandage on the knuckles of her left hand and a tetanus shot.

111. In September 2012, in Kamloops, British Columbia, a man on a bicycle was attacked by a coyote and forced to stop and fend it off. He used his bicycle to defend himself and stood his ground and behaved aggressively and the coyote soon ran off.

112. On May 21, 2013, in Kamloops, British Columbia, a coyote attacked a camper in a sleeping bag, but he was not in a tent. The man drove himself to the hospital to get his wounds stitched. The coyote was described as somewhat large and healthy-looking. Conservation officers began hunting for the coyote.

113. On December 11, 2013, in Summerland, British Columbia, a pack of three coyotes surrounded and attacked a woman walking her friend 's Labradoodle. Although her heavy winter coat took most of the damage, she suffered defensive wounds to the left hand. As a result of this attack, authorities began a cull of area coyotes.

114. On January 20, 2014, in Markham, Ontario, two women were bitten by wild canids. Coyotes were suspected.

115. On Monday, June 23, 2014, at about 4:00 p.m., in a residential area of Thornhill, Ontario, two women were attacked by two wild canids, thought to be coyotes, coywolves, coydogs, or lupine feral dogs, biting one of them on the leg and the other on the hip. Both were treated for injuries and began preventive treatment for rabies. Earlier that day, in

a nearby area, the same two coyotes had tried to attack at least three other people who escaped into their houses and called police, who arrived and shot at the animals, driving them off while perhaps wounding one of them. At last report, the animals had not been caught, and officials had canceled city-run outdoor activities and were advising residents to be careful when venturing outdoors, especially with children or domesticated animals.

116. On Saturday, July 19, 2014, at about 4:00 p.m., outside her home in Gravenhurst, Ontario, a woman was exercising her two American Bulldogs when the female dog, which had a neurological disorder, was attacked by an eastern coyote. The woman then attacked the wild dog, but it fought her off and returned to attack the dog three times. Then, the male dog managed to slip its collar and chase off the coyote. The woman suffered multiple tooth drags and scratches. After the attack, the doctor ordered the woman to begin a series of painful rabies treatments and had difficulty determining which authority or authorities to properly file a report to, and the neighbors began carrying clubs when outdoors. Before the attack, the wild animal had been following them for a short time.

117. On January 31, 2017, three coyotes attacked a man who took his dog for a walk in Alliston, Ontario. The man's dog was able to fend off the coyotes. Neither the man nor his dog had any serious injuries.

118. On February 27, 2017, a rabid coyote bit a man while jogging in Roswell, Georgia. While a neighbor called the emergency number, the man pinned the animal to the ground for twenty minutes until paramedics came to his aid. He went to the hospital for rabies treatment.

119. On August 1, 2017, a coyote chased a woman who was riding a bicycle at Holmes Lake in Lincoln, Nebraska.

120. On August 4, 2017, a coyote stalked a woman to the fence line to her house in Lakeview, New York. She subsequently shared photos of the animal as a warning to her neighbors.

121. On August 16, 2017, a woman was mauled by a coyote along the Glens Falls Feeder Canal in Kingsbury, New York. She was taken to the Albany Medical Center by a helicopter for rabies treatment due to severe injuries.

122. On September 5, 2017, a coyote stalked a man who was walking with his domestic dog at an archaeological state preserve in Glenwood, Iowa.

123. On September 8, 2017, two coyotes attacked a 43-year-old woman and her cat in Santa Cruz, California. They took her cat 's life, and the woman was sent to a hospital for rabies treatment.

124. On September 14, 2017, a coyote pack in Saddle River, New Jersey, ambushed a woman and tried to snatch her dog. A motorist in a sport utility vehicle honked the horn and stepped out to frighten the pack away.

125. On October 8, 2017, a rabid coyote in Gervais, Oregon, bit a man on a farm after walking up to him and sniffing him. After shooting the animal, the man was medically treated for rabies and released from a hospital.

126. On October 20, 2017, a 57-year-old woman in Apple Valley, Minnesota, was bitten by a coyote while jogging with her husband at Cedar Isle Park.

127. On October 22, 2017, a 22-year-old man in Ashburnham, Massachusetts, was bitten by a coyote when he mistook it for a domesticated dog. He was taken to Gardner 's Heywood Hospital for rabies treatment afterward.

Rabies, starvation, mange, and other diseases are signs of overpopulation—nature's way of curing the problem. The problem besides animals suffering is humans become targets. It is amazing to me how many people think coyotes are no threat. They are naturally shy of humans, they say. Really? So where did all these attacks come from?

It's the same old song and dance with coyotes as all predators—the thinking they should be left alone. What left alone means is no fear of humans and more attacks.

128. One of the most brutal attacks happened to Taylor Mitchell, a 19-year-old Canadian singer who was riding high on her one and only album *For Your Consideration*. She was on tour of eastern Canada. She was walking the Skyline Trail in Cape Breton Highlands National Park in Nova Scotia, Canada. Two American tourists heard what they thought were animals howling or a young woman screaming (or both) at 3:02 p.m. They immediately called for help using a telephone box and were able to alert the park personnel. They told other people in the car parking area. Others started off to see if they could help. They found Taylor's keys and a small knife on the trail. Next, they found torn pieces of bloodied clothing and a large amount of blood along the ground. At 3:25, they found Taylor with a bloodthirsty coyote standing over her body. Three young men charged the coyote several times before they were able to drive the animal off.

Taylor was still alive and talking to her rescuers. The coyote stayed in the area growling at the people, unafraid until the RCMP showed up and fired a shotgun, driving the animal out of the area. Taylor was covered in bite marks with serious wounds to her head and legs. She was rushed to Sacred Heart Community Health Centre and later airlifted to Queen Elizabeth II Community Health Centre. She had lost so much blood she was unable to recover and died twelve hours after being rescued.

Hours later, a game warden shot and killed an aggressive female coyote. Three other coyotes were removed from the area. Caught in a leghold trap later was a large male, forty-two pounds. Scientific investigation of the carcasses determined that three were linked to the attack on Taylor by her blood on their coats and other forensic evidence.

In April, the Nova Scotia government declared a bounty on coyotes of $20. But inside the park, the coyotes were still protected. Ten months later, a 16-year-old girl was bitten in the head twice by a coyote while camping. The coyotes were tested, and using DNA found these were a cross between coyotes and wolves. Was that what caused the animals to be more aggressive? Or is it the simple fact that mankind is no longer acting like the top predator in the area? Are predators viewing humans as weak prey animals to be killed and eaten?

129. On October 16, 2013, a man walking to work at 5 a.m. in Boulder, Colorado, found out that coyotes are not afraid of humans. Three coyotes decided to prey test the man. The battle was on; he had to fight for his life. For seventy long yards, he fought the beasts off, receiving numerous bloody gashes to his face, arms, and legs. He was taken to the hospital. Wildlife officials claimed they killed the larger coyote and one of the smaller ones from the attack, but one was still on the loose. (CBS, 2013)

Clearly, this is the bunny-hugging part of Colorado where coyotes are protected. Human safety is never a concern to the animal lovers. What is the common cause between the two cases? In both areas, the coyotes are protected, and no hunting is allowed.

Chapter 7
Black Bear Attack Victims

I vividly remember being bitten on the head and the sound that makes as her teeth were going into my head and running along the skull. It was just a horrendous fight. —John Chelminiak

By Jim Martin - Own work, Public Domain

The most dangerous month for black bear attacks is June. The second most dangerous month is August.

I will say this after studying hundreds of attacks from bears. If you are in a sleeping bag at night and a bear attacks, YOU have one choice—you better fight. I don't care if it's a grizzly, a polar bear, a black bear, a Carebear, or a large gummy bear—fight back. That bear can smell so good at a mile away, he knew what you had for dinner. At a half mile away, he knew what you had for lunch, and at a quarter mile away, he knew what you had for breakfast. If any bear attacks you at night, you better fight like the devil himself is trying to drag you straight to hell because you are about to visit hell as the bear claws and eats your flesh right before your eyes. Forget all the nonsense the so-called wildlife experts have told you. Bears are predators; they know you are human and they plan on eating you. Get that in your head right now. Don't let all this Disneyland "bears are cute cuddly friendly misunderstood animals" nonsense confuse you. Bears are predators that kill for a living.

A bear attacks you at night for one reason—you are made of meat and bears are predators. That means you're prey to be killed and eaten. At times, researching for this book was overwhelming. How many times do you read the same lame excuses? It was the person's fault because the woman was wearing lipstick. Food in the tent. Oh, my favorite, toothpaste was found in the tent. That must have been what attracted the bear. Anyone that says something that stupid is not qualified to speak as an expert. Really, did the bear tear into the tent and bite into the toothpaste tube or into the person? Come on, get real.

I think we should start with black bear attacks. A famous attack happened in Alaska in 1977. Cynthia Dusel-Bacon, a geologist, was air dropped to take samples. She ran into a predatory black bear. It wasn't even a very large bear, around 170 pounds.

As one Alaska wildlife biologist, John Hechtel, once famously observed about bears, "Don't kill; they eat. ' ' What this means is the bear could care less if you're dead before they start eating on you. Yes, tearing flesh from your body and consuming it as they hold you down. I can't think of a more horrible way to die than to witness your own flesh being eaten a few feet away in front of you. Smelling the blood, hearing the bear crunch and swallow your flesh. Yes, real life is scarier than horror movies.

When she first saw the black bear, it popped out of the brush ten feet away. She did as she was taught, waving her arms yelling at the bear. The bear circled around her knocking her to the ground.

The bear first tried to put her head in its mouth. She tried to reach her radio to call for help but it was inaccessible, buckled in a pocket on her pack. The bear attacked her right side, dragging her by the right arm. She played dead. At one point the bear took a break, so she could retrieve her radio and call for help. The bear seeing or hearing her movement attacked her left arm.

The bear had dragged her over rocks and brush and down a slope. The pilot was not able to locate her and flew back to pick up another geologist to help search. Fifty minutes later, the bear started searching Cynthia's pack for food rations. They would find her after she activated a homing signal. He buzzed the bear, driving her off. They landed and saved Cynthia, airlifting her to the hospital. Both arms were so badly torn up they had to be amputated. Alaska Fish and Game shot the bear.

Cynthia is the true spirit of endurance. Her advice: "Don't work alone." Her husband acted as her gun bearer as she continued her work until 2014 when she retired.

I always used to call the bear cubs that were kicked out two-year-old bears. The mommy bear has raised them until the second spring when she comes into estrus again. This is her signal to drive the cubs out to make room for the new ones.

I was curious about the age of the black bear that attacked Cynthia. Was it a three-year-old with a first-time encounter with a person? I was unable to find that data.

An old adage when I grew up in Michigan was that animals need to fear mankind. When hunting of large predators is stopped, apex predators lose their fear of mankind and humans become prey. Really, it's that simple.

A child was killed in the Upper Peninsula (UP) of Michigan. For decades, it was advisable to keep your mouth shut in the UP if you were a city person from Detroit saying, "stop the hunts, save the bears." The people would gladly knock some sense into you because it was their children's lives on the line.

How are bear harvest numbers set? It's based on sound science. For example, in Montana, there are an estimated 13,000 black bears in the state. Of which, hunters take 1,030 on the average per year. Real close to eight percent of the population. This will ensure a sustainable harvest forever.

California 's black bear population has increased over the past twenty-five years. In 1982, the statewide bear population was estimated to be between 10,000 and 15,000. Presently, the statewide black bear population is conservatively estimated to be between 25,000 and 30,000.

In 2014, the California black bear hunting season resulted in 1,439 kills. We called it 28,000 for easier math. A little over five percent harvest rate.

Minnesota has an estimated black bear population of 20,000 with an annual harvest of 3,000 bears. That is a harvest rate of fifteen percent.

Wisconsin is home to 28,000 black bears with an annual harvest of 4,643 bears. That is a harvest rate of a little over sixteen percent.

Michigan is home to 15,000 to 19,000 with an annual harvest of 1,625. Using the high number of 19,000, the harvest rate is 8.6 percent.

Keep in mind what the goals are of hunting bears—to help keep the species in a healthy population in relation to the carrying capacity of the land and reduction of the bear population when problem bears conflict with people. That includes human attacks, raiding livestock, destroying farmers' crops, and so on. What non-hunters don't understand is that the remaining population of bears has more food and is able to put on the needed fat to survive the winter.

Wikipedia list of Fatal Black Bear Attacks Between 2017 and 1991.

1. Erin Johnson, 27, female, Alaska, June 19, 2017. Bear spray failed.

2. Patrick Cooper, 16, male, Alaska, June 18, 2017.

3. Daniel Ward O'Connor 27, male, May 10, 2015, BC. Killed at campsite. Predatory attack.

4. Darsh Patel, 22, male, September 21, 2014. NJ predatory attack.

5. Lorna Weafer, 36, female, May 7, 2014,   Alberta, Canada. Predatory attack.

6. Robert Weaver, 64, male, June 6, 2013, Delta Junction, Alaska. Predatory attack.

7. Lana Hollingsworth 61, female, July 25, 2011. Died a month later as a direct result of the attack. Pinetop Lakeside, Arizona.

8. Bernice Adolph, 72, femaile, June 2011, Lillooet, British Columbia.

9. Donna Munson, 74, female, August 6, 2009, Ouray, Colorado. Feeding bears.

10. Cecile Lavoie, 70, female, May 30, 2008. Predatory attack.

11. Robin Kochoorek, 31, female, July 20, 2007, Uinta National Forest, Utah. Predatory attack.

12. Samuel Evan Ives, 11, male, June 17, 2007, predatory attack, American Fork Canyon, Utah.

13. Elora Petrasek, 6, female, April 13, 2006, Cherokee National Forest, TN. Maybe predatory.

14. Jacqueline Perry, 30, female, September 6, 2005, Missinaibi Lake, Ontario. Predatory attack.

15. Harvey Robinson, 69, male, August 26, 2005, Selkirk, Manitoba. Maybe predatory.

16. Merlyn Carter, 71, male, June 14, 2005, 270 miles southeast of Yellowknife, NW Territories. Predatory?

17. Maurice Malenfant, 77, male, September 29, 2002, Saint-Zenon-du-Lac-Humqui, Quebec.

18. Christopher Bayduza, 31, male, September 1, 2002, Fort Nelson BC.

19. Ester Schwimmer, 5 months, female. August 19, 2002, Fallsburg, NY. Predatory attack.

20. Adelia Maestras Trujillo, 93, female, August 18, 2001, Mora, New Mexico. Predatory attack.

21. Kyle Harry, 18, male, June 3, 2001, 25 miles southeast of Yellowknife, NW Territories.

22. Mary Beth Miller, 24, female, July 2, 2000, Valcartier, Quebec.

23. Glenda Ann Bradley, 50, female, May 21, 2000, Great Smokey National Park, TN. Predatory attack.

24. Raymond Kitchen, 56, male, August 14, 1997.

25. Patti McConnell, 37, female, August 14, 1997, Liard River Hot Springs, BC. Predatory rampaging bear.

26. Sevend Satre, 53, male, June 14, 1996, Tatlayoko, British Columbia. Predatory attack.

27. Ian Dunbar, 4, male, September 16, 1994, Mile House, BC.

28. Colin McClelland, 24, male, August 10, 1993, Fremont County, Colorado.

29. Darcy Staver, 33, female, July 8, 1992, Glennallen, Alaska.

30. Sebastien Lauzier, 20, male, June 14, 1992, Cochrane, Ontario.

31. Raymond Jakubauskas, 32, male.

32. Carola Frehe, 48, female, October 11, 1991, Algonquin Provincial Park, Ontario. Predator attack.

33. James Waddell, 12, male, May 26, 1991, Lesser Slave Lake, Alberta. Predatory attack.

Now let's add the non-fatal attacks for the same time period.

1. October 22, 2017, Mission, BC, Canada, Murray Smith, a 21-year-old woman. Her dogs were barking, so she opened her back door and came face to face with a black bear. The bear entered the house, attacking her,

biting her on the back. Her boyfriend chased the bear out of the house. A conservation officer was also bitten by the bear responding to the call. She needed stitches for her leg.

2. September 18, 2017, Clifton Forge, Virginia. Not much information on this one. Unnamed woman attacked by black bear hiking with her dogs. She suffered non-life-threatening injuries. That is a new phrase to cover up how serious the injuries truly are.

3. September 12, 2017, Santa Rosa Beach, Florida. Troy Roach's 9-year-old son, Jackson, took their dogs for a walk. As Jackson tells it, a "humongous" black bear attacked the dogs. Troy got in between the bear and the dogs. The bear took a single swipe with his powerful paw, knocking Troy to the ground. The bear grabbed one of the dogs. Troy retrieved a pellet gun and shot the bear. The dog broke free and raced for the house and they all retreated inside. The bear charged the house and climbed up four steps before retreating and running off.

4. September 7, 2017, Saskatchewan, Canada. A 39-year-old says he was bow hunting in a tree stand. A mother bear with three cubs climbed the tree attacking the man. He fought it off, stabbing it with an arrow. He suffered serious injuries during the life and death struggle.

5. September 5, 2017, Sudbury, Ontario, Canada. Two hikers with their dog were attacked. The bear attacked, biting and clawing both men. They fought it off taking turns hitting the bear until it stopped attacking and left the area. No list of the injuries.

6. August 25, 2017, Panther River, Alberta, Canada. A 32-year-old man was attacked by a bear while eating. He was taken to the hospital with serious but non-life-threatening injuries to his head, face, and legs.

7. August 21, 2017, Gibsons, BC. Eleri Froude had a black bear follow her 2 ½-year-old son into the house. Her friend drove the bear outside using a chair. He could not close the door because the bear's head was in the

way, so he punched the bear in the nose. The bear pulled back and the man slammed the door shut. He was able to get pictures of the snarling bear on the other side of the glass.

8. August 20, 2017, Bossevain, Virginia. Tony Yopp, 42. Returning home at night he came face to face with a black bear on his porch. The bear, standing on two feet, roared in his face from six inches and tossed him aside like a rag doll, then running off. He was treated and released at the local hospital.

9. August 8, 2017, Canmore Reservoir, Canada. An unnamed woman has been released from the hospital after she and her dog were attacked by a black bear.

10. August 1, 2017, Priest Lake, Idaho. Unnamed jogger. Charged by a black bear. He first yelled and waved his arms, but the bear kept coming. He dropped to the ground, played dead, and the bear swiped at him, He suffered lacerations to his lower leg. The bear ran off.

11. July 13, 2017, Ketchum, Idaho. A lady camping was woken up when she felt a bear mouth on her foot. The bear ran off after she yelled at it.

12. July 4, 2017, Priest Lake, Idaho, a 60-year-old woman. The bear first attacked her dogs and then turned on her. The bear knocked her down, biting and scratching her several times. She called for help on her phone and family members who were in the area came to her aid. The bear was still in the area. Luckily, they were able to drive the bear off. She was airlifted to the hospital. The bear stayed in the area for thirty minutes!

13. January 31, 2017, Gulf Breeze, Florida. No name listed, male. Defensive attack with dog.

14. Karen Osborne, Maryland, 19, November 2016. Maybe predatory.

15. Dan Richman, 54, Sierra Madre, CA. October 10, 2016. Predatory attack.

16. October 23, 2016, unnamed male attacked by a bear. Park County, Colorado. Defensive attack.

17. August 30, 2016, Judy Milden, Warren County, Virginia. Defensive attack, was attacking dog.

18. August 09, 2016, Cody Troxell, Sequoyah County, Oklahoma. Cody was clawed on one arm at night. Defensive attack.

19. Rick Nelson, July 6, 2016, Sudbury, Ontario. Prey testing.

20. June 29, 2016, Three Rivers, California, unnamed male. Defensive attack.

21. June 28, 2016, Karen Williams Valles, Caldera National Preserve, NM. Defensive attack.

22. Catherine Hanson, Sebeka, Minnesota, May 17, 2016. Defensive attack.

23. June 02, 2016 Young, AZ. Man in his twenties. Prey testing.

24. May 12, 2016, Garrett DeWitt, Brainerd, MN. Defensive mother with cubs.

25. May 10, 2016, Bradley Veeder, 49, Great Smoky Mountains National Park, TN. Predator attack.

26. December 20, 2015, Rockaway TWP, NJ, Christopher Petronino, 50. Defensive or predatory?

27. October 24, 2015, Charlie Griffin, Eastpoint, Florida. Defensive attack.

28. October 7, 2015, Alan Bryant, Orange City, Florida. Defensive, going after dog.

29. October 2, 2015, Stephen Vouch, 29, Frank Church Wilderness, Idaho. Predatory attack.

30. September 28, 2015, Kalispell, MT. Elderly woman, unnamed. Authorities believe she was feeding the bear when she was attacked inside her house.

31. September 19, 2015, Clarie, Michigan, Ron Davis, 46, male. Hunter attacked; he stabbed bear with a knife.

32. September 12, 2015, 60, male, unnamed, northern New Mexico. Defensive momma bear.

33. August 14, 2015, Larry Yepez, 66, Mariposa County, California. Predatory attack.

34. August 13, 2015, unnamed male, 55, Fulton County, NY. Defensive attack, dog first.

35. August 10, 2015, Laurie Cooksey, 52, Millboro, Virginia. Predator attack.

36. July 7, 2015, Raton, NM. Unnamed teenage girl. Prey testing through tent.

37. Fontana Lake, NC, male, 16, Gabriel Alexander, June 8, 2015. Predatory attack.

38. June 1, 2015, Amherst, Massachusetts, Carly Hall, 17. Defensive with dog. Joint Base Lewis-McChord, about 45 miles south of Seattle

39. April 16, 2015, Unnamed male Defensive attack.

40. September 25, 2014, rural area of central California, woman. Defensive with dogs.

41. September 06, 2014, Jerry Hause, 60, Washington State. Predatory attack.

42. August 21, 2014, Hardy County, West Virginia, Steven Krichbaum, 59. Defensive attack; dog attacked bear.

43. June 25, 2014, Morgantown, WV, Kelly Dale. Defensives attack.

44. April 13, 2014, Florida woman attacked in her garage. Defensive attack.

45. December 12, 2013, Camille Bomboy, 18, Lock Haven, PA. Defensive attack.

46. October 30, 2013, Phil Anderson, Barron County, WI. Defensive attack.

47. September 14, 2013, Sandpoint, Idaho, Doug Harlicker. Attacked by sow in tree stand with cubs.

48. September 12, 2013, Adirondack, NY, Amy Stafford, 22. Prey testing.

49. Abby Wetherell, 12, Cadillac, Michigan, August 20, 2013. Predatory attack.

50. June 18, 2013, Burnett County, WI, Gerald Brown. Defensive attack with dog.

51. June 5, 2013, woman, 72, northern Minnesota. Defensive attack with cubs and dog.

52. May 17, 2013, Gerre Ninnemann, northern Wisconsin. Defensive with dog.

53. Joe Azougar, 30, male, May 12, 2013, northern Ontario, Canada. Predatory attack.

54. December 13, 2012, Pitkin County, CO, unnamed woman. Predatory attack.

55. November 27, 2012, Gary Lininger, 62, Clinton PA. Strange one, maybe killed by bear.

56. June 24, 2012, Payson, Arizona, Peter Baca, 30. Predatory attack.

57. June 21, 2012, Payson, Arizona, Jason Amperse. Predatory attack inside home.

58. June 18, 2012, Grafton, NH, Tracey Colburn. Defensive attack, dog involved.

59. Woman sleeping in a tent, 74, May 31, 2012, Payson, Arizona. Predatory attack.

60. Gord Shurvell, 65, north of Sioux Lookout, Ontario, May 23, 2012. Predatory attack.

61. Woman, 57, Thunder Bay, ON, August 6, 2011. Predatory attack.

62. Nick Mish, July 2011, Algonquin Park, Ontario. Vicious predatory attack.

63. July 14, 2011, Colville National Forest, Washington, woman, 36. Prey testing.

64. May 30, 2011, Cabot, Vermont. Jessica Miller. Defensive attack.

65. Richard Moyer and Angela Moyer, October 4, 2011, Oliver Township, PA. Defensive attack, chased dog into house.

66. May 23, 2011, Jacqueline Berghorn, 57, Center Harbor, NH. Defensive attack.

67. October 21, 2010, Centre County, PA. Bowhunter reports bear attack. Game Commission would not release the man's name and said no injury from bear.

68. September 17, 2010, John Chelminiak, Lake Wenatchee, Washington. Predatory attack.

69. July 15, 2010, Montezuma County, Colorado, unnamed male, 14, and female, 12. Predatory attack.

70. Gerald Marois, 47, 30 km northwest of Orillia, Ontario, May 25, 2010. Predatory attack.

71. Tim Scott, Red River Gorge, Kentucky, June 29, 2010. Predatory attack.

72. April 5, 2010, Parkville, New York. Predatory attack.

73. August 28, 2009, male, 78, southeastern Utah. Predatory attack.

74. Evan Pala, 8, old Gatlinburg, TN, August 12, 2008. Predatory attack. June 30, 2008, Sandy, OR, Dora Sue Redford, 58. Defensive attack.

75. September 21, 2007, La Plata County, Colorado. Adult man. Predatory attack.

76. September 2, 2007, Anthony Blasioli, 51, Kitsap County, Washington. Defensive or predatory.

77. Chris Everhart, June 22, 2007, Georgia. Bear was threatening children; father killed it with a log.

78. Nick Talbot, Standish, Maine, February 1, 2007. Defensive attack.

79. April 24, 2006, Forks, Washington. Unnamed male. Predatory attack.

80. August 1, 2005, Mary Munn, 50, Carlton County, MN. Defensive or predatory?

81. Jul 31, 2005, Teller County, Colorado, male, 49. Predatory attack.

82. July 19, 2005, Keelan Patton, 14, Coaldale, Colorado. Predatory attack.

83. July 22, 2003, Grand County, Colorado, unnamed male. Prey testing.

84. July 20, 2003, Jeff Nissman, Girdwood Valley, Alaska.

85. July 10, 2003, Nick Greeve, 18, 120 miles southeast of Salt Lake City, Utah. Defensive attack.

86. July 13, 2002, Greg Stalnaker, Salmon River, Idaho. Predatory attack.

87. July 12, 2002, Kristy L. Abbott, 27, Petersburg Mountain Trail, Alaska. Predatory attack.

88. August 2, 2001, Chaffee County, Colorado, male, 17. Prey testing.

89. July 24, 2001, Chaffee County, Colorado, female scout leader. Prey testing.

90. Jeff Schoendorf Sr., September 21, 2000, Saskatchewan. Predatory attack.

91. Carrie-Lynn Fair, 19, Dawson City, BC, on July 9, 1999. Predatory attack.

92. August 10, 1999, Matthew Murphy, 14, Long Lake, WI. Predatory attack.

One hundred and twenty-six attacks.
One problem with researching for this book was a complete lack of records

kept on the animal attacks. Hundreds more attacks have happened, but stories are hard to find after ten years. Websites are updated and articles are removed to make room for new ones. Where did the attack take place and who investigated it? Was it BLM, USFS, USFWS, or state officials?

With modern technology, there is no excuse for not having a national database of all attacks. Why are we paying all these government workers their salary when they hide information from us? All attacks should be on a national database with the full investigation for the public to read. You should not have to request information under FOIA. These people work for "we the people."

In most cases, I found more information from newspapers than any government agency.

Nonlethal Failures

Limitations exist to even the most intensive barrier maintenance effort. Carnivores that have become dedicated predators on livestock or humans have not been impeded by most barriers for long. (Treves and Karanth, 2003)

Isn't that interesting? Once a large predator targets livestock or HUMANS, they will figure a way through the barrier to keep killing. So much for the government's preferred nonlethal methods.

Black Bear Attacks

This book is not a complete picture of what is going on. Several stories are never told to the press. According to *The Alaska Dispatch News,* "Nearly 4 times more bears were shot dead than in 2016." This was in Anchorage, Alaska, only! Seventeen bears were killed by people who said they were defending their lives or their property. The other half were killed by police, park rangers, or wildlife biologists.

In May, police killed a black bear that charged two elderly women in East Anchorage. In July, a resident shot and killed a black bear attempting to break into his house. In October, police shot a black bear inside the Anchorage Post Office building.

In 2015, it cost nearly $10,000 to relocate a black bear sow with cubs from Government Hill to the Kenai National Wildlife Refuge. The bears were later *spotted in the town of Hope, where they continued to dig into the trash and killed a few chickens. Officials eventually shot four of the five relocated bears after one reportedly got into a vehicle.*

There is no greater example of the need for hunting than the state of New Jersey.

Harvest of nuisance black bears in New Jersey reducing human-bear conflicts

November 28, 2016

"Our research indicates regulated harvest of this recovered black bear population represents a pragmatic tool to help control population growth and, when coupled with incident-response management and educational programming, reduced the number of nuisance bear reports because hunters are more likely to harvest those bears with a history of being a nuisance," says USU researcher Jarod Raithel. "For New Jersey, managed harvest appears to provide a balance, ensuring bear preservation and protecting human welfare and property."

A managed harvest means sport hunting. After four years of hunting, the nuisance complaints and human conflict problems dropped by almost half in New Jersey. Hunting equals human safety.

Here is a perfect example of the three phases.

Prey testing. May 31, 2012, a 74-year-old woman at Ponderosa Campground, Arizona. She was awoken when a bear was clawing at her tent. The bear ripped open the tent and stuck his head in, clawing at the woman. Her screaming drove the bear off. She had bruises and a laceration on her scalp.

Prey tasting. June 22, 2012, Jason Amperse, 29. He was working on his unfinished cabin. The bear entered the building and bit him as he slept. Yelling and fighting back drove the bear off. He had bite marks on his right leg and claw marks on his left leg.

Prey eating. June 24, 2017. Going out for the first time camping, one of the last things you probably worry about is getting attacked by an animal. Unfortunately, that 's exactly what happened to Peter Baca of Southern California.

Baca, his one-year-old son, and his girlfriend set up camp in Ponderosa Campground for what was going to be his first camping trip and a birthday celebration. He was unaware of the reported bear attacks lately around that area as no warning signs had been issued by authorities.

As night fell, they all crawled into the tent to get some sleep. In the morning hours, Baca awoke with a sharp pain in his arm. He looked at it through the morning light and could see flesh hanging from it. He then saw the predatory black bear in the torn window screen of the tent. His son was sleeping right next to them. The bear continued the attack. Baca yelled to his girlfriend to grab the child and get out as he tried to keep the bear at bay.

His girlfriend was able to get out with the child. Baca stood toe to toe with the bear as the bear continued to maul him, engulfing his head and ripping his scalp and ear half off. Baca had torn flesh hanging off his body as the bear was trying to kill him. A nearby camper saw what was going on and started shooting at the bear with his small caliber pistol. The gunshots, along with other campers throwing rocks and sticks at the bear, finally stopped the attack and the bear took off.

The attack was over, but Baca was still tangled up in the tent. He barely had enough strength to get the tent off him. He tried walking to his truck but was severely out of breath with no strength left. Campers ran over to apply medical treatment with an advanced first-aid kit and even putting in an IV. Without that advanced first aid, Baca most likely would have died.

Baca lost a lot of blood and was airlifted to the nearest hospital for treatment.

"I remember being under the blades of the helicopter. The paramedics started coming. They cut my clothes off. I remember being very, very cold and thought it was because they cut my clothes off, but it was because I lost so much blood." (Fox 10, May 4, 2016)

At the hospital, Baca would wake up still trying to fight off the bear so worried about his son. He is still trying to navigate the emotional and physical pain of the attack that forever changed his life.

If you have the stomach for it, you can see the pictures of Peter in the hospital. fox10phoenix.com/news/136866488-gallery

January 30, 2017, Florida (Defensive)

In the Florida panhandle, a man had let his dog out into the front yard, but he did not know that a bear was out there too. The bear immediately started attacking the dog. When the man tried to get involved he got too close to the bear and the black bear turned on him, mauling him.

The attack was short lived and the defensive bear took off. The man and the dog both had to have medical treatment for several cuts and bruises. Wildlife officials set traps for the bear. (News Channel 8, Associated Press 1/30/2017)

November 20, 2016, Maryland (Defensive)

A 63-year-old woman, Karen Osborne, was attacked by a 200-pound black bear with three cubs outside her home in the late evening hours. She had gone outside her home to investigate her daughter 's dog barking when the defensive bear attacked.

Ms. Osborne was able to call 911 during the attack. She survived by fighting back then playing dead. She was left with a broken arm and required seventy stitches in her head and torso. The bear was later located and destroyed.

"He's getting ready to attack me again, please tell my husband I love him," *on the 911 call played on* WBALTV. (ABC/AP News posted Sun Nov 20, 2016)

October 23, 2016, Colorado (Defensive)

On a routine scouting trip for an upcoming hunting trip, a man was attacked by a black bear. The defensive bear was startled by the man and it charged and mauled him. The man fought back, and the bear stopped the attack and took off. The attack left him with minor scratches and bruises.

Even though this was a minor attack, wildlife services will try to trap the bear at which point it will be killed if DNA from the victim 's wounds matches the bear's.

No update if the bear was captured. (CBS Denver, CBS4 10/23/2016)

October 10, 2016, Sierra Madre, California, (Predatory)

Hiking about two miles on the Mount Wilson Trail, Dan Richman came upon two black bears. One was standing on its hind legs on the trail ahead staring at him. The other, which he did not see, was on his left and attacked him without warning. As the bear attacked, biting his wrist, leg, and neck, Dan yelled as loudly as he could, disrupting the attack for a moment.

The bear attacked again in which Mr. Richman then decided to stay perfectly still and in doing so, the predatory attacking bear began to stop the attack and eventually got off him and walked away. Dan had several cuts and multiple superficial injuries as he made his way down the trail covered in blood. A local resident saw Mr. Richman and called 911. He was then transferred to a local hospital to treat his wounds.

"If the bite had been a millimeter more it would have severed my tendon," Richman said. *"I'm just really fortunate."* (KTLA 5, Oct 10, 2016)

August 30, 2016, Virginia (Defensive)

Judy Milden went outside her house to see what her dogs were barking at. What she found was a black bear and her two cubs with the sow bear attacking the dogs. Judy tried to get the dogs away from the defensive bear, but the bear hit Judy with such power it knocked her off her feet and down a hill.

Luckily the bear stopped attacking and left. Milden rushed herself and her dogs inside the house. Milden and her dogs were left with multiple cuts and lacerations from the attack, which will take a while to heal. (WHSV3, whsv.com 8/30/2016)

June 29, 2016, California (Predatory)

An unnamed camper was in the Angeles National Forest looking at his iPad in his tent when a black bear tore through the tent with his claws cutting the camper's forehead. It was a quick attack. The bear immediately ran from the area according to witnesses. No food was present. The predatory bear was trapped and euthanized after tests confirmed it was the bear in the attack.

The camper was taken to a hospital where they received twenty-five staples to close up the cuts. (89.3 KPCC 6/29/2016)

June 28, 2016, New Mexico (Predatory)

"I have a fractured right orbit from the mean left hook, missing parts of eyelid and eyebrow, injury to the belly of my left bicep, and a lot of punctures and lacerations. But I am alive." This is what Karen Williams had posted on her Facebook page after getting attacked by a black bear as she ran a marathon in the Caldera National Preserve. Williams was three miles from the finish line when the defensive bear mauled her. Williams tried to stop the mauling by yelling no at the bear and raising her arms up to look bigger, but that had no effect; the bear attacked. Williams ended up rolling into a ball and playing dead. The bear stopped attacking as she played dead and the bear went back to its cub that was in a tree a short distance away.

The bear had a tracking device on it and authorities were able to track the bear down and euthanize it. (Health.com, June 28, 2016) Fox News Health

June 2, 2016, Arizona (Predatory)

An unnamed man in his twenties was sleeping inside a tent in an Arizona campground when a black bear scratched and bit through the tent, leaving the man with superficial wounds. The predatory bear retreated only after the man deployed pepper spray on it. The bear was properly identified by authorities and euthanized per Arizona wildlife code. (12 News KPNX 6/2/2016)

May 17, 2016, Minnesota (Defensive)

At approximately 10:00 p.m. on a Friday night, Catherine Hanson walked out on her deck. That is when a black bear attacked her. Hanson was able to fight back and get away but not without suffering serious wounds across her body. Hanson was able to make it back inside the house and call 911. Hanson was taken by ambulance to the local hospital for her wounds and recovery.

According to evidence at the scene of the attack, the defensive bear was a sow with cubs and most likely after the bird feeders located on the woman's deck.

Traps were set to capture the bear. No update on if that happened. (TwinCities.com, Forum News Service 5/17/2016)

May 10, 2016, Tennessee (Predatory)

Bradley Veeder had been hiking in the Great Smoky Mountains on the Appalachian Trail when he came upon the park trail shelter. The trail maintainers had told him that the shelter was full and they suggested he pitch his tent a couple hundred feet from the shelter.

Veeder put up his tent, hung his bear bag on the shelter's provided bear cables, and finished setting up the rest of his small campsite. As evening set in, Veeder entered his tent to sleep. He had been asleep for about two hours when a sharp pain in his leg awakened him. Veeder immediately knew it was a bear clamping down on his leg like a vise. Bradley started yelling at the bear and hitting it. The bear finally let go but returned several more times, trying to enter the tent as he continued to yell at the bear.

He had thought the predatory bear had gone after several minutes of silence, but when he went to unzip the tent door, the bear attacked again almost biting his hand. Veeder screamed at the bear again. At that point, the bear left.

Bradley slowly made it back to the main shelter to get first aid and contact park rangers. He was driven to a hospital for medical treatment.

The next day, hikers found Bradley 's camping equipment torn apart about a hundred yards away from where his tent was originally located. Everything Veeder had, including tent poles, were torn and chewed up. He felt very lucky that he was able to get away before the bear came back again. (10 News. wbir.com 5/10/2016)

October 24, 2015, Florida (Defensive)

One of the last things you would think of when taking your trash out to a dumpster is a bear popping up out of the dumpster as you throw your garbage bag in, but that 's exactly what happened to Charlie Griffin.

Mr. Griffin had just opened the dumpster 's lid to throw in his trash bag when a 400-pound black bear jumped out and started chasing him. The bear chased him down and swiped at him, putting a severe cut in his arm. With his arm gushing blood, it ran down his leg, leaving bloody footprints. Griffin had just about reached his truck but slipped and fell. The bear turned around and headed off in a different direction.

Authorities believe it was a defensive attack based on the fact that the bear stopped the attack promptly and left.

Said Griffin, *"I don't know whether I was going to live or not, I'll tell you the truth, but I came through it."* (WCTV.tv Oct 24, 2015)

October 8, 2015, Idaho (Predatory)

Stephen Vouch was bighorn sheep hunting with his friends in the backcountry of the Frank Church Wilderness of No Return when a black bear tried biting his head while he was sleeping under an open tarp.

Vouch was awoken by something biting at his head. He reached up and felt his head and it was all wet. He heard the bear breathing behind him.

Vouch yelled out as he realized the predatory bear was biting his head. The bear jumped back, entangling himself in the tarp. His friend hearing the scream of Vouch and the commotion woke up. He realized it was a bear and shot it with his .45 caliber pistol, wounding the bear.

The 250-pound bear quickly ran up the closest tree where Vouch went ahead and killed the bear, not wanting to leave it wounded and have it attack someone else.

The experienced backcountry hunters had stored all their food and supplies correctly to keep bears and other animals from being attracted to the smells. This bear decided though that Vouch must have smelled tasty.

The injuries sustained were not life-threatening and it took three days for the hunters to get to a location to fly out. After getting back home, Vouch went in for medical treatment. (AL.COM, Associated Press 10/8/2015)

October 7, 2015, Florida (Predatory)

Alan Bryant let his dog out the front door to go to the bathroom. The dog then ran to the backyard. Bryant followed the dog to the back yard but by the time he got there a large black bear had already killed his dog.

The bear then charged towards Bryant. He tried running back into the house, but the bear easily caught up to him, swiping at his legs and knocking him down. Bryant's wife had been inside watching the whole thing, and as Bryant went down his wife came running outside screaming, scaring off the bear.

"My wife is thankful that he didn't get me. It's just a terrible thing," Bryant said.

(NBC News, Oct 7, 2015)

September 28, 2015, Montana (Predatory)

When wildlife officials say don't feed the bears, people should take that very seriously. Unfortunately, an elderly woman did not take that advice and continued feeding a black bear on a regular basis at her rural residence.

That led to an attack inside the woman's home as the predatory black bear tried to kill her. The bear did end up stopping the attack and disappearing but not without leaving her with serious wounds throughout her body.

No update on whether the bear was killed or the woman survived as she was in critical condition at a hospital. (Billings Gazette 9/28/2015)

September 19, 2015, Michigan (Predatory)

A man out porcupine hunting was attacked from behind by a black bear. The man was able to pull out a knife and stab the predatory bear. The bear then retreated into the woods.

The man was treated for minor injuries and traps were set to catch the wounded bear. No update on whether the bear was trapped. (USA News Today, Associated Press 9/19/2015

September 12, 2015, New Mexico (Defensive)

While sitting at a watering hole waiting for elk to show up, a bowhunter was attacked by a black bear. The man had seen a couple of bears that day and even took pictures of the bear that attacked him, which had a cub with her. Authorities believe the bear, feeling a threat to her cub, charged at the man. The hunter fired a warning shot with his pistol then climbed up a tree to get away. The defensive bear chased after the man up the tree, biting his foot. He then fired at the bear several more times scaring off the bear or wounding it.

The bowhunter radioed for help from a guide and when they showed up, the hunter was still in the tree almost to the top. That was the fourth bear attack on a person in New Mexico in only half a year. (Albuquerque Journal 9/12/2015)

August 14, 2015, California (Predatory)

At 4:00 a.m. in Mariposa County, 66-year-old Larry Yepez stepped out his front door to get some air. As he stood on his porch a black bear attacked him from behind with no warning, knocking him to the ground.

Mr. Yepez is a Vietnam veteran and a tough individual. He fought the bear off by using his reflex training and experience. The predatory bear bit into his head and other areas and left multiple deep cuts in his legs, arms, and abdomen.

Even with all the injuries, Mr. Yepez was able to get away from the bear and drive himself to the local hospital for medical treatment. Fish and wildlife were in the process of searching for the bear. No update on if they found it. (Sierra Sun 8/14/2015)

August 13, 2015, New York (Defensive)

A man in his fifties was walking his dog in the southwest corner of Adirondack Park when they encountered a black bear. Authorities were not sure if the bear attacked the dog first or the dog attacked the bear. As the attack was taking place, the man tried stopping the attack by hitting the bear with a stick. The bear then turned on the man, mauling him. The defensive attack was brief and the bear ran off.

The attack victim then made it back to a road where drivers saw him and stopped to render aid. He was eventually taken to a hospital to address his puncture wounds and scratches. The dog was taken to a veterinarian. Both had non-life-threatening injuries. (NCPR 8/13/2015)

August 10, 2015, Virginia (Predatory)

A family of experienced hikers was on a routine hike. Coming back down the trail, Laurie Cooksey, 52, and one of her sons, Ellis, walked ahead out of view of the two other family members. As they walked ahead, Ellis spotted the black bear just fifteen feet in front of them on the trail in a position ready to charge.

Laurie and Ellis tried to run but that was a mistake. The bear caught them within seconds clawing Laurie on the back. The two realized their mistake and started sliding downhill to get some type of an advantage, but the bear followed, latching onto Laurie 's leg behind the knee and shaking her. The mother kicked and hit the bear creating a moment where the bear let go, slipping down the wet hill a bit. The two attack victims ran as fast as they could back up to the trail towards the rest of their family.

Yelling as they approached the other two-family members, they first thought they were joking but soon saw the blood on their mom and the bear not too far behind. Blake, who was familiar with what to do during a bear attack, started waving his arms and yelling while the other family members threw rocks at the predatory bear, driving it away.

After getting back to the trailhead, authorities were contacted, and Laurie received medical treatment for several puncture wounds, cuts that required stitches, and rabies shots. The bear was found and killed per state policy.

For Laurie, the overwhelming feeling of thinking you're going to be killed by a bear has left her with no desire to go hike anywhere where there may be bears ever again. (People 8/10/2015)

July 7, 2015, New Mexico (Predatory)

A teenage girl was bitten and scratched as a predatory black bear tried to attack her as she was sleeping in a residential backyard. The bear had to be scared away twice by the homeowner by shooting towards the bear with his handgun.

The girl was treated at a local hospital and released.

(Ammoland.com, New Mexico Game and Fish 7/72015)

June 11, 2015, North Carolina (Predatory)

Gabriel Alexander, a teenage boy, was asleep in his hammock on a backpacking trip in North Carolina when a black bear attacked him by first grabbing him by the skull and dragging him out of the hammock. The boy's father, Greg, was awakened by Gabriel's screams. Greg could see the predatory bear attacking his son. He immediately rushed over and kicked and jumped on the bear until it finally released his son. The father continued to throw rocks at the bear to keep him at bay.

The two made it down to the lake where two other campers who had a boat took them across the lake to Cable Cove boat dock where they called 911 and received medical attention for the serious wounds.

"I just felt a lot of pain in my scalp," Alexander said. *"I had no idea what it was. I thought maybe it was a wild dog. I just remember my scalp tearing."* (Citizen-Times, June 11, 2015)

April 22, 2015, Washington (Defensive)

Being attacked by a bear once is horrific enough. But twice? That's what happened to a man in Washington named "Bob" (real name not given).

The first time he was attacked was four years ago in a location about an hour south of Seattle. According to Bob, he was walking his dog and ran into a black bear, startling it. The bear charged Bob and started mauling him. He ended up rolling up into a tight ball and the bear stopped the attack, leaving him with minor cuts and bruises.

The second time he was attacked was in the same location with the same dog. There was no rolling up into a ball in this attack. He grabbed a large branch and started hitting the bear as it attacked. The blows from the branch did not have a lot of effect on the bear as it continued to spin and attack several times, biting him at least forty times.

Eventually, the bear ended the attack and ran off, leaving him with several puncture wounds and severe cuts. Wildlife officials wasted no time tracking down the bear and killing it. Bob confessed his hiking days are over in that area. (ABC News, 5/22/2016)

September 25, 2014, California (Defensive)

East of Santa Barbara, a woman was walking her dogs when she was attacked by a black bear.

She was letting the dogs run around but had lost sight of them for just for a moment. Soon though, the dogs came running back with the bear chasing them close behind.

When the bear saw the woman it immediately started mauling her.

During the attack, the bear pushed the woman downhill. The defensive bear then ended the attack.

The woman sustained bites, deep scratches, and a broken rib. She was able to make it to a nearby house for help. An ambulance took her to a local hospital to receive medical treatment. She was released later that evening.

Even though it was most likely a defensive attack, traps will be set in the area and if the correct bear is caught it will be destroyed, according to fish and wildlife division. (Bangor Daily News/Reuters 9/25/2014)

September 6, 2014, Washington

A bowhunter by the name of Jerry House was resting against a tree when a black bear came charging him out of nowhere. House had no time to draw his bow and his reaction was to just climb up the tree he was leaning against.

House thought for sure he had climbed high enough to get away from the bear but the angry predatory bear had no problem climbing up that tree and biting into his leg. As the bear clamped down on his leg, House kicked the bear squarely on the nose with his other foot, hurting the bear enough for it to let go and climb down the tree. It ran off ending the attack.

House was able to make it to his vehicle and drive to get medical treatment for the deep puncture wounds the bear left. (Fox News 9/6/2014)

August 21, 2014, West Virginia (Defensive)

Steven Krichbaum, 59, was walking his dog in the national forest when they came upon a black bear and her two cubs. The dog chased the cubs, attacking them. That is when the defensive bear attacked Krichbaum, causing severe injuries.

After mauling Krichbaum and the dog, the bear left the area. Steven and his dog were able to make it back to their vehicle and drive to a local market to get help. Krichbaum and his dog were taken to medical clinics to get the required medical attention for the deep wounds. (localdvm.com, WHAG News 8/21/2014)

FOUR SECONDS UNTIL IMPACT

July 1, 2014, West Virginia (Defensive)

A woman, Kelly Dale, had yet to see a bear in the wild. When bears started hanging around the family's property she was excited to have a chance to see one. She had gotten several pictures when the bears would show up at night, but they would easily have frightened by clapping or other loud noises and take off.

However, on June 25, Kelly went out to get something out of her car and that is when she was attacked by the black bear. Kelly had just shut the car door when she heard a chilling growl. She turned around and saw a cub. She automatically knew she was in trouble.

The mother bear came out from behind the car and charged Kelly, attacking her. The bear started mauling Kelly, putting a gash in her head. The bear swung at Kelly's midsection severely bruising her ribs all the while Kelly is screaming from the attack. The bear turned with its mouth opened like it was going to bite Kelly in the neck. That is when she decided to fight back; she screamed directly at the bear and hit it. That was enough to disrupt the attack and the bear stopped, gathered up her cub, and left.

This was a problem bear that had already been tagged and designated as such. No report on whether the bear was caught and killed.

Kelly Dale was quoted, "I beg that I never ever even see a bear again." (July 1, 2014, MetroNews)

May 8, 2014 (Predatory)

Seven co-workers tried to fend off a deadly bear attack.

"It was ... seven people that were working in a group area and she was attacked by this bear out of that group and dragged off," said Scott Doherty, a spokesman for Unifor.

"People tried to stop it and do everything they could. Obviously, they are fairly horrified at what they saw and witnessed."

Actor Alan O'Neill, who has appeared on the TV show Sons of Anarchy, *wrote in a tweet, "Heartbreaking & devastating news for all my family at the very tragic passing of my beautiful vivacious cousin in Canada. #RIPLornaWeafer."* (The Globe and Mail Canada, The Canadian Press 4/8/2014 Updated 3/25/2017)

December 12, 2013, Pennsylvania (Defensive)

A teenage girl, Camille Bombay, was out hunting deer near her family farm when she came upon a black bear with cubs. The bear charged at Bombay, mauling her. As the bear clawed and bit Bombay, she screamed, frantically alerting the teen's father. The bear only stopped the attack and left after Camille's father shot his rifle in the air.

Camille was left with several cuts with her ear nearly torn off. After a brief stay in the hospital, she was able to return home.

The father, Michael Courter, told his wife, "Can't get her scream out of my head... I could see her face; it looked like she had been massacred." (Dec 12, 2013, Daily News)

November 1, 2013, New York (Predatory)

Amy Stafford was an experienced hiker having hiked all forty-six of Adirondacks' highest peaks. Amy was on the Northville-Placid Trail when she noticed three bears behind her. She wasn't too worried and even took a couple of pictures. She continued walking the trail but the bears followed. Amy tried everything you're supposed to do when confronting a bear: wave arms, scream at them, play music on her phone, try to look big. None of that had any effect on the bears and they continued following her, sometimes going around on the side of her and even in front of her.

At this point, Stafford became very worried and pulled her folding knife out of her backpack. A small weapon for a bear but that was all she had.

Amy understood she might be attacked from the behavior of the bears and was ready. A short time later, the largest bear charged at her. With knife in hand, Amy swung at the bear as it came within inches of her, stabbing it in the jaw. Blood gushed out of the bear's jaw and down Amy's hand and arm. The bear ran away as fast as it charged, meeting up with the other two bears.

After the attack, Amy started walking away. Not seeing the bears any longer she began to run down the trail until she got to Lake Durant State Campground. Once there, she knocked on the caretaker's cabin door for help. The knife was still in Amy's hand when a woman answered the door.

The sight of the woman helped Amy calm down from all the adrenaline, but she had a hard time speaking without starting to tear up.

State forest rangers arrived and took Amy's statements and she even took them to the place of the attack. Nothing she did could explain the exact cause of the attack other than they were predatory bears.

Amy was quoted as saying, "The whole time I am thinking, if this bear wanted me, it could have me, it could have me in a heartbeat." (Nov. 1, 2013, Adirondack Explorer)

October 30, 2013, Wisconsin (Defensive)

Phil Anderson was in the middle of hunting grouse at a wildlife refuge when he encountered a black bear.

Anderson heard branches cracking and then he heard his dog call out in distress. He ran over to his dog and saw a mother bear with cubs attacking the dog. He yelled at the bear hoping to scare it away but instead, the bear stopped attacking the dog and immediately charged at Anderson, knocking him down before he could even react. The bear quickly swiped, knocking him to the ground, and bit Anderson a few times deeply cutting him. The sow stopped the attack and went back to the dog.

Anderson regained his composure and got up on his feet. He yelled at the bear again trying to stop it from killing his dog and the bear once again charged at Anderson, but this time Anderson had his shotgun ready and shot it within three feet of him, killing it instantly.

Anderson and his dog limped back to his truck and drove home. His wife then took him to the local hospital for first aid but then had to be airlifted to a different hospital to close up his more extensive wounds. Both Anderson and his dog recovered. (WQOW News 18 10/30/2013)

September 14, 2013, Idaho (Predatory)

A deer hunter was about seven feet up in a tree stand when a black bear attacked him. Doug Harlicker saw a large sow black bear and two cubs on a game trail not far from him. He noticed the bear had caught wind of his scent and was following it back to his tree stand.

Once the bear reached the tree, it looked up at Harlicker and immediately pinned its ears back and shot up the tree. Harlicker had barely any time to react. Once the bear was on him he was able to strike the bear hard on the side of the head with his elbow, knocking the bear out of the tree.

The bear landed on the ground, got up, stared at Harlicker for about a minute, and then took off with her cubs.

"I wouldn't have time (to shoot) even if I had the gun in my hand — It was that fast," said Harlicker.

(Sept 14, 2013, Bonner County Daily Bee.com)

June 18, 2013, Wisconsin (Defensive)

Gerald Brown was tending to his backyard when a black bear entered his property and got into a fight with his dog.

Brown tried to break up the fight and in turn, Brown was mauled by the bear. Brown's brother was with him in the backyard and when it started attacking Gerald, his brother shot at the bear, scaring it away.

Gerald ended up with extensive injuries and had to be flown to a hospital for medical treatment.

Brown survived but no update on whether the bear was ever captured and killed. (Journal Sentinel 6/18/2013)

June 5, 2013, Minnesota (Defensive)

After checking outside her property to see if a black bear with her three cubs had left the area, a 72-year-old woman let her dogs out of the house. Soon though, three cubs came running out from under her deck. Her golden retriever gave chase after the cubs.

The woman ran down the stairs yelling for the dog to come back. That is when the sow who was heading towards the dog made a sharp turn and headed for the woman. Before she could even think what to do, the bear knocked her down and was mauling her. The bear stopped the attack and started walking away, but spun around and came back for another attack, biting the woman in several places. The bear stopped the attack and headed towards the direction of the cubs.

The woman was able to call 911 and was transported to a hospital for medical treatment for her serious wounds.

Conservation officers reported to the area and soon came across the bear. One officer shot and killed the bear after the bear saw the officer and started charging towards him. The three cubs were old enough to make it on their own, so they were not captured. (WCCO, CBS Minnesota 6/5/2013)

June 5, 2013, New Mexico (Predatory)

A black bear broke into a bedridden woman 's home through a screen door and attacked her. Fortunately for the elderly woman, the bear only scratched up her head and face.

The housekeeper found the woman in need of medical aid after coming to the house to check on the elderly woman. The bear was tracked down and killed per state regulations. (USA Today 6/5/2013)

July 15, 2011, Washington (Predatory/Prey Tasting)

A large black bear attacked a woman as she was running on a trail in Colville National Forest.

The woman was thrown down and she curled up in a fetal position. The bear scratched and pawed at her and left the scene.

The woman was treated at a local hospital and released that evening. Washington Fish and Game set out to find and kill the bear. No update was found as to whether or not the bear was located.

(Competitor Running)

May 17, 2013, Wisconsin (Predatory)

Gerre Ninneman was shocked when he looked outside and saw his yellow lab being attacked by a black bear. He ran outside yelling at the bear and raising his arms to scare the bear away, but instead of the bear running, it let go of the dog and came charging towards Ninneman.

Ninneman turned around and ran but the bear quickly caught up, tackling him to the ground, biting and scratching him. Ninneman was able to fight him off and get back on his feet and run towards a shed. Again, the bear quickly caught up to him and started attacking once more.

Marie, Ninneman's wife, was watching the whole attack from inside the house. She quickly ran down to their basement and retrieved a shotgun. Just one problem. She did not know how to load it. Marie ran outside with the shotgun and started hitting the bear over the head with the shotgun. The bear stopped the attack and backed off, letting the two escape into the house.

The bear did not give up though. It followed them to the house, pacing back and forth on their deck and looking into the windows. The couple called the authorities and a deputy arrived quickly. The deputy shot and killed the bear.

Ninneman was taken to the hospital for medical treatment for puncture wounds, scratches, and deep cuts that had to be stapled shut. The black bear was only a year old. (Fox News 5/17/2013)

May 12, 2013, Ontario, Canada, Joe Azougar, 30

"I could feel his teeth rubbing against my skull. That was the worst feeling ever," Joe Azougar, 30, said Sunday from his hospital bed at Lady Minto Hospital in Cochrane, Ont.

Joe was eating breakfast on the front porch of his cabin when the bear attacked. He was screaming for help when two "angels" driving by came to his recuse using their car to scare off the bear. Joe was seriously injured during the attack and required 300 stitches to close all of his wounds. (Toronto Sun May 12, 2013)

December 13, 2012, Colorado (Predatory)

Imagine taking a nice nap on your deck of your rural home only to be awakened by a black bear biting down on your leg. That's what happened to a woman in Pitkin County as she slept.

Of course, the intense pain of the bite woke her up screaming in pain and scared the bear away. She then went into the house to call authorities, but the bear remained in her front yard. As the authorities arrived, the bear climbed into a nearby tree where it was tranquilized and later killed. (timetoast.com)

June 18, 2012, New Hampshire (Defensive)

A woman who lives in Grafton, NH, was attacked next to her home by a black bear shortly after letting her dog outside.

The bear left deep scratches on the woman's arms before it took off. The bear had two cubs with it, so authorities believe it was a defensive attack spurred on by the presence of the dog. (CBS Boston)

October 11, 2011, Pennsylvania (Defensive)

Richard Moyer got up at his usual time at 3 a.m. to get ready for work. He let their dog out the front door where it immediately took off into the surrounding woods. Within a short amount of time, Richard heard his dog barking and growling. He knew something was not right.

Moyer got out his spotlight to see what was going on. That's when he saw the dog sprinting back to the house with a black bear right behind. The bear chased the dog into the house where it immediately started attacking Moyer. Moyer's wife, Angela, was awoken by the frenzy and came downstairs to help. The bear then turned on Angela and started mauling her. The dog then jumped on the bear's back attacking it. At the same time, Richard rejoined the fight by leaping into the bear, which apparently made the bear even more aggressive, biting and clawing Richard's back. As fast as the attack happened, the attack stopped. The bear just walked outside and sat down on the porch.

By the time authorities arrived the bear had left the area. The couple was then taken by ambulance to the local hospital.

Angela had several puncture wounds and a cracked vertebra. Moyer had to have thirty-seven staples in his back and head in addition to several puncture wounds.

Game commission officers put out traps for the bear but no update on whether it was caught or not. (CNN 10/4/2011)

The New York Public Library Digital Collections

Frost, A. B. (Arthur Burdett) (1851-1928) "Just in the Nick of Time."

September 17, 2010, Washington (Predatory)

John Chelminiak was out at his cabin in eastern Washington to get some work done on the cabin, listen to some football games, and get some much-needed relaxation. John's simple plans at the cabin took a horrifying turn.

The evening came around and at 8:30 p.m., he decided to take his two dogs for a walk. Chelminiak leashed them up and headed down the driveway. He was only seventy-five feet from his house when he heard a noise in the bushes and a huffing sound. Before he could even wonder what it was, he heard nails scraping on the paved road and the bear was on him.

Chelminiak, with dogs still in hand, fought back as hard as he could. The predatory black bear at only 150 pounds had no problems clawing, biting, and pushing Chelminiak to the ground. But Chelminiak kept getting back up, trying to fight back but not face the bear head on.

The attack paused for a brief moment and Chelminiak tried to run back to the house. The bear quickly gave chase, jumping on the two dogs. Chelminiak pulled on the leashes as hard as he could, freeing the dogs, but the bear quickly started attacking Chelminiak again.

Chelminiak, fighting the bear back, yelled to his wife to call 911. His wife heard the commotion outside and came outside to see what was going on. She then heard her husband say call 911. Their 11-year-old daughter was there and she quickly dialed 911. The motion detecting lights on the cabin switched on as his wife came out of the house and scared the bear off. Chelminiak's wife could see her husband on the ground but still did not comprehend what was going on, until she saw the bear. It did not go too far and was just down the street pacing back and forth.

Chelminiak laid there on the driveway with blood gushing from his face. He could not see, as the blood from his wounds poured into his eyes. The bear had ripped into his left eye requiring the doctors to remove it.

The flesh was torn or hanging off parts of his body with a gouge so deep in his neck you could see his spine. An ambulance was at the scene within fifteen minutes, taking Chelminiak to Central Washington Hospital and from there airlifted to Harborview Hospital where surgeons tried to put the pieces back together.

Chelminiak required several more surgeries and was fitted for a prosthetic eye. The bear was located and quickly killed. (Seattle Times 10/6/2010, updated 10/11/2010)

July 15, 2010, Colorado (Predatory)

Two siblings were attacked by a black bear as they slept in their residential backyard. The predatory bear bit the boy on the leg. The boy woke up screaming in pain. Grabbing his flashlight, he shined it on the bear and the bear ran away.

His sister had also been bitten but did not notice until her arm started bruising.

The brother and sister were treated by paramedics. No word on whether or not the bear was tracked down. (The Denver Post)

June 29, 2010, Kentucky (Predatory)

Tim Scott was hiking with his dog in the Red River Gorge area when he noticed something was behind them. As he turned, a black bear was in the middle of the trail. The bear eventually left but soon returned. Tim was a couple of hundred yards ahead of his wife and son and was just about to call them and warn them about the bear when the bear appeared on the trail. It began walking towards him. Scott tried to avoid the bear but the bear followed. The dog became very excited, so Tim decided to let her go. The dog took off away from Tim and the bear.

The bear came even closer. Scott decided to drop his belongings including his backpack, but this did not deter the bear. As Scott turned to try to get a foothold up the hill, the bear lunged, attacking him and biting down on his calf. The bear continued the aggressive attack by clawing, biting, and shaking him violently. Scott was on the ground with the bear's teeth deep into his body.

At this point, Scott remembered the knife he carried in his pocket but had to wait until the bear stepped off his thigh to get to it. He retrieved the knife and was about to stab the bear in the eye when a pair of hikers saw what was happening and ran over to help. Anthony Gobel, one of the hikers in the pair, slung his daypack at the bear striking him several times. The bear stopped attacking. That is when Scott's son and wife showed up yelling at the bear and waving sticks at it.

Had the attack not been stopped by the brave hikers and his family, Scott most certainly would have been mauled to death and eaten.

After the attack, Scott was bandaged up and he applied a tourniquet belt to stop the bleeding from the large holes the bear left.

With help, Scott made the long trek back down the trail with the bear still trying to follow them for much of the way, eventually disappearing. Shortly after making it back to the trailhead, an ambulance arrived to take him to the closest hospital. After medical treatment at that hospital, he was transferred to another one where he received sixty stitches to close all his wounds.

No update on if the bear was ever trapped or found.

"The bear was not interested in the man 's belongings. He was more interested in a predatory nature." (Herald-Leader, June 29, 2010)

August 28, 2009, Utah (Predatory)

During a rafting trip down the Green River, a 78-year-old man was attacked by a black bear.

A nine-member family group and four guides had set up camp on the riverside around 6:00 p.m. At that point, a bear was spotted heading towards their camp. When the bear got too close, one of the members fired a warning shot in the air, scaring the bear off out of sight.

Nightfall came, they were not really worried about the bear coming back. Some members slept in tents while others out in the open on cots.

At around 12:30 a.m., the bear came back. Members of the group awoke to the 78-year-old man being attacked by the bear. They quickly came to his aid with one of the daughters of the man jumping on the bear and hitting it. It took several family members to stop the attack and pull the man from the bear. As soon as everyone was clear, a family member shot the bear and it took off running. It was later found dead not too far from the attack site.

The man was left with puncture wounds throughout his body plus deep scratches. The guides radioed for help and the man was life-flighted out of the remote area to a hospital where he recovered.

The rest of the family members were flown out by airplane and the bear was retrieved by wildlife services. (Emery County Progress 8/28/2009)

June 30, 2008, Oregon (Defensive)

A woman went to investigate noises in the back of the house. She opened the back door and saw a black bear eating out of a garbage can that she kept bird seed in. The bear swiped at her, scratching her arm, and then ran off. The woman had to have minor medical treatment for her wounds. (Salem News 6/30/2008)

September 19, 2007, Washington (Predatory)

Mountain bike rider Anthony Blasioli was riding a trail he was very familiar with in Banner Heritage State Park with his two German shorthaired dogs when he was attacked by a black bear.

The dogs that Blasioli takes with him usually run a short distance ahead of him and warn him when there are other mountain bikers or horseback riders ahead. In this instance, the dogs barked a couple of times ahead of him. Blasioli got off his bike to let whoever pass.

It was not another mountain biker or someone on horseback that wanted to pass. It was a bear the dogs initially barked at and it headed straight to Blasioli at full speed attacking him. Blasioli was able to use his bike as a partial shield as the bear was mauling him.

Blasioli fought back, kicking the bear, hitting the bear, and anything else he could think of as the bear bit through his helmet, mangling his ear then biting and almost tearing off his lip.

The bear, deterred from Blasioli fighting back and dogs barking, stopped the attack and took off, leaving Blasioli with flesh hanging off his left arm and huge gashes in his back. Blasioli was able to climb back on his damaged bike and ride back down the hill where he met up with other bikers that helped him get medical care.

Doctors thought they may have to amputate the arm but they managed to put most of it together; he will never have full use of his arm again. No update on whether the bear was tracked down and killed. (Today 9/19/2007)

March 30, 2007: (GMU 391, Jefferson County, Colorado) Injury: A 38-year-old woman suffered a number of abrasions and cuts on the side of her body and legs when a yearly bear attacked her on her porch. At approximately 12:30 a.m. the woman was in the process of bringing her dogs into the house when the attack occurred. Jefferson County State Patrol deputies assisted a DOW officer in the search for the bear. A small (yearling) bear was tracked a short distance away from the scene and observed to be blonde in color. Two other bears, at least one being a yearling and black in color, were also observed close to the scene. The lone blonde bear began to walk down the hill towards the other bears but when it was approximately fifteen yards from the DOW officer it turned and began to charge in his direction. The officer shot and killed the charging bear. The black yearling bear then ran toward the blonde yearling. The officer fired a second shot in the second bear's direction. Both the black yearling bear and the third bear ran away from the scene. The woman was treated and released from a metro Denver hospital.

(Draft Colorado Division of Wildlife Reported Bear Attacks on Humans, 1990 to present)

February 1, 2007, Maine (Defensive)

Eighteen-year-old Nick Talbot got a rare visitor at his parents' house, a black bear. Talbot was pretty excited to see the bear, so he grabbed his camera and went outside to snap some pictures. Even though his dog was barking he did not notice the bear getting agitated or that she had two cubs nearby.

Before Talbot could react, the bear charged at him, swiping him down with just one paw. Luckily the bear stopped the attack, took her two cubs, and left immediately, leaving Talbot with just some scratches and bruises.

"It's unbelievable how an animal that big is that fast," Talbot remarked.

April 28, 2006, Southern Colorado

Harold Cerda, 29, just left the outhouse when the bear attacked, hitting him so hard he flew ten to fifteen feet. *"I'm used to hard falls because I used to ride bulls a lot. It's pretty much the hardest I've been hit,"* Cerda told the *Associated Press*. Seeing the bear walking off, he headed for the car and the bear started following him. Making it to the car, he quickly started the engine and closed the electric windows. He noticed his lunch had been eaten by the bear. The bear sniffed at the windows and bit the tires. Cerda took a couple of pictures and drove to the hospital. He had bruises and possible nerve damage to the neck and shoulder. (timetoast.com)

April 24, 2006, Washington (Unknown)

A hunter in the area of Forks, Washington, was attacked by a black bear. The details are vague about how the attack happened. A second hunter saw the attacked man being dragged by the bear and at that point, the second hunter shot and killed the bear.

The attack victim had a fractured arm, broken hand, and several cuts and bites to his body. The victim did survive. (National Geographic News 4/24/2006)

August 1, 2005, Minnesota (Predatory)

Mary Munn was walking back from a short hike from her house when she was attacked by a black bear.

Munn had just emerged from a wooded area when she saw the predatory bear standing on its hind legs staring at her. The bear immediately charged her. Munn was only able to take a few steps to get away, but the bear was already on her.

Munn had been holding a large stick and she broke that over the bear, but it had no effect. She punched the bear several times in the nose as the bear scratched and bit her. The dog distracted the bear but the bear would come right back to Munn and continue the attack.

The dog nipped at the back of the bear and the bear chased after it, letting Munn stand up and catch her breath. Her knee had been badly hurt and she made a groaning sound as she stood up. The bear heard her and ran back over, knocking her to the ground. It grabbed her by the waist, shaking her. The bear let go then bit her one more time in the armpit. After that, the bear turned around and took off. The attack was over about as fast as it began.

Munn was able to get up and walk back to her house. She never looked back to see if the bear was following her. She just concentrated on trying to make it home without dying. The dog joined up with Munn before she got back to the house. She then called 911 and waited for help.

The bear left her with multiple wounds that doctors had to repair but luckily there was no damage to internal organs.

Traps were set for the bear but no update on whether it was caught. (Minnesota Public Radio 8/1/2005)

July 19, 2005, Colorado (Predatory)

A fourteen-year-old Texas boy, Keelan Patton, was camping in Colorado with his family when a black bear attacked him through their tent.

The bear bit the teenager's head and put deep cuts in his hands that required fourteen stitches as he fought back against the bear. The attack was short lived. Once the boy fought back, the bear immediately stopped attacking and left.

Keelan said, "It was so unreal. It was like a dream - a very painful dream." (July 19, 2005, The Denver Post)

July 22, 2003, Colorado (Predatory)

A man was sleeping outside next to his truck when a noise awakened him. What he heard was a black bear standing over him. Startled, the man kind of jumped up and the bear swatted him, scratching his face. The man stood up and the bear backed off. He was able to get into his truck and honk the horn, scaring the bear away.

No medical treatment was required. The bear was not tracked. (timetoast.com)

July 20, 2003, Girdwood Valley, Alaska

Jeff Nissman had an hour-long battle with two predatory bears. The more aggressive one charged. He climbed on top of a downed tree and threw sticks at the bear. That didn't work. Next, he picked up a large stick and charged the bear, forcing it to climb a tree. As soon as he left, the bear would chase after him at full speed. He slowly made ground until he reached the road. That is when the bear stopped following him. That bear was in prey testing mode. (*Anchorage Daily News*)

July 10, 2003, Utah (Predatory)

Eighteen-year-old Nick Greeve from Oregon was on a five-day whitewater trip in Utah with an Outdoor Leadership Class when he was attacked by a black bear.

The group of fifteen campers was camped for the night, sleeping outside under the stars in just sleeping bags. The predatory bear grabbed Nick by the head and tried dragging him away from the other campers. The other campers awoke to Nick screaming. They quickly intervened, chasing the bear away.

Nick was able to be taken to a hospital to receive medical treatment for several puncture wounds on his head and neck. He was released the same day, heading back to Oregon with a horrifying tale. (Southeast Missourian, Associated Press 7/10/2003)

August 10, 2002, Idaho (Predatory)

A trip of whitewater rafting and fly fishing on the Salmon River took a horrifying turn for Greg Stalnaker of Idaho when a predatory large black bear attacked him.

On the second day of the trip, the group of adventurers set up camp along an embankment of the river. Mr. Stalnaker decided to get some peaceful fly fishing in.

As Stalnaker headed over some rocks and down to the river, he turned and saw that a large bear was staring directly at him. The bear made a false charge. Stalnaker put up his arms and waved and yelled at the bear. The bear turned around and seemed to be heading off. Stalnaker had seen lots of bears over the years so he was not that concerned. The bear turned around again, charging once again, and from the looks of the bear, Stalnaker knew this time was different.

Stalnaker began to run towards the river but the rocky terrain made it very difficult. He came upon a twelve-foot cliff and jumped as it was his only option. The bear came around the side off the cliff, still intent on attacking him. Stalnaker, now already hurt from the jump, headed into the water but the bear was already upon him, clawing at his legs. In the river, Stalnaker tried backing away from the bear into deeper water. He slipped and the bear was on him again, pinning him down trying to get a bite in. Stalnaker fought back the best he could, getting away from the bear and heading towards even deeper water. The bear was relentless, still coming after him by swimming.

The other campers and guides heard the battle and sprang into action. The guides rushed down to help Stalnaker in their kayaks. The other campers rushed towards him over the rocky hillside.

The guides reached Stalnaker just in time, smacking their paddles on the water and yelling at the bear. The other campers threw rocks at the bear. The bear turned around and swam back to shore but even then, it did not leave, pacing back and forth, waiting.

The guides finally did drive the bear off but it returned a couple more times and the guides had to drive it off again.

The guides quickly returned Mr. Stalnaker to camp. Applying first aid, they bandaged up his puncture wounds and scratches. Luckily an EMT and doctor were in the next group. From that point, they determined that Stalnaker 's injuries were not life-threatening and he decided to keep going on the trip. Forest service was contacted but they were unable to find the bear; however, they did have to kill another bear not too far from where this attack happened because of a separate attack. It was determined the bear they killed was not the one that attacked Stalnaker. (No info on this second attack.)

"Walking downstream to the river I was thinking, It doesn't get much better than this," Mr. Stalnaker recalled recently. (Aug 10, 2002, The Frederick News-Post)

July 12, 2002, Alaska (Predatory)

Kristy L. Abbott, 27. Kristy was jogging along a trail when she spotted a black bear in front of her. She sounded her air horn to scare the bear away but instead, the bear charged her. For an hour and a half, she traded blows with the bear. Using a stick to beat on the bear to keep it back, she hid behind a tree and for fifteen minutes they ran around it. She said the animal was thin. After hitting the bear in the head, maybe in the eye, the bear gave up. Kristy suffered bite and claw wounds. (*Peninsula Clarion*, Anchorage AP 7/12/2002)

August 2, 2001, Colorado (Predatory)

A 17-year-old Boy Scout was sleeping in the same tent at the exact location as the previous attack (July 24, 2001), when a black bear entered the tent, bruising the boy's back, resulting in some minor injuries. The boy's screams woke the scout leaders who then chased off the bear.

No word on if the bear was tracked and killed. (timetoast.com)

July 24, 2001, Colorado (Predatory)

While on a scout camping trip, one of the leaders was attacked by a black bear while she slept in her tent. The predatory bear entered her tent at which point she screamed for help, waking the other camp leaders who came and chased off the bear. The bear was later found and destroyed by wildlife officials. (timetoast.com)

September 13, 2000, Colorado (Predatory)

Four hunters were attacked by a large black bear while out hunting. The predatory bear managed to pin one of the hunters to the ground, biting him in the buttocks. Another hunter was knocked down, bitten on the hand and leg as they tried to fight off the bear.

One of the hunters was finally able to shoot at the bear with their pistol, injuring the bear and making it run away. The bear was later found dead by wildlife officials. (Summit Daily, The Associated Press 4/28/2006)

August 10, 1999, Wisconsin (Predatory)

Mathew Murphy was at a Boy Scout camping trip when a black bear attacked him.

The fourteen-year-old boy was sleeping in a tent at the campground when the predatory bear ripped through his tent and started attacking him. Murphy fought off the bear. The attack stopped about as quickly as it began but Murphy was left with serious wounds and had to be taken to a hospital for medical treatment.

Authorities were looking for the bear and if found, they will destroy it. No update was found about whether the bear was found or not. (Orlando Sentinel 8/10/1999)

August 14, 1997, Liard River Hot Springs Provincial Park, BC, Canada,
Reader's Digest

Two people would die before the rampaging beast was put down.

Patti McConnell and son Kelly were driving to Alaska from Texas. They stopped at the park. Patti spotted the bear first and warned her son. He at first thought she was joking.

Turning around, Kelly came face to face with a large black bear. He knew not to run. The bear snorted and lunged through the railing. Kelly yelled, "Run Mom." She ran to the end of the platform and the bear was on her. The 13-year-old charged the bear, kicking it in the face. "Get off my mom!"

The bear looked up, grunted, and turned back to the attack. Kelly, desperately searching for a weapon, grabbed a sawed-off branch and hit the bear in the head, screaming for help. The bear ignored him and continued with his captured prey. Kelly could see his mother's blood on the bear's teeth. Enraged, he took his best baseball stance and swung for the home run hit on the bear's nose. This drew blood and the bear had enough of this nonsense. With a single swing from his powerful paw, it ripped deep in the child's neck and shoulders. The bear charged the young man, grabbing the boy by the waist and picking him up, shaking him like a rag doll. He thought he was going to pass out. The bear stopped shaking him and slammed him on the deck. Kelly curled up in a ball. His mother laid on the platform, her skin gray, open eyes unblinking.

Ray Kitchen, a 56-year-old truck driver, heard the screams for help and ran over to see what could be done. He first saw the bear ripping and tearing at Kelly's body. He picked up a tree limb and started yelling and beating the railing with it. The beast ignored him. He tore off a larger limb and jammed the bear in its stomach, trying to get it off the boy.

This enraged the bear. It charged, hitting the man with such force the man broke through the railing, crashing down into the brush with the bear right with him. Dressed only in swim trunks, Ray crawled on his knees to a tree. He tried to protect his head with his hands and yelled for help.

Frank Hedingham, 71, heard the yelling, "Bear, help, get a gun." By now the word had spread and panicked people raced out of the area, adding to the confusion.

Ingrid Bailey, a wilderness firefighter and paramedic, with her friend Brad Westervelt, arrived on scene. They quickly saw two bloody bodies on the deck. Kitchen was being torn alive by the bear. The bear was holding him by his upper arm and shoulder ripping his body to shreds with its claws. The commanding strength of the bear was too much for Ray to overcome.

Hedingham and Westervelt picked up a large thick tree trunk and tried using it like a battering ram. Bailey joined them and the three kept hitting the bear but it refused to leave its prey.

Westervelt dropped his end of the tree trunk and said, "I am going for a ranger."

The bear suddenly changed his attack, grabbing Kitchen by the throat and throwing him in the air. Bailey yelled, "NO!"

The bear hesitated and dropped Kitchen to the ground. His windpipe was ripped out and his face torn badly. The bear had almost decapitated him. He was dead and the pain was over.

Bailey ran to Patti first. She was dead, but her paramedic training had taught her to try to resuscitate. Hedingham heard Kelly moan. Racing to his side, he couldn't even begin first-aid treatment before the bear claw appeared on the deck inches away from Kelly. Was he trying to retrieve his kill? Hedingham, a 71-year-old with a heart condition, was fed up, kicking the bear in vicious blows to drive him off. The bear walked off, heading toward the boardwalk where more people were still passing by. Kelly was crawling toward his mom saying, "Help my mother."

Hedingham knew by the sight that it was too late for Patti. "Don't worry. We're doing all we can. You mustn't move. Breathe slowly."

More help arrived. CPR was started on Patti. Another wrapped Kelly's wounds in a towel.

The quiet was suddenly shattered as a new scream rang out in the park. Arie Van Der Velden was hurrying down the boardwalk when he heard, "A bear is coming! Run for your lives."

In the ensuing panic, Arie slipped and fell into the brush. In seconds, the bear was on top of him slashing away. Arie grabbed both ears, trying to keep the bear back and kicking him in the nose. The bear was unbothered, ripping his flesh with his powerful claws and biting into this left thigh.

Dave Webb from Alaska had a bloody man come up to him and say, "We've got to do something, there is a bear up there." Dave nodded and ran for his motorhome. He carried a 30-30 and .223.

He yelled to a young man standing by, "Do you know how to use a gun?"

Duane Eggebroten, 27, said, "That 30-30 I do."

They loaded up and ran for the boardwalk.

The younger man reached the area first and heard moaning. The bear now had Arie propped against a log, feeding on him. Duane carefully aimed for the back of the neck of the bear and fired. The bear slumped. Duane thought he was dead but not taking any chances, pumped two more rounds into him.

When Ingrid heard the shooting, she yelled out, "Shoot it again. Shoot it again."

The death battle was over.

Patti McConnell and Ray Kitchen both died from the attack. Kelly McConnell and Arie Van Der Velden both made full recoveries.

Canada awarded Kitchen the Star of Courage posthumously in September 1998. Frank Hedingham, Kelly McConnell, Ingrid Bailey, and Brad Westervelt were awarded decorations for bravery.

It's one of the bloodiest multiple-victim bear rampages that has happened in recent history, but not the worst for fatalities. That award is for the next bear.

May 13, 1978, Forty-Nine Mile Creek in Algonquin Park, Ontario, Canada

Brian Morris, who taught history at General Panet High School, took Billy Rhindress, George Halfkenny, and Mark Halfkenny, on a fishing trip. Fishing along Lone Creek, Brian took a nap in the car as the teenagers worked the creek for trout. He awoke at 6:30 and was surprised the boys had not returned yet.

Calling their names, he walked along the creek but there was no reply.

He jumped in his vehicle and drove the road looking for the kids but discovered he had a leak in his gas line. He decided to go home and repair it. Stopping at Sand Lake gatehouse, he informed the ranger there were three boys still out fishing but he would be back. At 9:30 he returned, but still no sign of the boys. Police and park officials were notified.

The next morning, four hundred troops from the 8th Canadian Hussars started the search for the boys. Helicopters flew search patterns. Everyone must have been thinking they would soon find the boys hungry, cold, and a little scared.

Lorne O 'Brien, conservation officer, searched for the boys but fog and rain had hampered his search. He had seen twenty-nine bears in the area. He requested tracking dogs be brought in.

George 's khaki jacket was found first, with blood stains and turned inside out. His fishing pole was still on the bank with line in the water.

A hundred yards down on the other side of the creek, a trampled area was found with Mark's broken eyeglasses. Farther down, they found Billy's left shoe.

One searcher yelled out, "There's a bear!" Standing up over his kill stood a 275-pound black bear. More help arrived soon; forty soldiers were facing the bear. He was protecting his kill and would not leave. The bear dropped to all fours, walking away. It turned and headed for the soldiers. No one was armed! The soldiers had no choice but to retreat.

One of the helicopter pilots thought the noise from the blades could be used to drive the bear off. They blasted the bear downhill thirty yards from the wind. The stubborn bear recovered and returned to protect his kill. O 'Brien, armed with a carbine, said he would go kill the animal. Ontario Provincial Police Constable Ray Carson would be his back up, armed only with his service revolver.

The bear backed off and they sat back to back, ready to fight. The bear came out a few yards away; O'Brien fired three times and the bear dropped.

The bear was in predatory mode. It's believed he killed and cached one boy at a time as they walked into the area. Others thought maybe he attacked the first boy and the other two came to his aid. We will never know for sure.

With that many bears in the area, it's clear one bear decided to return to the old ways of hunting humans for food.

(The Daily Observer)

October 11, 1991, Raymond Jakubauskas, 32, and Carola Frehe

The two were camping in Algonquin Provincial Park, Ontario. While they were setting up camp on Bates Island, a black bear broke both of their necks. The bear then dragged their bodies into the woods and consumed the remains. When police arrived five days later, the bear was guarding the bodies. *A park naturalist called the attack "right off the scale of normal bear behavior."*

Right off the scale of normal bear behavior? Or normal bear behavior after losing the fear of man?

(Toronto Star*)*

Chapter 8
Wolf Attacks

We feel like we're trapped. The hills around us, they don't look safe anymore to the people in the village. —Virginia Aleck, 66, a village elder, said after the Candice Berner fatal attack.

Wolves Attacking The Family Of A Back-Settler. 1835
The New York Public Library Digital Collections

The most dangerous month for wolf attacks is September in North America. The second most dangerous month is August.

I found this in the New York Public Library Digital Collections. I would love to know the story behind this. I would imagine this is the true story of early settlers battling the wolves, the kind of facts that the animal rights groups will go to great lengths to hide from the public.

Perception of wolves is carefully cultivated in the public mind. Notice when Discovery Channel or National Geographic does a show on wolves, they are very careful to craft the show in propaganda format to make the wolves as heroes. At the same time, they deliberately hide the facts that show the truth about wolves.

Another way to hide the destruction wolves are causing is to lie to the public about the official wolf count. In 2008, Dr. Mech testified in federal court under oath that the Rocky Mountain wolf population was most likely double the official number or around 3,000 wolves.

I will give an example of the lengths the wolf lovers will go to hide evidence about wolves attacking people. Researching, I found a website that had historical accounts of settlers in the early 1800s Arkansas. One account was of a husband returning home at night. He never made it. His wife searching for him the next day found him hanging from the waist on a tree branch high in a tree. The snow around the base of the tree was covered by wolf tracks. It was believed the man climbed the tree to save himself from being killed by wolves. He used his belt to keep himself from falling out of the tree if he fell asleep during the night. Unfortunately, it was brutally cold that night and he froze to death.

This website was filled with simple historical accounts of other wolf attacks and the hardship of early settlers. The wolf lovers so attacked his website over this he shut it down. For the man's health and sanity, it was easier to close the website down instead of putting up with the terroristic threats.

But what these people think is very important to understand their motivation. Biologists and conservationists see wolves as impressive and fascinating, a social and intelligent animal; the very incarnation of "wildness." The illusion of pure wilderness because you may hear a wolf howl.

But the truth is wolves are dangerous predators. They clean out an area of wildlife; what do you think starving wolves are going to feed on next?

In France, historical records compiled by rural historian Jean-Marc Moriceau indicate that during the period of 1362–1918, nearly 7,600 people were killed by wolves, of whom 4,600 were killed by non-rabid wolves.

Wolves: the power of the pack
Nov. 12, 2017, by The Brain Bank North West
A reputation which appears well founded as there have been at least 14 wolf attacks this year alone, injuring almost 30 people.

By National Park Service -
http://www.nps.gov/media/photo/view.htm?id=E6FE02AF-1DD8-B71C-07270855E406666C, Public Domain.

WOLVES are to blame for mauling death of retired university professor, 62, in Greece, says coroner. September 25, 2017, By Charlie Bayliss Daily Mail

She was attacked by a pack of wolves and was able to call her son, stating, *"Tell them it's wolves not dogs. I know the difference."* Her son in the UK called for help in Greece. She made her frantic call for help on Thursday. Her body and remains were not found until Saturday morning. The coroner ruled her cause of death was wolves.

Ten Attacks in Four Months: Brazen Wolves Preying on Children in Israel 's South
Haaretz News, Nir Hasson, September 22, 2017

On May 10, a wolf entered a tent holding two children, a one-and-a-half-year-old, a three-year-old, and their mother. She screamed and kicked at the wolf who would not leave. Other people rushed to her aid and were able to drive off the wolf. The wolf returned two hours later and attacked the daughter. The wolf had tried to pick her up and run off with her. The child suffered puncture wounds in her back.

The attacks continued throughout the summer. Bet you never saw that on the evening news.

How many wolf attacks have you heard about? One or two I bet. The rest are quickly covered up and hid from public view. Here is a recent attack.

November 2016, Canmore man attacked by wolf. Canmore is a town in Alberta, Canada, located approximately 81 kilometers (around 50 miles) west of Calgary near the southeast boundary of Banff National Park.

"I am definitely sure that it was a wolf that I saw," he said, noting he's still *nursing some bruises and cuts from trying to get away. "It was lucky that I got out of there. It was definitely a terrifying experience."*

The man was shocked there was no public warning out about vicious wolves in the area. Can't tell the public the truth about wolves, can we?

Wolf attacks Canadian mine worker.

August 29, 2016

The incident happened Monday morning at 12:05 a.m. CST at Cameco's Cigar Lake uranium mine, about 600 kilometers north of Saskatoon. Cameco spokesperson Rob Gereghty told the CBC News that a contractor at the mine was mauled by an unprovoked wolf while taking his lunch break.

"The injured contractor received immediate medical attention from a security guard who interrupted the attack and scared the lone wolf away," Gereghty said.

"He wasn't more than about 50-60 meters away from our main campsite. He was airlifted to the hospital and was expected to make a full recovery."

Canada's Occupational Health & Safety Magazine said, "The attack victim appeared to be recovering in good spirits." Struthers added, "He's obviously had a pretty frightful experience, but he underwent surgery and that went well."

I went to great lengths to try and track down this man to interview him. I was blocked every step of the way. No one would even release his name.

Worldwide exclusive: Wisconsin Deer Hunter Fends off Wolves with Walter PK .380

NRA Hunters by Jon Draper- Wednesday, September 30, 2015

Matthew Nellessen was scouting for the upcoming deer season. Thirty yards away he saw a wolf. He pulled out his Walter PK .380 and chambered a round. As her racked the slide he noticed two more wolves flanking him on his left side.

"It all happened so fast," said Nellessen. "It was maybe 3-4 seconds and the wolves were on me."

The first wolf came in from the right, mouth open, fangs ready to rip into Nellessen's leg. A swift kick from the man's boot landed square on the wolf's face and deflected the bite.

The other wolves moved in to press the attack. The next wolf leapt at Nellessen. He jumped back firing a single round into the animal. The other two wolves ran off at the sound of the gun shot and the third limped after them.

He was using full metal jacket ammunition and the wounded wolf was never found.

The Weather Network
Rabid wolf chases two families on snowmobile trip in Labrador

Saturday, January 31, 2015 - Two families say they're grateful to be alive after a frightening run-in with a rabid wolf in Labrador last Sunday.

Sexton says the interaction lasted about 20 minutes.

"There was nowhere you could put your kids safe enough or get away fast enough because he was right behind you," said Sexton in an interview with CBC. "He came directly at the Ski-Doo, right for us, showing his teeth."

The two families began fearing for their lives as the wolf began lunging at the snowmobiles, standing up on its hind legs near the children.

"I screamed in my helmet, but no one could hear me," said Patey.

Eventually, the families were able to get away and track down wildlife officers, who immediately sprang into action. After a 25-minute hunt, officers tracked down and killed the rabid wolf, staring death in the face.

Five persons injured in a wolf attack in Hashampur village
Posted on: September 26, 2014, News18

Five persons were seriously injured in a wolf attack when they had gone to collect grass from a jungle here, police said on Friday.

The incident took place on Thursday when Khem Chand, Kamlesh, Rita, Baljore, and Maksood had gone to collect grass from a jungle at Hashampur village under Ramraj police station in the district, they said.

Horrific wolf attack in Chinese village leaves six people disfigured and one missing an ear after pack of five 'starving mad' beasts surrounded small farming community. August 13, 2014, Daily Mail

Horrific wolf attack in Chinese village leaves six people disfigured and one missing an ear after pack of five 'starving mad' beasts surrounded the small farming community.

In September 2013, Noah Graham, 16, of Solway, Minnesota, was bitten in the head at a Chippewa National Forest campground near Lake Winnibigoshish. The wolf tested negative for rabies. That attack occurred at night while Graham was lying on the ground, but not inside a tent.

Attacked By a Wolf! What One Smart Cyclist Did to Save His Life, *Readers Digest* July 12, 2013

On a bright, warm July afternoon, Mac Hollan, 36, an elementary school teacher, was cycling along Route 1 in Canada's Yukon, midway through a 2,750-mile bike tour from his home in Sandpoint, Idaho, to Prudhoe Bay, Alaska.

Mac's heart jumped. He reached into his handlebar pack to fish out his can of bear spray. With one hand on the handlebars, he fired the spray at the wolf. A bright red cloud enveloped the animal, and to Mac's relief, it fell back, snorting and shaking its head. But a minute later, it was by his side again. Then it lunged at the back of Mac's bike, tearing open his tent bag. He blasted the wolf a second time, and again, it fell back, only to quickly resume the chase.

Mac was pedaling hard now. He waved and yelled at passing motorists but was careful not to slow down. He rounded a bend in the road to see a steep uphill climb before him. He knew that once he hit the hill, he'd be easy prey. Mac imagined the wolf's teeth tearing into his forearm as he tried to fend the animal off.

Paul and Becky Woltjer were driving their RV down Route 1 on their way from Pennock, Minnesota, to Alaska. They didn't think much of it when they saw two cyclists stopped on the side of the road. A bit later, they spotted what they, too, assumed was a dog loping with immense strides alongside a man on a bike. As they got closer, they realized the dog was a wolf.

He escaped into the RV saying, "I thought I was going to die."

CTV Winnipeg
Woman says timber wolf attacked her while she was near side of road helping motorist
March 15, 2013

"The wolf jumped at my neck and took hold," said Dawn Hepp. *"His whole jaw was wrapped around my neck."*

She survived because she was wearing a thick scarf. She froze and didn't fight back. The wolf was confused and let go. She suffered wounds to her neck. This was prey testing.

Daily News-Miner, **Fairbanks, Alaska, December 17, 2012**: A wolf attacked a Tok trapper on his snow machine last week about thirty miles off the Taylor Highway, biting through the man's parka and three layers of clothing to put a 3-inch gash on his arm.

Lance Grangaard, 30, said he was "puttering along" on his Ski-Doo Tundra on Thursday afternoon, coming down a frozen creek, when he saw the wolf out of the corner of his eye.

"I turned in time to stick my arm up," said Grangaard, who was trapping with his father, Danny, in a remote area off the Taylor Highway known as Ketchumstuk. *"A single black wolf grabbed my arm and started jerking on me."*

Findings Related to the March 2010 Fatal Wolf Attack near Chignik Lake, Alaska

Candice was a young small woman, 32 years old, 115 pounds, four feet eleven inches. She was hired as a school teacher in Chignik Lake, Alaska, population seventy-three with seventeen students. She spent the day teaching school children and after school, she told a co-worker she was going for a jog.

On March 8, 2010, the weather was 24 degrees and the wind blowing at 35 mph with gusts up to 53 mph. Snow and blowing snow periodically reduced visibility to one mile. Candice jogging in this weather indicates she was in excellent physical shape.

At 6 p.m., four snowmobiles were returning to the village when the lead snowmobiler spotted blood on the trail. He stopped to investigate. He walked downhill and discovered a human body. All four snowmobilers returned to the village to report the incident to the Alaska State Troopers.

The wind was blowing into the wolves and they knew Candice was a human. This was no chance encounter. Candice came around a bend; seeing something caused her to turn around and run back toward the village. Was it the lead wolf, a healthy hundred-pound female wolf on the trail, showing aggression? Or was it the two other wolves flanking her? We will never know for sure. The wolves now were in sight knowing full well this was a human. Later DNA testing confirmed the fat healthy female wolf was the main attacker on Candice.

Tracks indicated she traveled 360 feet from where she turned around to the point she died. One mitten was found and believed to be the first attack on her. Her second mitten found sixty-three feet later had one thumb torn off. From the first traces of blood in the snow, she would have fought or run another forty feet. The next attack came with several wolves at once converging on her. It is believed she was knocked to the ground. A second spot where she fell or was knocked down was ten feet from the last attack site.

It appeared she was crawling, trying to get away from the bloodthirsty attack. It appeared the wolf or wolves grabbed and dragged her down the hill. The extent of blood in the trail now indicated she was severely wounded. There was no more sign of struggle and it 's believed to be the place she died. In the snow, this would look like a slasher film with blood covering large portions of the area.

The next part is very graphic. We as humans have forgotten an important detail in the wilds. We are meat to a predator. Prey to be eaten. The photo at the scene indicated the wolves dragged her farther downhill. How much they ate at this spot is unknown.

The three snowmobilers returned to preserve the scene and the body. When they returned, the wolves had moved the body another seventy feet. Two of the snowmobilers returned to the village for warmer clothes. The lone man circled 200 feet downhill from the body using his headlight on the snowmobile to look for the wolves. When a wolf was spotted, the man left and returned to the village. Three men returned, and the body had been moved again and more of the body was partially consumed. The wolves were moving the body to protect their "kill" the same way they would protect a caribou kill. When this event was reported to AST (Alaska State Troopers), they instructed the residents to move the body to the community for safekeeping until investigators arrived (AST report).

Nine different wolf tracks were recorded within thirty feet of the body. All nine wolves are thought to have been killed in the cull that lasted until March 26, 2010. One was wounded and never recovered; the other eight were sent in for testing.

Reading this report is heartbreaking. We know for sure that wolves were attacking a human; they could smell her long before they saw her. If wolves are shy and exclusive, why didn't they take cover as soon as they smelled her? If the wolves were starving, why was the female that did the main attack called a fat healthy wolf? None of the normal excuses for animal attacks work here.

There were only seven wolves per 1,000 km with plenty of moose, caribou, and snowshoe hares in the area. Two of the wolves were in poor condition. It appears they were two and three years old, a male and female, and may have broken away from the pack or were following to be able to feed on scraps. The rest of the wolves were considered in good health.

One of the pups that was shot weighed 100 pounds and was considered fat. The female pup may have weighed more because it had a full belly of moose meat. She was shot March 25, 2010, fifteen days after the attack on Candice.

Prior to the attack, a lone wolf was spotted at distance watching people. The uninformed would think this is great. I saw a wolf, how thrilling. But to someone who understands wolf behavior, this is a clear danger zone. The wolves were studying humans as prey. How to attack and escape. No one in the village actively trapped or hunted wolves.

Why do I bring up no hunting pressure? You must think like a predator. How much can they get away with? They come closer to the village and nothing bad happens. They watch and study humans and nothing bad happens. Their courage is built up. Who knows, they may have closed in on humans several times and were not seen? The wolves could clearly see the humans and were studying, wondering, what do they taste like?

Wolves can hear as far as six miles away in the forest and ten miles in the open. The wolf's sense of smell is a hundred times greater than a human's; the wolf possesses as many as 200 million olfactory cells. The wolf has extremely powerful jaws that can generate 1,100 psi of pressure, almost twice that of a large dog. Nature provides these for breaking moose bones.

The vegetation in the area was small shrubs with a height of ten feet. No tall trees to climb. This could have saved Candice's life if she could have climbed a tree.

Because of their highly developed nose, I believe they can smell fear. When you're scared, you put out pheromones, sweat. If you run, you act and smell like prey. A pack of wolves can drive a grizzly off a kill. A lone human stands no chance against these vicious predators unless they are armed.

Candice Berner, rest in peace.

Does this mean every single wolf you come across is planning to attack you? Of course not. But what it does mean is active hunting protects human life. When one wolf is shot, the remaining pack members smell the spot. They understand a human did it. Humans are something to fear and avoid. The female will teach their young when they smell humans to run and hide.

When wolves become brave and stop to study humans, if they are shot they quickly learn this is a bad idea. The idea that you can coexist with large apex predators like wolves is beyond normal thinking. More on the verge of insanity. In the lower 48, attacks on people by wolves are quickly covered up and hidden from public view. The propaganda machine is never ending when it comes to wolves.

People have a hard time understanding the size of wolves. They try to compare a hundred-pound dog to a wolf. The truth is, a hundred-pound wolf is almost twice the size of a hundred-pound dog. The Canadian monster they put in the lower 48 from the Yukon is a great example. These wolves stand at the shoulder almost the same size as a full-grown buck deer.

People have been bombarded with wolf propaganda for so long, they no longer can think for themselves. The so-called experts have said over and over again that wolves have never attacked anyone in North America. This misinformation was put out mostly by David L. Mech.

Painted by Richard Ansdell, May 6, 1854, "Travelers attacked by Wolves."
New York Public Library Digital Collections

Mech wanted to erase 300 years of history in North America. He set rules for wolves to be listed as killing a human. The list requires certain things to be met, one of which was that all attacking wolves had to be tested for rabies. Therefore, all the attacks on humans prior to rabies testing did not happen.

Journalists did not fact check the historical record and took his word for it and the propaganda was spread throughout the land. The only record I could find when rabies first started being tested was in Texas in 1943. The laboratory at Houston's public health department became the first laboratory in Texas other than the Texas State Department of Health to conduct rabies testing.

It appears that prior to 1943, all wolf attacks on humans were swept under the rug and magically didn't happen. Why is this important when thousands of attacks and over a hundred fatalities by wolves are in the historical record?

Kayaker fights off hungry wolf on North Coast
Larry Pynn, CanWest News Service
Published: Wednesday, August 01, 2007

VANCOUVER — A Port Moody kayaker 's recent life-and-death struggle with a hungry wolf on B.C. 's remote North Coast — the second wolf attack in the province in seven years, and the first thought to involve predatory intent — has prompted a conservation officer to warn against taking wolf encounters too lightly.

This is a predatory attack when the man stopped on an island for the night. The wolf grabbed the man's arm and held on. The man fought him off, punching and kicking but the bloodthirsty wolf would not let go.

Dragging the wolf over to his kayak, the man was able to retrieve his knife and stabbed the wolf several times before the wolf ran off.

The man's legs, hands, and arms were too torn up to continue kayaking. He radioed for rescue. A nearby fishing boat arrived and the men tracked down and finished off the wolf with a single shot.

Bet you never saw that on the evening news, did you?

A Canadian newspaper offered a $100 reward for any documented wolf attacks. They soon had to pay out and quickly dropped the offer when six people were attacked by a lone healthy wolf.

The Hamilton Spectator wrote this story in September 2006.

Six injured in rare wolf attack

Her son, Casey, 12, noticed a black, doglike animal running across the beach. She said the animal nipped the ankle of her 13-year-old nephew, Jake, then clamped down on her son 's buttock, carrying him about half a meter before dropping him and lunging at her.

The wolf's teeth tore into her hands and her leg as she fought back, and the group raced into the shallow swimming area. Wright said the wolf followed them, this time going after Emily Travaglini-Wright, 14.

"(Emily) was a real fighter. . . She got mostly claws in her head and her arm," her mother said.

Leah Morgan from Marathon, Ontario, was attacked by a wolf at

Katherine 's Cove, Lake Superior Provincial Park. She was with her grandparents who rescued her from the wolf as it tried to drag her away.

Anchorage woman attacked by wolf.
State wildlife biologist says there 's little doubt about the attacker.
Posted: Thursday, July 13, 2006
Wanamaker was walking along the Dalton Highway northwest of Fairbanks on Friday when she saw the gray and white wolf about 20 yards away. That 's when the animal ran at her.

"It sunk its teeth into the back of one of my legs and I kind of stumbled, but I kept running toward the outhouse," she said, referring to an outhouse at the highway pullout. "I was pretty scared and I remember thinking, 'Don 't fall. If you 're down on the ground, you 're toast. '"

The wolf bit her again. But she managed to escape into the outhouse calling out for help. Other campers came to her aid. They helped bandage her up and gave her a ride back to her friend's camp. They quickly left for the hospital.

State wildlife biologist Mark McNay had little doubt it was a wolf that attacked Wanamaker.

The case of Kenton Joel Carnegie (February 11, 1983 – November 8, 2005). This heartbreaking case and the corruption that followed included National Geographic and many major news outlets, all trying to hide the facts that a pack of vicious wolves killed Kenton. Six weeks after the attack, a "so-called" wolf expert flew up to examine the site. He claimed he saw a bear track in the snow in one of the pictures. You got it, six weeks later, he ignored all the eyewitnesses including the RCMP report of only wolf tracks at the scene and claimed a bear killed Kenton. This set off a firestorm of problems.

Kenton's father did not rest until the case was settled in court. The court ruling was wolves indeed killed Kenton Carnegie.

Having spent a lot of time in the woods, I knew right away it wasn't a bear attack. There was ice on the lake. People failed to grasp the significance of ice on the lake. Trapping and hunting for a long period of time in Upper

Michigan, once ice had formed all the way across the lakes, you would never see another bear track until spring. Especially in February. To believe this, you have to accept that a bear woke up from hibernation months early, just happened to come out right where and when a pack of wolves was chasing Kenton off the lake, then ambushed and killed the young man, leaving the body for the wolves to eat, and then went back to hibernation without leaving bear tracks clearly in the snow. Must be a magic bear. Kenton's remains were later found in the stomach of two of the wolves in the area.

(See Doctor Val Geist's written statement on Kenton wolf attack at the end of this chapter.)

National Post: 'The bear hunted him ': BC camper killed by black bear didn't stand a chance. May 12, 2015.

The bear believed responsible for the attack was located and destroyed.

His fiancée, Jami Wallace, said he fell asleep by the campfire and she went to bed in the RV around 1:30 a.m. The next morning, she could not find Daniel Ward Folland O'Connor, 27. Searching for him she found a blood trail in the woods, and 200 yards later she found his body. She called the BC Conservation Office. Arriving on scene, the first animal seen was a wolf; they shot and killed it. Only later was a bear shot.

Did the Canadian authorities remember the uproar from Kenton's death and simply blamed it on the bear? We can only guess.

Wolf attacks Saskatchewan man Jan 4, 2005, CBC News Canada

On New Year's Eve of 2004, a wolf lunged at Fred Desjarlais while he was on his way home from the Cameco uranium mine in Key Lake.

The lone wolf bit him on the back, arms, legs, and groin. Grabbing the wolf by the neck, he tried to wrestle it to the ground with no success. Luckily for the man, a busload of miners came down the road and stopped. They were able to chase the wolf off. Without help he could have been a fatality.

Desjarlais survived the attack but required stitches and rabies shots.

Wolf attack in Palampur area
Times of India | August 19, 2003

In the past six months, the animals have cleverly managed to kill ten children in villages of Balrampur while the last four killings have been reported in the month of August itself from villages near Laliya and Araiya thana.

Wolf attack has science community mystified. July 5, 2000, The Globe and Mail

Mr. Langevin told rescuers he was awakened by something pulling at his sleeping bag. When he saw it was a wolf, Mr. Langevin covered his head with his arms and tried to roll away, but the wolf clamped its jaws around his hand. Soon the animal was gnawing at Mr. Langevin's head.

How bad were his wounds? Fifty stitches were required to sew up all the wounds. Other campers in his group drove the wolf off or he would not be alive. As stated under bear attacks, the same applies to wolves. If a wolf attacks you in your sleeping bag, you better fight with everything you have. They know you're human and this is a predatory attack, meaning they plan on eating you.

Deadly attack of a wolf upon a man, and heroic conduct of the man's wife. 1859
The New York Public Library Digital Collections

Wolf attacks boy in Icy Bay
Posted: Thursday, April 27, 2000, Juneau Empire

YAKUTAT —A six-year-old boy was bitten three times by a wolf on Wednesday at a logging camp in Icy Bay, according to Alaska State Troopers.

The wolf apparently was trying to drag the child into the woods when it was driven off by an adult. The wound in the small of his back was the most substantial bite, with puncture wounds and some tearing. The wounds to the buttocks were only puncture wounds. ``He was aware of the other people around him, but his whole intention was trying to take off with the little boy. He had literally picked the little boy off the ground, and this little boy is probably about 70 pounds. ''
The wolf, an adult male weighing about 75 pounds, was then chased into the woods by a dog. The father shot the wolf 10 minute later it was wearing a radio collar.

The seventy-five-pound wolf picked the boy right off the ground. If there weren't other people in the area to save the child, the wolf could have easily run off and devoured him, never to be seen again.

Synopsis of survival encounter with a pack of twenty wolves in Ontario w/ Kellie Nightlinger

https://www.youtube.com/watch?v=FdOXiGOgrwE

September 27, 1998, in Algonquin Provincial Park, Canada, a 19-month old boy was grabbed by a wolf and tossed three feet. A Case History of Wolf-Human Encounters in Alaska and Canada By Mark McNay

Man-eating wolves terrorize Indian villages
July 22, 1997, CNN

UTTAR PRADESH, India — *What happened to 10-year-old Manwati sounds like a nightmare.*

But the small child has the scars to prove a vicious wolf really did snatch her from her bed and attempt to eat her.

A man says he heard Manwati cry out and hurried to see what was causing the alarm. What he saw was the shadow of a creature dropping the girl and disappearing into the night.

Wildlife officials say they 'll continue killing wolves until the attacks on

children stop. If they fail, Singh fears, the people will take the law into their own hands, "and they will start killing each and every wolf."

Until the man-eating wolves can be killed, children in the villages will continue to fear the predators. And every night will bring a new danger.

In India, Attacks by Wolves Spark Old Fears and Hatreds
By John F. Burns SEPT. 1, 1996 *NY Times*

Since the first killing five months ago, 33 children have been carried off and killed by wolves, according to police figures; 20 others have been seriously mauled along this stretch of the Ganges River basin, 350 miles from New Delhi. A hunt by thousands of villagers and police officers has killed only 10 wolves so far.

On August 18, 1996, Algonquin Provincial Park, Canada, a wolf seized the head of a 12-year-old boy who was sleeping without a tent. The boy was dragged an estimated seven feet before the wolf was driven off by his father. The boy suffered a broken nose and six lacerations to the lower face that resulted in eighty stitches. (McNay)

In August 1994, Algonquin Provincial Park, Canada, a fearless wolf was observed by many campers in the park. It seemed uninterested in food but growled at people in a seemingly aggressive manner, tore up camping gear, and bit two people. On August 3, a nine-year-old boy suffered a single tooth puncture wound and a skin tear on his side. On September 1, a woman suffered a similar wound on the back of her leg. The wolf was shot eight days later and it seemed normal and tested negative for rabies.

(McNay)

In 1987, a 16-year-old girl in Algonquin Provincial Park, Canada, was briefly seized on the arm after she shined a flashlight in the eyes of a wolf at close range. The bite was interpreted as a "disciplinary or "annoyance reaction to the light." The wolf was shot the next day and tested negative for rabies. The girl received two slight scratches. (McNay)

People think that hunting wolves will cause them to become extinct. *Wolves have high population growth rates – litter sizes average five and survival can be high where prey is abundant. As a result, annual growth rates for wolves can exceed 50% per year (Fuller et al. 2003). Thus, wolves can sustain very high harvest rates (Fuller et al. 2003). Management Plan for the Grey Wolf April 2014*

Hunting season on wolves is common sense. Hunting will not in a million years wipe out wolves. It took a host of tools last time to wipe out wolves, with poison being the main tool. Without poison, wolves are safe from being driven to extinction level. All hunting does is stabilize the population. People who say hunting can wipe out wolves simply have to check Idaho Fish and Game harvest numbers on wolves. The number of successful wolf hunters is 1.6%; that is the lowest success rate of any animal in America.

Draft April 22nd, 2008.
Essay no. 2. Fair Chase
Death by wolves and misleading advocacy. The Kenton Carnegie Tragedy.

On November 8, 2005, a 22-year-old honors and scholarship student in Geological Engineering, Kenton Joel Carnegie, from the University of Waterloo, Ontario, Canada, was killed in northern Saskatchewan by a pack of wolves. While he was almost certainly not the only victim of wolf predation in North America in the past century, judging from conversations with native people, and a closer review of case histories, this was the best-investigated case to date. In the process of that investigation, matters were uncovered that need to be discussed as they have significant policy implications for wildlife conservation and human safety. However, we need to review what happened to Kenton Carnegie, as it is relevant to considerations following.

Mr. Carnegie was in a university co-op program that allowed students to gain hands-on experience from visits to mining operations. He was flown into Points North Landing, a mining camp close to Wollaston Lake in northern Saskatchewan. Bad weather delayed his return. On November 4, 2005, Todd Svarchopf, an experienced bush pilot, and Chris Van Galder, a geophysicist, two of Kenton's camp companions, had an encounter with two aggressive wolves on the airfield close to camp. The two young men beat back the attack, photographed the wolves, and told everybody in camp. The incident was apparently belittled, even though two days before Kenton was killed, the young men were warned at a dinner at a local lodge by an experienced northerner, Bill Topping (a part-time car pilot, that is, a guide who leads heavy trucks through the labyrinth of dirt roads in northern Saskatchewan). He admired the pictures and told his guests that they are lucky to be alive!

In fall and early winter of 2005 at Points North Landing, there was evidence for circumstances facilitating an attack on humans by wolves, followed by the predictable exploratory attack by wolves on November 4. That is, the events leading to the death of Kenton Carnegie follow the pattern predicting attacks on humans as described for wolves and earlier for urban coyotes targeting children in parks. It is a pattern of increasing observations of and habituation to humans followed by boldness and attacks on pets and livestock, followed by closing in and testing humans with skirmishes prior to the fatal attack. Both species of canids explore alternative prey in much the same manner.

Unfortunately, nobody recognized the growing danger. Moreover, how wolves target people was not a question asked by current wolf biologists, probably due to the overriding belief that wolves do not attack people. Four wolves at Points North Landing had begun feeding on camp refuse that fall and were habituating increasingly to human activities.

November 8, 2005, at about 15:30, Kenton Carnegie notified Van Gelder that he was going for a walk along the lake and expected to return by 17:00. Kenton had gone to the west shore of Wollaston Lake before when going fishing. This area is isolated and not open to unauthorized traffic. At about 18:15, because Kenton failed to appear for dinner, Chris Van Gelder and Todd Svarchopf searched for him, but could not find him in camp. Todd saw Kenton's tracks in the fresh snow leaving camp, but not returning. About 18:30, Chris, Todd, and Mark Eikel, co-owner of the camp, drove out in a truck searching for Kenton. Fresh snow had fallen, and the party followed the clear footprints, which headed south from camp. Because of the fresh snow, the tracks were easy to follow (this accounts for the crisp footprints of wolves etc. as photographed the following mid-day by Royal Canadian Mounted Police [RCMP] Constable Alfonse Noey). Kenton's tracks headed towards the shore of the lake.

When Eikel and companions encountered wolf tracks, they reversed and headed back to camp for Eikel to get his rifle, a more powerful flashlight, and a radio. (There were no domestic dogs at Points North Landing). The party then drove to a nearby cabin, thinking Kenton might be there, but found none of his footprints. They returned by truck to where they had left off and soon saw that Kenton's footprints left the road and headed down a trail toward the lake. There were wolf tracks on the trail. Then they saw Kenton's footprints doubling back and found a concentration of wolf tracks. Mark Eikel shone about with the flashlight and saw what he thought was Kenton's body. He ordered everybody back to the truck, not wanting the others to see the sight. (Neither Todd nor Chris saw Kenton's body.) On the way to camp, Mark Eikel called on the radio Robert Dennis (Bob) Burseth, an employee of the camp, a long-term resident of the north, and an experienced hunter. (19:00 hours)

Burseth realized something tragic had happened and contacted his wife Rosalie Tsannie-Burseth, who is the local coroner at Wollaston Lake, and asked her to contact the RCMP. Next, Chris Van Gelder called the RCMP from camp and the company office was notified. About 19:30 Eikel and Burseth returned by truck to check on Kenton. Eikel believed that Kenton was dead, but he wanted to make sure that his mind was not playing tricks on him and he wanted to get a second opinion. They parked the truck and walked down the ridge on the edge of the lake noting many wolf tracks. Mark Eikel shone with the flashlight and both could see Kenton's body. They saw exposed flesh and ribs, from the belt up. The pants appeared to be on. Eikel and Burseth approached within thirty feet. They stayed only a couple of minutes and returned to camp to await police and coroner, which arrived about 21:35 p.m.

Neither Bob Burseth nor Mark Eikel returned to the body till they went there with RCMP constable Alfonse Noey and coroner Rosalie Tsannie-Burseth. Kenton's body had been moved from where Mark Eikel and Bob Burseth had seen it some two hours earlier. The distance moved was about twenty yards. Officer Noey 's hand-drawn map indicated the body was dragged twenty meters, a distance which he paced out the next day. (Wolves readily move their kills—even over a mile—as I can personally attest to having observed what they do with domestic sheep carcasses. That wolves move carcasses and human victims is well established in Eurasian experience). Much more of the body had been consumed (there was no clothing down to the knees).

Asked by Constable Noey what had consumed the body, Burseth stated wolves. Asked by Constable Noey what kind of tracks Burseth had seen on location, Burseth replied that he had seen only wolf tracks. There had been four wolves running together about camp earlier (a black one, a white one, and two gray-tan ones). The four had been seen on the runway (close to camp) on the day before, on the seventh of November. Burseth also saw three wolves running across the lake towards the kill site at about 7:45 a.m. on the morning following Kenton's death, that is, on the ninth of November. Eikel confirmed that four wolves had been seen near the camp and garbage dumpsite.

About 21:50, Constable Noey and coroner Rosalie Tsannie-Burseth began securing and inspecting the site. Constable Noey took the lead, and the coroner and Bob Burseth and Mark Eikel followed him in single file. (This minimizes disturbance to the original tracks). As Constable Noey approached the site of Kenton's body, he saw two wolves near the body (he refers to sighting these two wolves repeatedly in his report and in conversations with others). He discharged two rounds from his shotgun into the air to scare away the wolves from the body. Constable Noey noted many wolf tracks on the land and on the snow of the frozen lake. Constable Noey ordered Burseth and Eikel to remain on the trail, while he and the coroner went in to examine Kenton's body. Eikel was instructed by Constable Noey to discharge his rifle into the air, as the wolves could be heard in the bushes near to the body. Bob Buresth made a fire on the trail, certain it would keep the wolves away.

Constable Noey and Mrs. Tsannie-Burseth examined and photographed the body and surroundings for forty to forty-five minutes. Then Constable Noey called Constable Marion on a satellite phone and advised him of the condition of the body, and of the wolves in the area, at which point Constable Marion authorized the removal of Kenton's body and the return of the party to Points North Landing. With the assistance of Eikel and Burseth, the coroner and Constable Noey placed Kenton's body into a body bag, which was tagged by Constable Noey with time and date. At that time, Constable Noey discovered that his GPS unit was missing, and searched the immediate area of the last resting site (disturbing site – after the fact!). He instructed Eikel to ensure that nobody be allowed to enter the area and was assured by Eikel that only Cameco employees may use the road between their mine (Cigar Lake Mine) and the Points North Landing, and that they have been instructed not to get out of their vehicles close to the camp. Constable Noey next took down witness statements.

On the following day, November 9, 2005, at 13:00-14:14 Constable Noey, coroner Tsannie-Burseth, and Bob Burseth attended again to the scene in daylight, taking pictures, and analyzed the scene. Here are their joint results as summarized in the report by Constable Noey:

1. The footprints of Kenton heading south were followed by a wolf who stepped into Kenton's footprints (this wolf had thus cut off Kenton from the camp, as the two wolves had tried to do on November the 4th with Chris and Todd). Constable Noey surmised that this wolf was following and possibly stalking Kenton.

2. Constable Noey followed Kenton's footprint south past the kill site, which went for a distance of about 60-80 meters (undisturbed by previous day's activities). Here Kenton was on the shoreline. Noey surmised that Kenton, at this point in sight of the camp, may have been trying to get somebody's attention at the camp as there was a clear line of sight to the camp.

3. At this point, more wolf tracks converged on where Kenton stood, so the report by Constable Noey. The wolf tracks were coming from the south along the lake shore. (Several wolves approached from the south while one wolf approached Kenton from the north. That looks like a hunting strategy executed by the wolves. Since several wolves approached Kenton from the south, and one wolf from the north, there must have been more than two wolves involved. He was thus killed by at least three wolves and possibly by all four!)

4. Here Kenton's footprints turned back towards the road (that is up the trail, heading north toward the camp).

5. From here it is 10-20 m along the trail before the snow is disturbed, indicating an altercation. Constable Noey noted that the snow was disturbed as if somebody was rolling in the snow.

6. Footprints now headed across the trail a little way into the muskeg-shrub. The footprints indicate that Kenton was running. He was half on the trail, half on muskeg. There was a lot of disturbance of the snow.

7. From here it is a short distance north to the kill site, where the body was first discovered along with pieces of clothing. When seen a second time the body had been dragged about twenty yards.

8. In between were two sites where the tracks indicated that Kenton stood and shed a lot of blood. (Photos indicate considerable blood loss.) A third place indicates he stood and dripped blood. The search party found the body there.

Constable Noey photographed till the battery of his camera gave out and collected all clothing pieces not found previously.

At 14:31, Constable Noey received a CD with photos of Van Gelder and Svarchopf interacting with two wolves on the previous Friday, November 4, from Christy Oysteryk, and expresses surprise that neither had informed him of that attack. (In short, this attack by wolves, which the two young men were able to beat off—and photographed—was belittled. It was only post hoc, after Kenton's death that the scary significance of that attack did sink in.)

Two conservation officers from the Saskatchewan game department (SERM), Kelly Crayne and Mario Gaudet, arrived on the tenth in order to do their investigation. They stated in their report: "Officers investigated the site and found numerous wolf tracks in the area. No other large animal tracks could be found."

In the light of what was to follow, it is important to examine the nature and qualifications at tracking of the eight witnesses who were on the scene after Kenton was killed.

Mrs. Rosalie Tsannie-Burseth is not only the coroner for Wollaston Lake, but also the Chief of the Hatchet Lake Band, and the Director of Education. She has three university degrees, is working on her doctorate in sociology, and has a long career in the public service. She grew up in the northern bush when her family was still nomadic and fully dependent on their skills at hunting, fishing, and trapping, and was tutored by her father in tracking. This articulate, humorous grandmother still goes hunting.

RCMP Constable Alfonse Noey is, like Chief Tsannie-Burseth, a native, a hunter, and a long-standing northern resident. (He produced a detailed report, based on his and Mrs. Tsannie-Burseth's on-the-spot investigations, as well as questioning all witnesses to the scene.)

Robert Dennis (Bob) Burseth is an employee at Points North Landing, with seventeen years of experience in the region. He is married to the local coroner and chief, Mrs. Rosalie Tsannie-Burseth. He is an avid hunter. (He killed the two wolves [at the dump] after Kenton's attack. He shoots the bears that become a nuisance at the camp.)

Todd Svarchopf is an aviation officer and well-known bush pilot, employee of Sanders Geophysics, Ottawa, working out of camp. (He testified at the coroner's inquiry that he had warned Kenton against going out.)

Mark Eikel, the co-owner of the camp, Points North Landing, is an experienced outdoorsman and hunter. He shot the third wolf (250 - 300 yards away) after Kenton's attack. He claimed he would have seen a bear if it had been in the area. None had been seen for at least a month (inquiry testimony).

Chris Van Gelder, geophysicist, employee of Sanders Geophysics, Ottawa, working out of the camp. Kelly Crayne and Mario Gaudet, conservation officers, also examined the site on November 10, 2005. (Any black bear moving in or out of the site of Kenton's body would have been detected in the crisp snow by these men.)

Please note: the tracks and signs at the scene were thus examined by two senior native persons highly experienced in tracking, by two experienced northern hunters, by two conservation officers, by a seasoned bush pilot, and a highly trained physical scientist. Svarchopf, Van Galder and Eikel, who were first on the scene, identified only wolf tracks. They were vindicated by Bob Burseth, as he insisted that he saw only wolf tracks. He, in turn, was vindicated by RCMP constable Noey and coroner Tsannie-Burseth, who not only saw only wolf tracks at the site but also saw and heard wolves so close to Kenton's body, that Constable Noey fired his shotgun twice to spook the wolves away and asked Mark Eikel to discharge his rifle. Conservation officers Crayne and Gaudet also saw only wolf tracks. In addition, Constable Noey and coroner Tsannie-Burseth, not merely identified wolves as the killers of Kenton Carnegie, but deciphered the track pattern left by wolves, showing a classic hunt pattern by wolves. The wolf pack had split and the wolves approached their prey from the back as well as from the front, cutting off any possible retreat. They documented multiple attacks and a progression of the victim to final collapse. Moreover, four wolves had been for weeks habituating to camp activity, ran in anticipation towards garbage disposal units, and tore apart plastic garbage bags in the presence of humans, observed humans, and staged an unsuccessful attack on two camp residents four days before they killed Kenton Carnegie.

Then came a surprise: The Saskatchewan coroner asked for the case to be re-examined by scientists, Dr. Paul Paquet, a wolf researcher, and Professor Ernest G. Walker of the University of Saskatchewan. Before their confidential report was submitted, Paquet informed the popular news media that he recognized immediately that a black bear had killed Carnegie. In pp. 29-30 of National Wildlife, February/March 2007 edition in an article entitled, "Sexy Beasts" by Paul Tolmé we read: "Wolves remain a bogeyman today, as illustrated by the death of a Canadian man in 2005. When Kenton Carnegie's mangled corpse was discovered near a remote Saskatchewan mining camp of Points North Landing, the Royal Canadian Mounted Police immediately blamed wolves. The story made headlines around the world. But when noted wolf biologist Paul Paquet of the World Wildlife Fund investigated, he recognized immediately that a black bear killed Carnegie. 'The problem was bias right from the start,' Paquet says. 'When I looked at the photos, I immediately saw bear tracks,' Paquet says.

The National Geographic Society sent a team to film and re-enact Kenton's death. Dr. Paquet acted as a consultant. (Kenton's parents were so upset by the resulting "documentary" that they wrote a letter of protest to the society. Mrs. Tsannie-Burseth told me that she was upset and offended by the manner the camera and interview crew of National Geographic had treated her. She told me she tried to speak to Paul Paquet at the inquest, but that he would not speak with her or even make eye contact with her). Victims of wildlife tragedies in North America tend to be blamed for the event, and it was not different in Kenton's case. It greatly upset Kenton's family, as did the brazen whitewash of wolves that could not only mislead the public, but also the judiciary.

Distraught by the treatment they had received and the misattribution to their son, Kenton's parents turned to four scientists and asked them to do independent investigations. Three agreed: Mark McNay, a senior biologist from Alaska, Brent Patterson, as a seasoned scientist from Ontario with considerable wolf experience, and the third was myself. All three wrote reports concluding that Paquet's claim that a bear had killed Kenton Carnegie was untenable and that wolves had killed Kenton Carnegie.

Paquet claimed the eyewitness accounts were unreliable and biased, an unsupported claim contrary to all evidence.

Paquet examining the photos of the site as photographed by RCMP Constable Noey mistook the tracks of wolves heading across an overflow on the lake ice (where the wolves stepped through a thin layer of snow resting on water, and which consequently distorted their tracks) as bear tracks. McNay and I used colleagues highly experienced with wolves (he from Alaska, I from Finland) to double check on our identifications. All concluded that the tracks in question as photographed by Constable Noey were wolf tracks, and McNay demonstrated that the pattern of the distorted tracks on the overflow was of a regular canid trotting pattern, and quite different from the track patterns left by bears. That is, three independent peer reviews confirmed what the eight eyewitnesses on the site had observed.

Paquet claimed that a number of forensic signs identified the responsible predator as a bear. These were that:

(a) wolves do not drag their prey from the kill site but consume such in situ. Yet Kenton's body, he claimed, had been dragged some 50 paces (In North America

the experience of wolf biologists studying free-living wolves in wilderness areas is that wolves feed on their prey in situ. In my personal experience here with wolves killing my neighbor's sheep is that they always move their kills into cover, up to about one mile from the sheep pasture. The European accounts of how wolves deal with prey, livestock and humans included, is that they carry or drag such into cover away from where they attacked the prey close to human habitations. The resolution of what appears as opposites is quite simple: wolves, undisturbed, consume their kill at the kill site. Wolves, disturbed or close to danger, move their kill. And that 's what happened in the Kenton Carnegie's case. The wolves fed at the kill site till they were disturbed by the first search party. When the second party arrived, the wolves had dragged Kenton 's body about 20 m – not 50 m.).

(b) Paul Paquet is quoted in the National Wildlife article p. 30 "The clothes and skin been stripped away, indicating the so-called banana-peel eating technique common to bears"). (How could Paquet know that? How many clothed human bodies handled by wolves have been available for examination in North America? Moreover, he ignored that the four wolves in question had plenty of experience ripping apart and peeling back the plastic of plastic garbage bags, saturated with human smell, in order to reach discarded camp food).

(c) The wolves had not consumed the victim's liver and heart, which is also very uncharacteristic of wolves. I quote from National Wildlife: "Carnegie 's heart and liver -"the most desirable morsel for wolves" Paquet says - were left intact" (Internal organs had been consumed - namely the ones surrounded by fat. And that fits with my own observations how wolves, disrupted by approaching humans, "scheduled" their feeding on sheep they killed: fat first. Paquet did not take into account that the wolves had been disturbed twice and were not able to finish with the corpse. Furthermore, on p. 48 of Will Grave 's book on the Russian experience with wolves a Russian scientist reports that wolves, in feeding on a freshly killed moose, the heart, lungs, and liver had not been touched. Dr. Kaarlo Nygren from Finland made similar findings.

However, ALL forensic signs of a "bear" presume that the bear was standing or moving in about 1.5 inches of fresh snow. For instance, if a bear peeled away the clothing, then the bear must have had his paws on the ground in the snow. Also, the bear must have moved in on the kill site, leaving tracks, dragged the body, leaving tracks, ran away when the first search party arrived, leaving tracks, returned to the carcass, leaving tracks, and left again when the second party arrived - again leaving tracks. And he would have done so all on land. There would have been massive bear track signs of multiple entries and exits and massive trampling around the body. There were no bear tracks!

My Finnish colleagues, spontaneously, identified a lonely fox track beside the abundant wolf tracks. If they found the track of a fox, would they have missed the tracks of a bear?

All the forensic signs pointing to "bear," as proclaimed by Paquet, are thus misidentifications, as the only bear that could have left such signs at the site of the tragedy must have been suspended in mid-air, as none of his paws reached the telltale snow. Furthermore, Paquet's repeated insistence that his approach alone was in the spirit and methodology of science, and was supported by superior experience, has demonstrably no basis, as shown by three peer reviews and the coroner's inquest.

Moreover, Paquet failed to notice that the wolves involved were not merely habituating, but were targeting people as prey. Wolves do this in the very same manner as coyotes do in urban parks when targeting children. Both canids explore humans very cautiously and over a protracted time period before mounting the first, exploratory attack, which two wolves had done four days before Kenton's death. Ironically, while coyote biologists recognized that the smaller coyote will target people as prey, those studying free-living wolves were denying that wolves were a danger to people. While the behavior of wolves thus signaled a disaster waiting to happen, nobody recognized it as such even after the failed wolf attack on Van Gelder and Swarchopf four days prior to the attack on Kenton. The belief in the harmlessness of wolves was that firmly entrenched.

The coroner ruled that only one expert witness would be allowed to testify on behalf of the Carnegies and chose Mark McNay. After listening to eyewitnesses at the scene, to Paul Paquet and the presentation by Mark McNay, the six-person jury rejected Paquet's presentation, unanimously, despite his being assisted by counsel. The jury ruled that the cause of Kenton Carnegie's death were wolves. There have been other victims such as five-year-old Marc Leblond, killed Sept. 24, 1963, north of Baie-Comeau, Quebec Gerard McNebel, November 18th, 1963, Winnipeg Free Press, p. 12.

The following draft of a paper on wildlife habituation I presented at a symposium entitled "Wildlife Habituation: Advances in Understanding and Management Application" by The Wildlife Society in Madison, Wisconsin on Sept. 27th, 2005. Due to personal circumstances, I was not able to finish this paper for publication. It is entitled: Habituation of wildlife to humans: research tool, key to naturalistic recording and a common curse for wildlife and hapless humans. I published the relevant excerpt on wolves as Appendix B pp. 195-197 in Will N. Graves 2007 Wolves in Russia. Anxiety Through the Ages (edited by V. Geist). Detselig, Calgary. Baker, R. O. and R. M. Timm 1998. Management of conflict between urban coyotes and humans in southern California. Pp. 229-312 in R. O. Baker and A. c. Crabb eds. Proc. 18th Vertebrate Pest Conference, University of California, Davis).

The advocacy in favor of the "benign wolf" hypothesis is so powerful, that the better educated the persons, the more likely it seems that they are to become true believers and endanger themselves. So far exceptionally well-educated people have become victims of lethal attacks.

Kenton Carnegie is not the only victim of the "harmless wolf hypothesis." So was 24-year-old Wildlife Biologist, Trisha Wyman, who was killed on April 18th, 1996 by a captive wolf pack in Ontario. I had a long phone conversation with Dr. Erich Klinghammer of Wolf Park. He was called in as an expert witness to examine the Wyman case and discovered quickly that there was great surprise at her death, as wolves are not supposed to attack people. Ms. Wyman had visited the park previously and spent some time studying the wolves. She was given the dream job of looking after and interpreting the wolves. She lasted three days! She and the people surrounding her, just like Kenton and the people surrounding him, were imbued by the myth of the "harmless wolves" as advocated by North American wolf specialists in the late 50s and 60s. Keepers of wolf packs can inform themselves by turning to the people running Wolf Park. These have been researching wolves for decades and have detailed advice on how to handle captive wolves and wolf-dog hybrids. They would have been quickly disabused of any naive faith in conventional, but mis-presented science about harmless wolves. (James Gary Shelton 1998 Bear Attacks. Pogany Productions, Hagensborg, BC.)

Shelton makes a point of how viciously victims of predatory attacks have been pursued and maligned in Canada and the US by enumerating such in some detail. In an e-mail of March 28, 2007, Dr. Nygren wrote to me:

"They (the wolf pack) ate one ear and tip of the tongue when waiting for their turn in the abdominal cavity. The fore-stomachs were left largely untouched until almost all the good stuff was taken from the intestines. So did the liver, heart, and lungs. They were taken out almost ten hours later when all the pups and their mother were lying flat around the place with their stomachs full. Then, almost in the midnight, the male came in starting to rip the carcass in pieces. A bite and a kilogram or two. He ate as much as he pleased, then pulled out the liver, ate some of it and dropped. Soon, he started to walk towards the sleepy pups who immediately jumped up and hurried to meet him with cheerful faces, tails wagging and showing submissive gestures. They looked funny with their round bellies and saw-buck like appearance. A roundish white spot cranially from their thighs on the belly coat had appeared and was visible even in the dim light of autumn. This seems to be a good visual sign of a well-fed wolf. When they poked the father's lips with their noses, he threw up everything that was in his stomach. The pups immediately ate up it. and returned to their beds. The male walked back to work, filled his stomach and did the feeding procedure several times. He seemed to have a pet among the pups. It was the smallest, a female always chased out first by the mother and siblings. The female never fed the pups like the father. In the next morning, the flesh of the prey was practically stripped off with bare bones protruding and some legs completely cut off the carcass. So, the fat reserves seemed to be the preferred bits, not the liver, heart, and lungs. We have seen the same many times in the field. Guts first. Even the dogs are usually first opened from the belly and the abdominal cavity emptied. I have seen many dogs cut in two around the diaphragm, caudal halve eaten completely or transported somewhere. Heart and lungs are, in many cases, were left inside the breast cavity." (Baker, R. O. and R. M. Timm 1998. Management of conflict between urban coyotes and humans in southern California. Pp. 229-312 in R. O. Baker and A. c. Crabb eds. Proc. 18th Vertebrate Pest Conference, University of California, Davis).

A potent feature of the North American Model of Wildlife Conservation is its transparency and public accountability, a feature not prominent, for instance, in the management of national parks. What happens to hunted wildlife is very much a public concern annually, and citizens participate avidly in discussions about hunting regulations and their justification, holding managers and public officials accountable in a very public process. Because of the openness, the concern, and the fervor, those that make decisions must explain themselves in detail, and must reach for knowledge from all quarters. Knowledge pertaining to wildlife flows from three sources, science, history, and professional knowledge as it pertains to wildlife. In North America science carries most prestige, in central Europe, it is knowledge that is enveloped by a historic corps of hands-on wildlife managers, science being a relatively recent interloper.

It must, however, be stated from the outset that while accumulated professional experience is not science, it is nevertheless rooted in reality, and some of it is of excellent scholarship. European professional knowledge pertaining to wildlife is not publicly circulated but is vital to managers which are normally owners or lessees of hunting territories, as well as a small crop of professional hunters and foresters. In North America, while wildlife science is strong, history, unfortunately, is very weak, while accumulated professional knowledge is struggling to be recorded and heard. Nevertheless, all three channels provide vital information that is tested in the public domain as the need arises. In the wolf issue, neglect or disdain of the historical information, labeling such unjustly as biased myths and fairytales, mixed with perfectly good science, has nevertheless generated flawed scholarship, and – consequently – flawed legislation.

The proud and one-sided emphasis on science has ensured that, as the philosopher Emanuel Kant put it, we again learn from history that we do not learn from history! At this point, the science/history conundrum pertaining to wolves is not resolved. However, it will be someday, as deficits in scholarship do not sit well with scholars regardless of background, and pressure from the grassroots, the stakeholders, for resolution will drive the agenda. And that is the strength of our system of conservation based on accountability and grassroots democracy.

Chapter 9
Other Animal Attacks

I was bleeding everyplace. If that cat (Bobcat)had attacked a child, it would've been really bad. It wouldn't have quit." —Dale Rippy told The Associated Press

February 03, 2016, New Jersey ABC 7 news report. Boy and family speak out after raccoon attack in New Jersey

"He screamed, 'Mommy!' I turned around and I saw that something was on his back," said Monali Galavi, Aryan's mother.

His mother tried desperately to fight off the creature, frantically looking for a stick or rock. Fortunately, neighbor and Good Samaritan Danny Walls grabbed a tool from his truck and beat the animal off Aryan.

The first grader has deep cuts on his face and scratches on his head. He's gotten his first round of shots for rabies.

Our children are paying the price for the "save the animal" groups. As we become weaker, with animals being given more rights than American citizens, these types of attacks will only increase.

The horrific injuries sustained by woman, 28, after she is knocked down and mauled by RACCOONS while out walking her dog. Daily Mail Reporter 11 July 2012

"They were on top of me, just biting my arms and legs and sides. I was just trying not to let them get to my face.

"I was trying to run to a neighbor's front door but the raccoons were between my legs and they tripped me and I fell," she told KOMO News.

Raccoons are predators, not cute little cuddly animals. They can be quite vicious. But God forbid anyone hurt the animals or there would be marches from the drama queen screamers.

ABC Action 30 News August 22, 2015
Raccoons attack couple, dog in San Francisco

Suddenly, Upsavs says, a pack of raccoons pounced…and the woman and dog weren't the only victims.

"I started swinging the dog around trying to get [an attacking raccoon] off,…And then I got another one on my other leg. And so at this point, I'm in the middle of the street and I look up to see, 'Where is my husband? How come he's not helping?' And I look and he's throwing…raccoons are just jumping on him."

The couple was saved when their neighbor, Brian Wong, raced from his house yelling and banging on the trash can with a golf club. This frightened the raccoons who ran off. The couple had alarming numbers of scratches and bites. They now had to undergo the rabies treatment shots.

You never heard about cases like this in the 1960s because we still had men around that controlled wild animals. Trapping the problem animals is illegal in California without a special permit.

Nine-month-old baby in Georgia nearly eaten by raccoons; animals chewed on face, head, hands. November 4, 2010, NY Daily News

This was an extremely brutal attack on the child. Apparently, the father found the cute little baby raccoons and raised them for months in the house. When they became unmanageable, he tossed them out of the house but the raccoons would not leave. They broke into the house and attacked the child.

When are people going to learn they are wild animals? Endangering your own family so you claim you care about animals is asinine.

August 9, 2016

SPRINGFIELD, VA (WUSA9) - Fairfax County Police warned residents about a potentially rabid fox on the run after it attacked two elderly Springfield residents.

Both victims have already started a series of four vaccines to prevent them from contracting the disease.

WUSA9 learned that rabid foxes attack in Fairfax County about six times a year. Once a fox shows symptoms of rabies, it is expected to die within about a week.

An 81-year-old woman was viciously attacked by the fox. Using a lawn chair to keep the fox from biting her anymore, she was able to drive the animal off.

The fox raced around the corner and attacked an 84-year-old man mowing his grass.

An official came in and set traps for the animal. The victims were treated and started on rabies vaccines.

Man Survives Bobcat Attack by Choking Animal to Death
Published June 19, 2007, Fox News

WESLEY CHAPEL, Fla. – A 62-year-old Florida man depended on his instincts when a bobcat attacked him, and it paid off — he survived, the bobcat didn't.

When it growled, I knew it was going to jump and bite me," he said.

The animal then jumped on him and began to scratch and bite. Rippy said he knew if he could get a good hold on the animal, he would be able to choke it, even if that meant letting the bobcat take a couple of bites

Resort Arizona town on alert after rabid bobcat attacks, injured 4 people
Published January 18, 2017, Fox News

Authorities killed the rabid animal after it injured four people, a dog, and a house cat in three separate attacks last week in Sedona.

Mass. Pair Attacked By Bobcat in Garage
January 8, 2013, ABC News

Rounding a car, he heard a hissing sound and Mundell says that without warning, the bobcat pounced on his head, sinking its teeth into his face and clawing his back.

"It got me just like this and gave me a bear hug right here," Mundell said

while pointing to his scarred face.

"All of a sudden, he's just looking at me. Just giving me the death stare and you can tell he's meaning business," Granger said.

His nephew came to his rescue and the bobcat attacked him. His wife brought a gun out and he shot the enraged cat twice, ending the battle.

No word on if the animal was rabid.

Bobcat That Attacked People This Weekend Was Rabid: Officials
Sep 1, 2014, NBC Connecticut

Summer and Tom Berube were out for a walk with their newborn daughter, Neeve, the area of Norwich Avenue and Waterman Road in Lebanon around 7 p.m. on Sunday when the bobcat approached Tom, who was carrying the baby in a sling, Summer Berube said.

"It started running toward me. It made like a hissing noise. I stomped my foot, but it didn't do anything," Tom Berube said.

Tom fought the cat with a mailbox he saw laying in the ditch. Hitting the cat and knocking it down, it recovered and circled the couple. Summer flagged down a truck for help.

Bobcats Attack Two at Death Valley National Park
By Kurt Repanshek on December 31st, 2007 National Parks Traveler

Park officials say that on December 17th a bobcat attacked a visitor at the Furnace Creek Inn. Rangers found that a 64-year-old woman had suffered scratches and bites on her hands, face, and scalp.

On Friday, December 21st, rangers responded to another report of a bobcat attack at the inn. A male employee of the resort had reportedly been smoking outside the building when the bobcat attacked him, inflicting bites and lacerations to his head and neck.

Fish and Game officers asked the park to euthanize the bobcat to ensure public safety. Necropsy results, received last week, revealed that the animal was not suffering from rabies.

Holden Man Kills Bobcat That Attacked Him In Driveway
By Ken MacLeod, WBZ-TV *June 19, 2013* By Ken MacLeod

Michael Votruba thought the animal lurking around in his driveway Monday night was his neighbor's cat, but he soon found himself backpedaling and reaching for his pistol.

"I kicked him off twice and he was still coming," said Michael. "That is the first time that I have had to draw my weapon, period."

As he was backing away, he tripped and the 25-pound animal pounced on him.

The bobcat made a mess of his clothes, but only inflicted a few small scratches on him. He couldn't help but notice that the bobcat had a face full of porcupine quills.

He said, "I'm not sure whether he was rabid or if he was just angry because he messed up when he went to hunt the porcupine."

Maybe both.

Bobcat attacks 3 women in Connecticut:

The attack occurred at around noon on the property of the Caring Community of Connecticut, a social service agency.

WFSB-Channel 3 reports the three women, all clients at the program, were in a greenhouse on the property and having lunch when the bobcat walked in and attacked them.

About 20 people were having lunch in the area at the same time.

The station also reports the bobcat appeared aggressive and attempt to go after first responders. The animal was put down by police.

It was taken away to the state Department of Health lab for tests to determine if it was rabid.

Bobcat attacks dog, teen, in southern Florida January 05, 2017
Isabel Mascarenas and WTSP

Karen says, "All of a sudden I heard a terrible awful noise. I came running out. The bobcat was right here on the dog. I screamed at my grandson, 'Pick Sammy up, pick Sammy up.'"

The bobcat had grabbed Sammy by the neck and left 5 puncture wounds also scratching the teenager in the leg.

Karen says the bobcat walked into the home, right past her and jumped on the dining room chair.

Karen says, "He lumbered through the living room coming out here. My son bursts out of the bedroom opens the lanai door, bobcat goes out. … He jumped on the glass see him wandering around."

Karen's son Robert captured video of the wildlife officer trying to catch the bobcat.

Karen and her son's family — all 6 — are getting shots for rabies as a precaution.

Karen says, "The next day I find out it's rabid."

Bobcat Attacks Multiple People in Albany, Shot And Killed By Homeowner
Conceal Nation Posted by G. Halek, July 2, 2016

NEW SCOTLAND, NEW YORK — A couple visiting the beautiful countryside outside Albany got a bigger taste of the wild than they would have liked. A bobcat viciously attacked a woman before her husband and the homeowner could come to her rescue. The husband was attacked as well before the men pinned down the wild animal and put it down with a close-range shot.

UPDATE: Bobcat that hurt two at New Scotland home, tested positive for rabies.

Plano Man Fights Off Bobcat During Dog Walk
NBC 5 Reports October 21, 2016

Ortolf says his 10-month-old Blue Heeler mix named Harley was off the leash at the park when the encounter happened. "It jumped on her and I grabbed it by the back of the neck and tried to throw it into the woods, but it kind of latched onto my arm," he said.

"I had her by the neck and I kind of grabbed her by the back of the tail and flung it into a tree and then it ran off," he said.

Bobcat attacks woman in Show Low
Associated Press
Posted: April 29, 2013, Posted by Phil Benson

A *bobcat like this one attacked a woman in Show Low Sunday night. (Source: KPHO-TV)*

A *necropsy and rabies testing are being performed on a bobcat after the animal was seen acting aggressively near the site of an attack in Show Low.*

A *woman was scratched and bitten on her thigh by a bobcat Sunday at about 10:30 p.m. behind a Lowe's store, the Arizona Game and Fish Department said in a press release.*

She *was given rabies vaccines and anti-rabies serum as a precaution. A bobcat was spotted nearby by a Navajo County deputy sheriff, who killed it.*

"*Bobcats rarely attack people, but when they do, the animal is often rabid,"* said Bruce Sitko, a department spokesman.

Rabid bobcat attacks people, killed by tire iron
Star News August 23, 2012

The *bobcat charged a second man in his yard and tried to attack him. The man grabbed a tire iron, threw it at the animal and killed it, the release says.*

The *bobcat was sent to the N.C. State Laboratory of Public Health in Raleigh for testing, where it was found to be rabid.*

Bobcat, not bear or mountain lion, culprit in attack near Humpback Rocks
By Rob Longley, The News Virginian, July 4, 2016

Kyle Houghton was hiking with his girlfriend Katie. They stopped for a break and Kyle spotted the bobcat. The cat was laser-focused on Katie. When it started trotting at her, Kyle stood up and placed himself in between the two. The cat charged in, leaping upon Kyle. He knew it was going for his neck and he placed his arms up to protect himself.

The cat bit down on his left arm, raking his claws on his right arm. Kyle slammed the cat to the ground and started stomping on it. The bobcat fought while Katie retrieved the bear spray, spraying the cat who finally ran off. Kyle claimed the cat was huge, seventy-five to eight pounds. But it was most likely around forty-five pounds.

They hiked out and sought medical aid. Kyle was given rabies serum.

Do you know rats injure people too?

Rats Chew Off Newborn Baby's Nose, Upper Lip in Kansas City, Mo., Apartment, February 28, 2007, Associated Press.

A small 4-week-old baby was attacked by rats in her crib. The rat or rats chewed off her nose and upper lip. Three years earlier, the city stopped rat control in budget cuts. The vast majority of Americans are very ignorant of what is really going on in pest control.

There are plenty of other examples of rats attacking people, mostly children and older people. If you have seen HBO's *The Iceman Interviews*, Richard "The Iceman" Kuklinski 's mafia hitman talked about taking one victim to an area infested with rats, leaving the person duct taped to a chair. He came back later and the rats had killed and eaten the person.

Two-week-old baby "needed surgery after being bitten up to 100 times when rats attacked cot." May 18, 2017 Independent Magnolia, Arkansas

This is a sad story of teenage parents that had no clue of what to do. They were raised in the modern age of do nothing to animals. Protect your children; kill animals. That should be common sense. Any real parent would kill any animal harming or about to harm their children.

Chapter 10
Unreported Attacks

"They got me set up now like I'm some kind of murderer. And then the environmental guy told me 'You should have called me instead of shooting it.' What was I going to do, say 'Mister Bear would you excuse me please while I go make a phone call?'"

Richard Ahlstrand as told to CBS News

After years of talking to hunters and rural residents around the country, there is a common message. Keep your mouth shut. I would say only one out of every four attacks are reported. The American people are fed up with defending their lives from vicious predatory animals. Federal law enforcement will gladly arrest you and put you through hell for killing one of the king's special animals. What person in their right mind would report killing a precious wolf or grizzly bear in the lower forty-eight? Or any large predator? Who wants to spend days on end waiting to hear if they are hauling you to jail and waiting months on end for your day in court to learn how corrupt our court system is? Any predator that enters my thirty-yard safe circle is a threat to my life. I will kill them without a second thought. Your right under the endangered species act is to defend yourself. But the courts and the federal LE can spin a tale that will make the best fiction writer pale in comparison.

I have this chapter to show what is happening that is never reported as attacks. Remember, not all attacks that are turned in to fish and game departments are ever told to the newspaper to begin with.

The reason I bring this up is undocumented attacks happen all the time and rarely get reported for the simple reason of all the hassle you must go through. There was the case in Bonner Ferry, Idaho. A family man was in the shower when his wife started screaming there was a grizzly bear in the yard. A father with small children. Like any real man, he grabbed his rifle to protect his family and shot the bear dead. Being an honest Christian, he called the authorities to tell them what happened. It was the worst mistake of his life.

Statement of Jeremy Hill Regarding Resolution of Grizzly Confrontation on May 8, 2011

"I am thankful that the government has dismissed all criminal charges against me in this case. I received a federal civil ticket and have paid the $1,000 fine to avoid putting my family through the emotional strain and the cost of a trial. I am glad this issue has been resolved out of court and I am looking forward to putting this unfortunate incident behind me.

"My family and I are very thankful for the support of our family and friends during this difficult time. We have been overwhelmed by the outpouring of concern from the many people who have contacted us. We are also grateful for the support of our state and local elected officials. We could not ask for better friends, neighbors, and supporters. Thank you again from all of our family."

Idaho Fish and Game officer Craig Johnson was literally trying to make a federal case out of it. The female DA was ready to hang the poor guy. You must wonder if she had a conflict of interest. I believe the members of the Sierra Club, Defenders of Wildlife, or any of the other "save the animals" groups cannot be unbiased and will use the government's power to abuse the American citizen. Whether this was the case, I don't know.

Undocumented Attacks

Here is a story from an avid hunter and fisherman. While elk hunting in 2015, a cougar came up the hill towards him, growling and snarling at fifty yards. For five to ten minutes, it stayed at fifty yards. As darkness was falling, the man lost sight of the animal in the brush. The next thing he knew, a cat was on the trail fifteen yards behind him, ears down in attack mode. The cat pounced at the man. He fired with his bow, hitting the animal in the chest area. It was too dark to track the wounded animal. He estimated the cat weighed about 150 pounds. Now imagine a missing child. An eighty-pound child or smaller could have been killed and carried off in seconds.

Unreported Wolf Attack

It was the last weekend in September 2010, I think. We had gotten up to go fishing early in the morning and had only been back long enough to get the fire going and the polish dogs over the fire when Theodore, my little shitzue, started a deep growl. I looked up and he was standing about ten feet in front of the car looking at us over the hood of the car easily. It stared long enough for me to un-holster my 9mm that I just carry in the field. I unloaded two in its chest and two hits in the head. It hit the ground within five feet from us. Scary as hell. If I hadn't been packing it would have been real, real, bad.

Undocumented Cougar Attack

I know for a fact; a menstruating woman should not go hunting (for any game)! I had a 7 '9" Tom cat stalking me while hunting elk (my 30-06 in hand and my husband with his rifle also). When I discovered what was making the noise (after hearing strange noises behind me for two hundred yards) there stood a cougar; he was about thirty feet behind me! My husband said, "Shoot him." I missed the shot. The strange part was the cat didn't run off in fear. Instead, he crouched to pounce. I will never forget the cougar's eyes were wide open about the size of silver dollars, hair standing up down his back, and ready to leap. His tail twitched like a housecat. My husband shot him in the chest as he was ready to leap! He 's hanging on the wall as a reminder of that day! I don 't go walking in the woods without a weapon.

How did national parks keep attacks down to almost zero? I heard a rumor that Yellowstone and Glacier National Park used to control bear populations in the fall. Back in the 50s and 60s, after the park was closed to visitors, certain park rangers would hunt the bears and teach them to fear humans. Some were killed, and others were simply shot at and harassed, teaching them to fear humans. I must stress this was simply a rumor. The National Park Service being very unwilling to be transparent would never admit to this or would deny FOIA requests unless you have a high-dollar lawyer to take them to court to get the FOIA information.

I did learn about a policy at Yosemite National Park from reading the book *Off the Wall: Death in Yosemite* by Michael Ghiglieri and Charles Farabee Jr. In 1910, the US Army was the park rangers for Yosemite. Major Forsyth was in charge. A park ranger suggested keeping the bears out of Yosemite Valley to protect the tourists. He requested and received permission to hunt bears with birdshot, light tiny BB-size shot intended for small game. The idea was to teach the bears to avoid humans and drive them out of the valley. How well did it work? The man in charge of the shooting and hunting the bears admitted to killing eight to ten bears in self-defense. I would imagine that large powerful black bear didn't take it lightly being peppered with birdshot like hundreds of stinging bees. Something to keep in mind for self-defense, birdshot will work at killing a bear when you are shooting from less than ten feet before the shot spreads out. Or it just might make him mad enough to kill and eat you.

"Words can't even describe my hunting experience yesterday. I was an hour over a vertical mountain before it got light. I got to the other side and was sneaking through the timber then suddenly I hear something to my left. I turned and it was a lion! No more than five yards away. Right when I turned, she hissed and came at me. I killed her at eight steps away from me. It's one of the scariest things that's ever happened to me. I took these mountains for granted.

"All the way down that mountain, all I could think about is I was one moment away from never seeing my family and my two little girls again. I killed the lion at 7:34 a.m. then came all the way back down that mountain. I reported it to DOW (Department of Wildlife). I showed them all the video evidence and GPS coordinates and they said it was all legal. Unfortunately, I wasn't able to keep the lion.

"One of the biggest things for me was I turned my scope down to low power when I got into the thick trees and was sneaking around. If my scope had not been on low power I would have never found the lion in it. Most hunters should have their scope set on low power anyway because I was hoping to jump a deer or elk. Other than that, reaction time was key. Every situation like this is going to be different because there's no actual way to prepare yourself for it."

Dylan Ross, Colorado

September 28th, 2016, Wolves don't run away when you shoot

"I spotted a lone wolf on the road and thought maybe I can call him and fill my wolf tag. Parking the vehicle, I walked up to where he disappeared in the brush about a ¼ mile off the road. I set up and started calling. I was by myself. The woods lit up with wolves howling, a whole pack. This huge monster came in right in front of me, way too close for my rifle that was set up for long range shooting and on ten power, it was worthless in the thick brush. I don't know if he heard me move or saw me, but he charged. Having no choice, I pulled my handgun, a .357 Sig. I fired my handgun three times and the one that came in on me was still on his feet. The first shot was at twenty-five yards. It was hit in the head. That knocked him down. Then he got up and charged me again. The second shot was closer, third was about six feet. All three shots hit him. The third shot turned him enough that he passed to my left. At that point, my handgun jammed so I picked up my rifle and hit him again. That put him down for good. About four seconds after the fourth shot, one howled about forty to fifty yards uphill from me. Before, all the wolves were below me on the hill. At least two more continued to howl below me on the hill. They surrounded me and I wasn't sure if I would be shooting my way back to the truck. Luckily the rest kept their distance.

"It happened on the east side of Hungry Horse Reservoir in Montana. He weighed in just under 110 pounds.

"I 've since put together a new rifle for wolf and coyote hunting that is much more suited to closer ranges with a 4-power scope. Don't think for a minute that gunfire causes these wolves to run off."—Jair Park

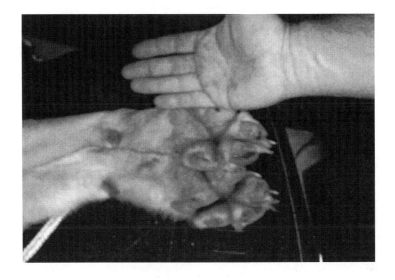

If you have the chance, go to bearspray.com, where UDAP company sells bear sprays. Read the testimony. I would bet the vast majority of those people never reported the attacks. There is one from Canada that the bear was in predatory mode. Four people and the bear kept approaching. They pepper sprayed it and drove it off. The next day it was back and had to be pepper sprayed again. That bear had no fear of humans whatsoever.

Start adding this all up. Newspapers are great; in fact, they are the main source on attacks to warn the public. But they don't get all the stories, or they received pressure not to run too many animal attack stories, bad for tourism don't you know. Fish and game departments are sure as heck not going to tell you about all the attacks that make them look bad.

There are unreported attacks from bear spray users, unreported attacks from hunters or armed hikers who killed the problem animal, picked up their brass, and left the area. There are missing never to be found hikers and hunters. What is the real number of attacks? One writer thought it would be four to one. Four attacks the public has no idea on to one that is reported.

Add the numbers up; that is truly a phenomenal amount of attacks. If the four to one is true, that means in this time period we are talking about 368 cougar attacks, 424 grizzly bear attacks, 500 black bear attacks, and 520 coyote attacks.

Let's be clear on what is being said here. Are the attack numbers this high? Is it possible when you factor in everything? Now take all the bear spray companies out there and all their testimonies. Considering most newspapers only keep articles up for a ten-year period, that is why so many attacks are missing from 1990 to 2007. Can the numbers be this high? I believe the answer is yes. Is it provable? No, the missing hikers and hunters, even when their bodies are found, have had other animals scavenge on them so much it's impossible to tell the cause of death. Or the authorities report as being killed by an animal but not which one. Hunters and hikers who kill in defense of life don't always report attacks.

Westword reported "Visit the Bear-Human Conflict Capital of Colorado"
Michael Roberts | November 27, 2017

As we've reported, at least 168 bears have been euthanized in Colorado so far in 2017. The troubles are so frequent that they seldom make headlines, even at times when bears rip apart homes with residents hiding inside them.

Bears are breaking into houses for food. Once they find food, they keep breaking into more houses. It's truly amazing to read all the excuses. It was a bad crop year; people are not keeping their trash properly. How about the real reason, we have too many bears that they have lost their fear of mankind? The carrying capacity of the land is at maximum level. Increase the tags; encourage more hunters to thin them out.

Seriously, if we bring the numbers down in the state to 15,000 from 19,000, the bears would have more room and more food to survive, hence fewer human-bear conflicts. Maybe the game department needs to look at an increased hunter harvest every five years to keep the bears in check. The current system is not working.

We have a major problem, Houston!

Chapter 11
Animal Rights Activists

Greenpeace's admissions in a recent lawsuit make it clear that environmentalists will spout baloney to make money in ways that no major company would dare.
—Kevin Libin

What is the foundation for the anti-hunting agenda? We must understand the basic concept or psychological profile of the people running the animal rights movement. They have a hive thinking and hate literally independent self-reliant individuals that can provide for their family. It's almost like they are the Borg. Resistance is futile. We all must be the same in a collective. Therefore, we must all buy our food from the store. A feeling of inferiority is so ingrained that they hate people who are strong and can hunt their own food. They aren't living around the large predators but if they can end hunting, these people are all for it.

It's self-hate from their own failure in life. They claim they are motivated by compassion or by moral principles. Save animals for future generations. Or hunting is morally wrong. The general public who is far removed from the natural world believes their high-dollar propaganda. The national media says, "Oh look, an easy feel-good story." They never bother to fact check and do in-depth research to learn the facts. Emotions over reality.

Today's media is filled with man-hatred that has metastasized into hunting is bad. No longer do we need the strong male that can handle and stop attacking animals. Oh my God, do you mean kill animals? Yes, killing the attacking animal is one sure fire way to stop the attacks. The truth of the matter is we need strong males more than ever that can handle guns and save his family life. As more and more predators increase, it's mathematically guaranteed that attacks will increase every year.

A great example to illustrate how insane these people are, is Christopher Ketcham's opinion article in High Country News. People are grizzly food — and that's OK! April 20, 2017

We cannot lament when a hungry grizzly enjoys extra meat. Meat is meat, Homo sapiens or otherwise. For the sake of the grizzlies, we should place a sign on the stone arch entrance to Yellowstone "Stop, you are entering the empire of death." Henceforth it is park policy that anyone killed by animals should be honored as food.

Christopher, please go forth and set the example. The grizzlies will honor your death. The rest of us can dismiss you as another mentally ill animal rights person that watched way too many Disney movies. Let the park service know that you don't want any help to stop the attack. You can start a new trend of death by grizzly bear. Go to the backcountry, cook up five pounds of bacon, and pour the grease all over yourself. We can find out quickly if you have real conviction to your words.

An excellent story about WWF *"funds anti-poaching squads in Cameroon and elsewhere in the Congo Basin," explained Survival International director Stephen Corry. "Baka and other rainforest tribes have reported systematic abuse at the hands of these squads, including arrests, beatings, torture, and even death, for well over 20 years," Corry said.*

Summarizing a Survival International media release, "Survival submitted the complaint in February 2016, citing numerous examples of violent abuse and harassment against Baka 'pygmies' in Cameroon by WWF-funded anti-poaching squads. Survival also alleges that WWF failed to seek communities' freely given, prior, and informed consent for conservation projects on their ancestral land."

This report is not getting much press. Who owns the land? The actual people who have lived there for thousands of years or the WWF?

The average public or even the average hunter has no idea how evil some of these animal rights activists truly are until you confront them. I will give you some examples of their insane ranting so you may get a clear picture from their own words.

These are unedited, printed with all the misspelling and errors as they were posted on Facebook. They were attacking a lady bear hunter.

Dawn P.: WELL THEN I SHOULD BE ABLE TO KILL YOU BECAUSE ACTUALLY WE ARE A FORM OF A ANIMAL ARE SELF BUT I THINK I WILL SKIN AND COOK YOU FIRST JUST FOR THE FUN OF IT.

Muriah H: WHAT MAKES ME SICK IS PEOPLE BRAGHING ABOUT KILLING INNOCENT ANIMALS THESE BITCHES NEED A PIECE OF REALITY BY BEING TORTURED THEM SELVRS

Alexx E: I don 't like people who kill animals for fun, hope your shotgun hits you one time with the bullet instead of the animal you want to kill

Wilcher C: Shoot her and hang her by her tits

More attacks on women hunters.

Shannon S.: I 'd like to shoot her pussy

Rachael G.: She needs to be buried

Samuel P.: Kill that bitch!

George B.: Someone should shoot her…Evil little Girl :-(

Ria Z.: I wish it would 've eaten her skanky ass instead.

Michael S.: shoot that hoe.

Josefine F.: Burn Bitch Burn !!!

Terry M.: Killer bitch…we want your head..

Martina P.: I hope someone soon schoots her ass, I will gladley pose next to here like sche dus now, the bitch :-(

Jan J.: i would scalp her if i got my hands on her

Kelly M.: You need mental health your fucked in the head. Hopefully someone might come and blow you to pieces. People like you have no place in our world. Karma bitch.

Carolyn G.: WHY DON 'T YOU COME HERE WHERE I LIVE AND I WILL TEACH YOU HOW IT FEELS TO BE HUNTED!!!! If I ever see you I have something thay will wipe that grin off your face!!!! You are a waste of skin and air!!!

Jannie K.: i like to kil you bitch

As you can clearly see, these people are sociopaths. I could write a full book on their insane ranting.

The ARA (Animal Rights Activist) cult is an INSANE breeding ground of mental illness and psychological dysfunction. Most ARA cultists are living in a psychological slum. Because they have no close family ties of their own, they are extremely jealous of families that hunt together. They attack these families with a viciousness normally only seen on movies like *The Silence of the Lambs.* For example, on a picture of a woman hunter holding her kill, rants can be found from killing her, to raping her, to slicing her children's throat.

Here are a few examples of the mentally disturbed sociopaths found on Facebook. These terroristic threats are found under a picture of a disabled wheelchair-bound man that is holding a deer he harvested.

"I hope his arms get cut off."

"Should have lost his (the hunter) fucking head."

"pls kill that disable (hunter)."

This is clear for any mental health expert that the people in this radical ARA cult are insane and need professional help. Most should be locked up for public safety reasons.

Female hunter is found dead after apparent suicide 'following online threats from animal rights activists '
By Rory Tingle For Mailonline, July 21, 2017

Even after her death, her Facebook profile was inundated with messages praising the tragic news.

One person wrote: 'You have done a favour to humanity! Bye Bye. '

Another commented: 'She is alive, do not worry, what happened is that she left hunting and now is in the casting of the series The Walking Dead. '

One internet user added: 'She was so bitter that she had to pay her hate killing innocent animals, thank God she killed herself, the only good thing she did lately.'

Another wrote: 'Ciao Mel! You made a favour to nature. '

Understand this is very much like a cult. Reading their ranting really makes you wonder how they survive in the real world.

CBC News Alberta, 'We want this bear alive ': Thousands rally to save grizzly that 's chased humans. July 14, 2017

"She is just as much of a local as I am, or Stacey is, or anybody else in this town," said Todd, who has lived in the area for 11 years. "And she deserves the same respect as everybody else."

The bear had charged a man with a baby stroller, chased hikers, and wandered through a high school rugby practice. But thousands of people signed a petition to save the bear known as Bear 148. Bree Todd and Stacey Sartoretto started a petition to save the bear.

Would someone please tell these two that bears are not people? When did human safety become second to animals? There are thousands of bears; killing one to protect the citizens is common sense.

When some people say they are happy when animals kill people, we are dealing with something very bizarre. It's important to understand what misanthropy is. Misanthropy is a dislike for humankind. People are being taught to hate their own species. After reading thousands of animal rights comments, I would define it as a hate of mankind to the point of cult-like thinking. This is very important to understand. Someone will say, "I researched this on Google and could not find what you're talking about." Google searches are based on money. The top ten positions are normally paid Google placements. With hundreds of animal rights groups flooding the internet, they can control what people see.

Date issued 1878 to 1891, Artist Stanley Berkeley Title: The enraged animal hugging him close in his huge paws. The New York Public Library Digital Collections

Terrible Animal Rights Activist Tries to Hire Hit Man to Kill Someone Wearing Fur
Jezebel Cassie Murdoch 2/22/12

Meredith Marie Lowell, a 27-year-old from Ohio, was arrested yesterday by the FBI after she tried to hire a hit man on Facebook.

She said the killing should take place across from a playground near her house, and she wanted to be there when it happened to hand out "papers" about the fur industry.

As for the intended victim, she asked that it be someone "older than 12 — preferably older than 14 years old."

Yes, you read that right. This insane animal rights psychopath wanted children to be murdered on a playground.

The Enraged Animal Hugging Him Close In His Huge PawsThe Enraged Animal Hugging Him Close In His Huge Paws

What we have is generations far removed from the land. In the 1930s, twenty-one percent of the labor force worked on farms. Today less than one percent live on farms. People don't understand where food comes from or what it takes to raise it. Protections from predators have been dated in mankind's history as far back as Greece in AD 46-120. The first wolf bounty was reportedly opened when Solon of Athens offered five silver drachmas to any hunter for killing any male wolf, and one for every female (Mech, 2003).

Simple bounties were used to protect a nation's food supply from predators. Utah today still has a bounty on coyotes of $50. The bounties in most states on predators have ended. An interesting fact is that California had a mountain lion bounty from 1907 to 1963. Records show 12,462 mountain lions were killed (more than any other state) and turned in for the bounty. These bounties were repealed in the sixties, then in the nineties the cougars were protected from hunting. How many mountain lion attacks happened to people during this time before they were protected? That would be zero. Even with the bounty and heavily hunted, they were never wiped out. But they highly feared humans.

Animal rights groups don't want to talk about human safety. Or they try to blow it off, saying more people are hit by lightning than attacked by whatever animal. While that is true, I have never heard of a grizzly bear walking downtown New York City. But lightning most certainly can hit someone living there. I've never seen a wolf stalking people in downtown Miami, but lightning can hit people there.

What we have with groups of people raised on Disneyland talking animals is they are very uneducated on wildlife. I am sure you have all heard of the tourist in national parks taking pictures too close and being attacked by bison. Even elk and deer have attacked people. This trend is causing a lot of stress in the park workers. How do you keep the Darwin award contestant from killing themselves?

With that in mind, how can someone living in a big city having no connection to wildlife have a voice on wildlife issues? The proper term for these people is drama queen screamers. They have the same chant. Save the animals, we are taking all the land. There are too many people in the world. Ranting like that is fine but when they take it into terrorist threats, we as a society must stand up and stop it.

Julie Faith Strauja in California had a 400-pound black bear tearing into her trash. Thinking to stop the animal, she moved it inside. The bear broke into her house. When the animal attempted to enter her property a third day in a row, according to wildlife officials, Strauja's friend shot and killed the bear July 31.

Strauja told the *Sun* she hasn't regretted her decision. But others in Forest Falls, California, — a community of about 1,100 people in the San Bernardino Mountains, seventy miles east of Los Angeles — certainly do.

"I've had death threats and my address posted all over social media," Strauja told the Sun.

She showed the newspaper an image of a Facebook post published Wednesday—but later taken down—that included Strauja's address.

"Contact me if you want to legally make their life a living hell," the Facebook post said.

As you can see, protecting your family from a bear breaking into your house causes death threats from the mentally unbalanced animal lovers in California. If a 400-pound man broke into someone's house you would think nothing for a homeowner shooting the person. What happened to common sense? When a bear enters your home, you kill it to protect your family. Anyone sending death threats to the family should immediately be arrested for sending terrorist threats.

This is not only in California; a group in Nevada put a family through hell over having the fish and game department kill a problem bear.

A Lake Tahoe woman is suing a longtime bear protection group for publishing her personal information and receiving death threats from the drama queen screamers. Adrienne Evans, a high school science teacher, accuses the BEAR League of starting an ugly social media campaign that turned into a vengeful attempt to run her and her husband out of town. She stated she loves bears and wasn't trying to get the animal killed.

The lawsuit seeks up to $50,000 in damages from the nonprofit bear group and its founder, Anne Bryant, for engaging in a "libelous smear campaign" putting the family through hell.

Why was the bear killed? Because it was a repeat offender that continued to be aggressive toward humans. The game department put the bear down.

That's when the Evans' family says the nightmare began.

"BEAR League volunteers (drama queen screamers) began to make false and malicious statements, a very vicious and calculated effort to damage her reputation and instill fear in Adrienne. They were trying to make an example of this poor family to instill fear in anyone else who might dare called the game department to protect their property from bears. A common tactic is to have the drama queen screamers call the employers to get the person fired, forcing them to leave the community."

"...The court finds that clear and convincing evidence exists to support the Evans' claims that the Bear League conspired with its followers to accomplish the unlawful objective of cyber-stalking/cyber harassment, causing harm to the (Evanses)," Stiglich wrote.

I have not been able to find the outcome of this case.

Environmentalists admit you shouldn't believe what they say—but they want your money anyway.

Financial Post by Kevin Libin, March 8, 2017

What a relief to hear that Greenpeace now says that we shouldn't seriously believe its claims.

After enduring a years-long campaign where Greenpeace publicly trashed Resolute's reputation and intimidated its customers into canceling their paper-supply contracts, the Montreal-based forestry company began fighting back with lawyers, alleging Greenpeace is a "global fraud" that "duped" its donors with "materially false and misleading claims." In the U.S., Resolute sued using the Racketeer Influenced and Corrupt Organizations Act (RICO), which was both a strikingly menacing tactic and an absolutely inspired idea. Since a racketeering suit can bring triple damages, and since Resolute claims Greenpeace's harassment campaign has cost it upwards of $100 million, the gravity of the threat has motivated Greenpeace to come up with the best defense it can muster.

Look at the fear mongering Greenpeace used. "forest destroyers," responsible for a "caribou death spiral and extinction." Greenpeace claims no big deal, it was only marketing hype.

But Resolute's allegation is that Greenpeace is practicing a form of fraud, outright lying for their own enrichment. The cult members of Greenpeace who believe every word put the company and employees through living hell.

When are these groups going to be held responsible for their actions?

Chapter 12
Missing Hunters and Hikers

Before I blacked out, the only emotion I felt was anger. I was mad. Because I thought I was going to die, and I didn't want to die. —Patty Miller as told to Darlena Cunha, *Backpacker Magazine*

You have to ask yourself what is happening to these people that are never found. Loved ones are left behind, wondering for years on end. Frustrated authorities do not have the answer or may even be looking for a human criminal element, ignoring the animal attacks completely.

Dead Men Walking: Search and Rescue in US National Parks. Travis W. Heggie, Michael E. Amundson. DOI: http://dx.doi.org/10.1580/08-WEME-OR-299R.1
Wilderness & Environmental Medicine, Vol. 20, Issue 3, 244–249
National parks suicides accounted for only one percent of all SAR incidents. During the sixteen-year period there was an average number of 4,090 SAR operations per year. Admits two and half percent of people are never found or around one hundred and two people a year. Note this is national parks; this doesn't include forest service land, BLM land, or other lands open to the public within each state.

Human Attacks by Large Felid Carnivores in Captivity and in the Wild Suzanne M. Shepherd MD, DTM&H Wilderness and Environmental Medicine June 2014 Volume 25, Issue 2, Pages 220–230
The bodies of victims of large feline carnivore attacks are often missing, making closure difficult for survivors.

The experts are finally admitting some of the truth. Large feline carnivores like to eat in private. That means it's very difficult for search and rescue to locate them or their body. Mountain lions and bears like to cache their kills, burying the body.

The Big Timber Pioneer, REMAINS OF MISSING HUNTER FOUND August 10, 2016

Aaron Joseph Hedges, 38, reported September 2014 as a missing bowhunter.

A local rancher found the remains and called the Sheriff. Other items had been found within sight of buildings he easily could have walked to.

Local law enforcement officers believe Hedges may have passed up the opportunity for shelter out of fear of getting caught trespassing.

Once on scene, law enforcement was shown the "skeletal remains of a skull" and then began a systematic search of the area where they uncovered less than 80 percent of Hedges' skeleton.

"The skeletal remains that we were able to recover were all within about 50 to 70 yards from the first one to the last one," Ronneberg said.

Or was something chasing him to prevent him from reaching the building? Or attacked him and he died in the fight?

September 7, 2014, Rick Cross was reported as a missing hunter.

Kananaskis Country, Alberta, Canada. A search team found his body. It's believed he walked into a kill site of a sow grizzly with a cub that had just killed a deer. No details on if he was fed on or cached.

NamUs Missing person database
Status Missing

Jerry Lee McKoen

Date last seen: September 21, 2002

Date entered 12/12/2008

Age last seen: 48 years old

Age now: 63 years old

Vehicle was located on October 8, 2002, just west of Medicine Lake Rd. in a heavily wooded area south of Door Knob Snowmobile Park in Siskiyou County, CA. Told his family he was going bow hunting. Over one hundred searchers were unsuccessful in locating him. The area is loaded with cougars and bears.

Idaho police search for missing retired Massachusetts Trooper
By Associated Press Thursday, October 2, 2008

GRANGEVILLE, Idaho - Authorities and trained volunteers in northern Idaho are searching for a 62-year-old Massachusetts man who went missing during an elk hunting trip. He said Gray had a GPS unit, a solar-powered radio, warm clothing, and enough food and water to last more than a week. He added local outfitters have stashed caches of food and supplies throughout the area where he was hiking. Gray also may have to contend with grizzly bears, mountain lions, and wolves.

Human remains those of hunter missing for 23 years
Sep 8, 2006, The Associated Press

Investigators said they found the driver's license of Grant C. Rice in the remains, along with a watch and other belongings believed to be his. Jay Hansen said authorities did not recover a complete skeleton and may never be able to determine how Rice died.

North America Missing Person Network
Jeromy Ivan Childress
Missing Since: October 17, 2004 from Tillamook, Oregon
- Classification: Missing Hunter
- Date of Birth: September 15, 1973
- Age: 31
- Height: 5 '10"
- Weight: 175 lbs.

Jeromy was on an annual hunting trip when the hunting party lost sight of camp and continued on foot to find their camp. The two other hunters returned to the truck; however, Jeromy did not. He was reported missing on October 17, 2004, and still no sighting or clues of Jeromy 's disappearance. He was carrying a rifle, a silver watch, a gold wedding band, wallet, his car keys, and possibly a pocket knife. None of these items have been found.

He was last seen at approximately 4.30 p.m. on Trask Mountain near Tucca Creek Road and Boundary Rd.

Allen Theis

Missing Since: November 25, 2003, from Lewistown, Montana

- •Classification: Missing
- •Age: 52

He disappeared into the Missouri Breaks on a planned hunting trip. His pickup truck was found in the Stafford Ferry area. Officially pronounced dead in 2011 but his remains have not been found.

Washington hiker battles bears while awaiting helicopter rescue on Pacific Crest Trail

Wednesday, June 25, 2014, by Nicole Hensley, New York Daily News

An injured hiker told a U.S. Navy rescue crew that he fended off bears after he fell and broke his leg along the Pacific Crest Trail.

The unnamed hiker, 50, luckily had a can of bear spray to fight off the predators during several hours of waiting as rescuers tried to get him out of the North Cascades in Washington Saturday evening.

This last one is an example of what might be happening. You get injured in the wild, especially if there is fresh blood, and that is a long-distance call lure for predators to come a knocking. Most people understand blood in the water attracts sharks, but they have no education on blood in the wilderness. Fresh blood is one of the best attractions for predators.

I was hunting in Hawaii and shot an Axis deer. We skinned and gutted it. The next day we checked the spot the remains were left at. The feral pigs had come in during the night and not a single piece of hide or guts was to be found. In fact, even the legs and hooves were missing. Just a trampled area and a blood spot. An injured hiker bleeding would be in serious trouble with feral pigs around. My first thought was if you had a broken bleeding leg and could not walk out or climb a tree, they would never find you.

There are several cases in this book where hunters were attacked either cleaning an elk or trying to retrieve the elk. Fresh blood in the air means a grizzly can zero right in. Not only bears, but all the other predators like cougars, wolves, and coyotes.

Missing hikers

Is it reasonable that animal attacks are causing people to disappear? Is there scientific evidence to back this theory up? Yes, people have been killed and eaten. Their bodies have been found in cache. This is well documented as in the case of John Wallace. After the grizzly bear killed and partially ate him the body was cache and buried. The man died relatively close to the trail in an area that is fairly open.

The New York Times wrote an excellent article that has some insight. "The Tale of Three Bad News Bears Who Became Killers" By Mark Derr August 18, 1998. The story is about a female bear with cubs that attacked and killed a man in Glacier National Park. Now here is the interesting part. Matthew Truszkowski, 25, of Michigan is reported missing July, 1997. A bear known as chocolate legs was seen in the area by searchers.

Craig Dahl, a 26-year-old park concessions worker was reported missing. His body was found three days later on May 20,1998. Using DNA evidence, it was positively identified as chocolate legs and her cubs as the killers. They not only killed but fed on Craig Dahl.

Now the question remains of what happened to Matthew Truskowski? I could find no report saying his body has ever been recovered. Bears have a history of becoming serial killers. But what we as humans tend to forget is that animals don't think like we do. A serial killer bear doesn't mean the bear is constantly stalking and feeding on humans. Predators are opportunist hunters. If the bear has plenty of natural food to eat, he or she might not touch another human. But if food is scarce and hunger is calling the bear, it may very well kill again when the opportunity presents itself, i.e., a lone hiker.

Bears can't explain why they do things. As humans, we try to explain things in easy terms and we want fast answers. This is more complicated. Don't think serial killer bears only feed on people. Bears are predators and when they are hungry, this triggers predatory attacks.

If you're wondering why bodies are rarely found, the book on Forensic Taphonomy, *The Postmortem Fate of Human Remains*, by William D. Hagland and Marcella H. Sorg, tells us of a coyote study. What the researcher found was extremities are removed and missing. It only makes sense that wolves would do the same thing.

Here is what they found. "*Dogs and coyotes are the most frequently reported canids responsible for scavenging human remains.*" Please remember this was done in the 80s and early 90s. Way before wolves were in the area. Today no doubt wolves would be added to this list.

Make sure you have the intestinal fortitude to deal with what I am about to describe. If you have lost a loved one, you may want to skip this section and jump to the next chapter.

Haglund (1991) did a report on fifty-three canid-scavenged human remains. What he found was dismemberment of human remains taking place in a relatively consistent sequence.

Table 1: Stages of Canid-Assisted Scavenging

1. 4 hours to 14 days: Early scavenging of soft tissue with no body unit removal.
2. 22 days to 2.5 months: Destruction of ventral thorax evisceration and removal of one or both extremities including scapulae and partial or complete clavicles.
3. 2 to 4.5 months: Lower exterminates fully or partially removed.
4. 2 to 11 months: All skeletal elements disarticulated except for segments of the vertebral column.
5. 5 to 52 months: Total disarticulation with only cranium and other assorted skeletal elements or fragment recovered.

What this means in laymen's terms:

1. The coyotes and or dogs are feeding on the soft tissue.
2. The thorax is the superior part of the trunk between the neck and the abdomen. Clavicle is the collarbone. Scapula: The shoulder blade.
3. Both legs are removed or partially removed.
4. The bones are being carried off.
5. Only the skull and or fragments are recovered.

Keep in mind this was not done for bears, cougars, or wolves. My guess is there is not enough left most of the time to perform a study when it comes to the larger predators.

Stage 1: This case involved a 22-year-old who died from a drug overdose in the woods. His body was found five days later. Upper portions of the coat and collar had been torn by animals. The skin muscle including the tongue had been removed on the left side. The right eye had been removed. There was other trauma on the upper body. Finding something like this would be difficult to determine the cause of death without blood work to identify the drug overdose.

Stage 2: A 19-year-old woman was reported missing in late December. Her body was found in mid-February. To explain the extensive feeding on by coyotes would easily be shown using her body weight. Her last live weight was 120 pounds. At the time of the autopsy, her remains weighed sixteen pounds. Without getting into the gruesome details of the autopsy, I'm confident that readers can fill in the details.

Stage 3: Major segments of axial skeleton are scattered. A case of a 49-year-old man last seen in August and found in April. Death was due to a gunshot wound to the head. All remaining skeletal elements were disarticulated (separate bones at the joints) and scattered.

Stage 4: Extensive gnawed scattered bones. A case of a 19-year-old woman believed to be deposited in the woods in September and discovered two and half years later. Most bones were found scattered over a ninety-yard area.

Coyotes have a consistent pattern of feeding on bodies. Porcupine, mice, rats, and squirrels all carry off bones and teeth. Some teeth have been found in mice burrows. I was really hoping and trying to find a study on large predators. Wolves have powerful jaws and most likely are breaking and eating the bones much like a house dog chewing on a bone until there is nothing left but chips. Bears have the jaw strength to crack human skulls, explaining why pieces are sometimes the only thing left at the kill site. Cougars feeding on children have the jaw strength to break open the skull.

In the book, *The Cost Of Being Green Before Green Was Cool*, TJ Elsbury gives a great example of the raw power of a cougar.

"A second large male (cougar) carried a 140-pound dog after ripping its chain loose from the siding of a secluded Jacinto Mountain cabin in Pine Cove, down two flights of stairs, and a quarter of a mile into heavy brush **without any trace of drag marks or blood.***"*

California fish and game biologist Sallie Reynolds in Outdoor California claimed: *"All big cats seem unable to resist children."*

A small 60-pound child would be easily carried off without leaving a trace.

The author also talks about how he called police detectives and asked if they were checking for animal attacks on missing children. An editorial in *Western Outdoors* claimed, *"Dozens of missing children reports have pointed toward mountain lions in the past few decades but due to their small size, there were not enough remains located to determine the means of death or they simply were never found."*

We must help the public to understand. Blood in the air currents has the same fatal attraction as blood in the water bringing the sharks to you. The land shark might be a 500-pound grizzly bear.

Chapter 13
Staring Death in the Face!

All I could think about was this bear is so close to me I can see its teeth, I could have kissed it. I wished I had a gun. —Allyson Jones Robinson as told to KOMO news.

Yes, guns are permitted in national parks. Park visitors are able to openly carry legal handguns, rifles, shotguns, and other firearms per a federal law approved by Congress and signed by President Barack Obama in February 2010. Concealed weapons are allowed by state statute.

One point I cannot stress enough here is to hell with warning shots. I have read too many cases where the warning shot failed to scare the animal off and the gun jammed. In high-stress situations, people do unexplainable things like unloading the gun thinking they are actually firing and working the action, tossing out live rounds. Once a large predator charging you is under the thirty-yard mark, you're talking four seconds before impact. Don't waste what might be your one and only shot.

I was hunting around Hungry Horse Reservoir, Montana, near where David Buckallew and his son, Rory, were attacked by a grizzly bear. I was carrying a new unproven 12-gauge pump action shotgun. An unproven gun meaning I had never fired it before. It was loaded with buckshot and slugs for bear protection. I saw a grouse and put in a birdshot round. I fired one shot and had the grouse for dinner. The gun jammed; it would not eject the empty shell. The action came back about halfway and stuck, refusing to open or close. Now it was a very expensive club. Mailing the gun back to the manufacturer, they were able to repair it. If a bear had charged me I would have had one and only one shot. Don't carry unproven guns, depending on them to save your life. Talking with victims of attacks, the one common thing they all say is, "I could not believe how fast they are."

So what guns should you use against bears? This topic I'm sure will get everyone talking. Bullet choice I believe is almost more important than caliber. For example, would you believe a 9mm was used successfully in stopping an enraged Alaskan brown bear? For the inexperienced people that get their gun information from television, would say oh yes makes sense. But for anyone who understands guns, the tiny 9mm round is not the gun of choice for bears.

Statement from Phil Shoemaker.

Two days ago, I was guiding a couple from NY on a fishing trip and decided to pack my S&W 3954 pistol. When we were approaching the stream, we bumped into a large boar who must have been sleeping as we were talking loud just so we wouldn't surprise one.

Over the past 33 years I have lived and guided here on the Alaska Peninsula; I have never had to kill a bear in defense of life but this bear was different.

ALASKAN GUIDE, PHIL SHOEMAKER, USES 9MM OUTDOORSMAN ROUNDS IN A S&W 3954 TO STOP AN ATTACKING GRIZZLY

Tim,

We were in thick brush and I was only eight to ten feet from the bear when he started growling and huffing. I began yelling and it eventually ran around, behind my two clients, into the brush. But within fifteen seconds it came charging back from the area behind us and popped out of the brush ten feet from me! I had the little S&W in my hands and was thinking I was probably going to have to shoot it but as it cleared the brush it headed toward my clients. The man had enough sense to grab his wife and fall backward into the tall grass. The bear seemed to lose track of them, even though it was less than three feet away from them and it was highly agitated! It then swung toward me, I was six to eight feet away, and I fired the first shot into the area between the head and shoulder. It growled and started wildly thrashing around, still basically on the feet of my clients. My next shot hit it in the shoulder and it began twisting and biting at the hits and I continued firing as fast as I could see vitals. Five shots later it turned into the brush and I hit it again and it twisted and fell twenty feet from us!

We hiked out and I flew back to camp to report the incident to F&G and pick up my daughter to go back and skin the bear for F&G.

You are the first person I have told this story to as I haven't decided whether to write it up or not, or where, but thought you should know that your ammo WORKS. We recovered four of the bullets and I took a photo of the back of the bear after the hide was removed that shows an entry on one side of the back and the tip of the bullet on the off side …

Phil Shoemaker
www.grizzlyskinsofalaska.com

He was using Buffalo Bore Bullets, hard cast lead flat nose bullets. Why this is important is bears are large, tough animals. Thick bones make it hard to penetrate and get into the vital area to do damage. A hollow point is the worst choice because they are designed for light-skinned animals and to rapidly expand. A bear has a thick hide to get through first, next a layer of fat, and third bone before you can reach the vitals. A hollow point might expand too fast stopping in the fat. This would just make the animal mad. Not to mention do little to save your life.

Round nose bullets can deflect off the bone. Some will get in but when seconds count, I want every bullet reaching inside the vitals. Full Metal Jacket is a better choice than hollow-point or a soft-point. But again, it has a round nose. FMJ are military rounds and were design not to expand.

If all you have is a little .22, you can still kill a bear. In fact, at the end of this chapter, you'll see the story of how one was used to successfully kill a record size grizzly. I read a bear attack story back in the 1970s where a man was attacked by a grizzly bear in a national park. He was mad because he was not allowed to carry a gun in the park. (This was before the law had changed.) He said even a .22 pistol could have saved him from the brutal attack when he was on the ground and the bear was mauling him. "I could have shot him in the ear, straight to the brain."

Of course, a good choice is the .12-gauge pump or semi-auto shotgun. The first round being 3-inch magnum buckshot followed by slugs. Don't be afraid to keep shooting. Even if you knock the bear down, put another round in him. Once the bear is down, a great kill shot is to get to the side and put one right in the ear. The skull is very weak at this point allowing the bullet to penetrate the brain stems.

With rifles, you want a short barrel, easy-to-handle rifle with no scope because you don't have time to try and find a charging bear in your scope. A 30-06 is considered the minimum rifle for grizzly. The .338 is a great choice. A .300-win mag, .375 (an Alaskan favorite), .45-70 (for those who like lever action), and .458 are all great choices. But as one guide said, "I would rather have a man carry a 30-06 that he can hit very well with than a client carrying a .458 that makes poor shots." That .458 is a real mule kicker and people flinch, causing poor bullet placement.

You have four seconds to shoot at the charging grizzly bear. You have to draw, aim, and fire. I did a training course where we had to draw and fire three rounds in five seconds. It sounds hard, but with practice, you can do it in three seconds. The trick was shooting from the hip. You clear the holster point and shoot. No aiming. With a little practice, you can become very accurate.

The equipment you choose is very important. Have a snap on your gun holster that you can pop off as you reach for the gun. You must put the time in practicing to do it. You should be shooting at least once a month until it becomes second nature to draw and fire. Of course, I must put a warning out. When you first start, go slow. YouTube is full of people shooting their foot or leg when they practice the quick draw. You're not Wyatt Earp. Practicing with an empty gun is the way to start this process. After you get that down, you can go to the range with live ammo.

When a bear is charging, you're in panic mode—fight or flight. You're not thinking clearly. Your breathing rate increases; that is where training kicks in. READ ABOUT police officers in shootouts sometimes having their first shot hit the pavement in front of them. They are trained. So, are you an expert trained to draw and accurately fire at a moving target coming to kill you?

Take a friend to the gun range. Do ten push-ups, stand up, have your friend play a tape of a bear growling at high volume, then draw and fire at a target. You will be shocked at how badly you do until you have gone through it repeatedly.

Now saying all that, what pistol are you going to carry in grizzly country? I would say a .357 magnum as a minimum, loaded with hard cast flat nose like Buffalo Bore Bullets.

The .44 mag is a great choice but just because Clint Eastwood said it will blow a man's head clear off doesn't mean that one shot is going to stop a charging grizzly bear. I think you should practice three shots when you are training. The .454 Casull is a hand cannon. Another mule kicker. The Desert Eagle .50 caliber is a great round but the gun loaded is close to five pounds. Do you really want a heavy gun strapped to your leg as you hike for miles?

You are far better off carrying the .44 mag or .357 that you can draw and shoot rapidly and is comfortable to carry. Ammo is more reasonably priced, which hopefully will allow you to practice more. Since we're talking ammunition, you can practice with any of the cheap ammo in your caliber and save your better ammo for defense.

If you want a semi-auto, choose a .40 caliber SW or 10mm. A Glock 22 in .40 caliber is fifteen rounds with 200-grain flat nose and has some impressive power. The Glock 20 in 10mm has more power and still holds fifteen rounds. Here is a quick chart to help you decided.

9MM +P Hard cast 147-grain bullet 1,083 feet per second. Muzzle Energy 394 ft. Pounds

.357 Hard cast 180 grain 1,400 feet per second. Muzzle Energy 783 ft. pounds

.40 cal. 200 gr. Hard Cast 1,000 feet per second. Muzzle Energy 537 ft. pounds

10mm 220 gr. Hard Cast – FN (1,200 feet per second. Muzzle Energy 703 ft. lbs.)

.44 mag 305 gr. Hard cast 1,325 feet per second. Muzzle Energy 1,189 ft. lbs.

454 Casull Ammo - 360 gr. Hard cast 1,425 fps/M.E. 1,623 ft. lbs.

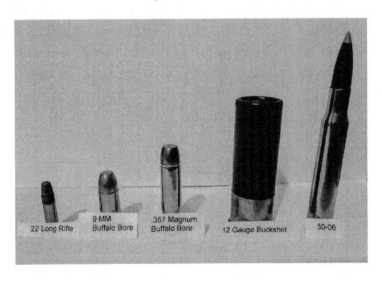

What does this all mean in layman terms? 9mm is the diameter of the bullet. .357 is the actual diameter of the bullet. Grains is the weight of the bullet. Feet per second is how fast the bullet is traveling. Now the important part is muzzle energy. That is how much energy you are transferring into the target. The higher the muzzle energy, the more knock-down power you have.

Now compare this to a rifle.

30-06 180 grain 2,700 feet per second. Muzzle Energy 2,913

.300 Winchester mag 180-grain bullet 2,960 feet per second. Muzzle Energy /3,501

338 225 grain bullet 2,920 feet per second. Muzzle Energy 4,259

375 Ruger 270 grain bullet 2,840 feet per second. Muzzle Energy 4,835

45-70 300 grain bullet 2,275 feet per second. Muzzle Energy 3,449

458 Win mag 500-grain bullet 2,090 feet per second. Muzzle Energy 4,850

12-gauge slug 550 grains 1,620 feet per second. Muzzle Energy: 2,488 ft. lbs.

As you can clearly see, a rifle or a 12-gauge shotgun is far superior to any pistol for stopping power.

Because a grizzly is a big dumb animal that can still kill you after being hit, even with a .458 Winchester Magnum, you must have it in your mind to keep shooting until the threat is neutralized. Like I already said, just because you knock the bear down doesn't mean it's dead; keep shooting.

There is literally a ton of other handgun and rifle rounds I didn't even mention. Clearly, that would take a book to explain it all. I just giving some common calibers for examples. The .454 Casull is one hell of a pistol round at $96 for a box of fifty rounds. You're not going to be practicing much with it. One thing you will find is the more common a caliber, the cheaper and more availability of the ammo. How accurate are you with your weapon of choice? How much do you practice?

A duck or pheasant hunter would be far better off carrying a 12 gauge with slugs simply because he/she has one heck of a lot of experience shooting it rapidly and accurately. Guns and caliber choice can be debated for years on end. It comes down to what you are good at shooting with. You are far better off with a rifle you are very familiar with and use often instead of upgrading to a large caliber. Same with pistols if you 're used to carrying a .40 SW, you are far better off carrying it for bear defense instead of upgrading to the .454 Casull. But that is a decision only you can make. If you believe the larger caliber is the best choice for you, go for it.

While we are talking about this, your gun and bullets of choice are your life insurance. Don't be cheap. Spend the money for quality firearm and ammunition.

It should be mentioned that the coastal brown bears of Alaska and British Columbia are much larger and harder to kill than an inland grizzly bear. They are notorious for taken a lot of lead before they die. You might have seen the internet hoax of an enormous Kodiak grizzly claiming it was 12 feet 6 inches tall, 1,600 pounds, and a man shot it after it charged him. The story claims it had killed five people.

Anchorage Daily News reported in December 2001 the true story. Within a year, the pictures were flowing around the internet with a different twist. The latest hoax on this bear was they found a partially eaten body the bear had killed and fed on. The truth is the bear measured 10 feet 6 inches and estimated weight was 1,000 to 1,200 pounds. He was using .338 not a semi-auto 7mm Mag. The bear was not known to have killed anyone.

Every few years, the pictures and a new story float around the internet. The pictures are a great learning tool to see how huge these bears are.

There is an old tale about a greenhorn in Alaska that goes to the gun store and buys a .44 magnum revolver for bear protection. The clerk, a grizzled old man, tells him to make sure to file off the front sight before going in the woods. The greenhorn asked, "Why? Is it some kind of Billy the Kid trick for firing quickly?"

"Nope," the old man replied. "It's so it doesn't hurt as much when the bear shoves it up your behind."

The joke is told a lot to newcomers to Alaska. But it's also a great reminder that guns are not going to save you one hundred percent of the time.

Did you ever wonder why bears and wolves attack the head of a person? In the predator world, the teeth are the deadly weapon. They are attacking your head to disable what they perceive as your best weapons to fight back with.

An example of the amount of lead a bear can take is in Don Zaide's book, *American Man-Killers*. He tells a story of BC hunting guide Roy Pattison who had a run-in with a grizzly. Tracking the wounded beast in the brush, he saw the bear laid up. He put a 180-grain bullet in the bear. The bear, not thinking this was funny, charged. He gave the bear hell with his 30-06. His second shot hit the bear behind the ear, putting the beast down. But after a moment, it was back up. His third shot hit the bear in the lower jaw. The bear hit him so hard with his shoulder he sent Roy flying through the air to land ten feet away. The bear tore him up, shaking him like a rag doll. His dog, a large German Shepard, came to his aid, driving the bear off. He survived. Now here is the twist of fate.

The following year, he was guiding the same client in the same area. He was again tracking a wounded bear when they spotted a second large grizzly. Roy thought that bear looked familiar. The bear charged again. This time there were three shooters. The two guides with 30-06 and the client's husband with a .303. It took fifteen rounds to put the beast down. When skinning the bear's hide, they found two bullets from the previous year, one in the lower jaw and one behind the ear. This happened in 1987. Today, thirty years later, bullets have vastly improved. The new Barnes copper bullet is an excellent choice. Checking with Alaska Fish and Game, the Nosler Partition®, the Swift A-Frame®, and the Trophy Bonded Bear Claw® are excellent bullets with the only downside being cost. Practice with cheap ammo. Carry for protection premium ammo.

Bear spray is covered in detail in the safety chapter.

Remember, if all else fails, climb up a tree. If the bear climbs up after you and eats you, it's a black bear. If the bear knocks the tree down and eats you, it's a grizzly.

Here is a great video why you don't want hollow points for bears rounds:
10MM and 44 MAGNUM vs Grizzly skull plate https://www.youtube.com/watch?v=eCUFzNLHP2Q

Let's look at a couple pepper spray failures.

Brown Bear Charge on Montague Island
By AKJournal

https://www.youtube.com/watch?v=4Dry7aDm6ws

Bear spray failed. The 30-06 saved the day. A brown bear sow charged a couple who were deer hunting. They heard the bear and made further noise but then the bear charged anyway. They hit the bear square on with pepper spray, but it did NOT stop her charge.

The husband fired one shot from his 30-06 "from the hip," hitting the bear between the eyes killing it instantly.

KOMO news reported on July 14, 2012, of a grizzly attack on three people.

"It was kind of trotting around me, and then it would charge and growl," *said Alyson Jones-Robinson, an English professor at the University of Alaska Fairbanks. "It charged, and I used my bear spray when it was about four feet away and then I fell with my pack on and dropped the bear spray."*

Using her walking stick next, she broke if over the bear's head. It was a small bear, she guesses two to three years old. The bear bluff charged several more times after being pepper sprayed. There were no injuries; she and her nieces made it out safely.

Alyson's final comment says it very well. *"All I could think about was this bear is so close to me I can see its teeth,"* she said. *"I could have kissed it. I wished I had a gun."*

Todd Orr's Facebook post:

I yelled a number of times so she knew I was human and would hopefully turn back. No such luck. Within a couple seconds, she was nearly on me. I gave her a full charge of bear spray at about twenty-five feet. Her momentum carried her right through the orange mist and on me.

The only cases I could find of firearms failing to save a person was when a gun misfired. I could find only two cases of firearms failure to save a person in defense of life in an unexpected attack. Both were misfires. Lack of evidence is not proof that firearms are 90% sure saviors either.

CHARACTERISTICS OF NONSPORT MORTALITIES TO BROWN AND BLACK BEARS AND HUMAN INJURIES FROM BEARS IN ALASKA
STERLING D. MILLER, V. LEIGH TUTTERROW 1999

These threats frequently result in bears being killed to minimize these dangers to humans. In Alaska, these mortalities are termed kills "in defense of life or property." Data on injuries from bears, however, are minimal figures because not all injuries are reported, and some newspaper accounts were probably missed. No agency in Alaska is charged with maintaining records of human injuries caused by wildlife.

Interesting in this study is the peak month for both grizzly and black bear attacks was July for Alaska. But in this book, including all of North America, the peak month was September for grizzly bears.

Miller and Tutterrow examined more than 2,000 incidents from 1970 to 1996 when people killed bears in defense of life or property. In reality, less than two percent of the people involved reported injuries. The Smith and Herrero study ignored this previous study. They pushed their new study widely touted in today's press, that bear spray is 90% effective. I have learned when it comes to favorite species of certain scientists, hiding or bending the truth is the norm. Endangering human health and safety for political agenda of saving the bears is not ethical.

Efficacy of firearms for bear deterrence in Alaska
Tom S. Smith & Stephen Herrero, The Wildlife Society. February 6, 2012

Red pepper spray stopped bears' undesirable behavior 92% of the time when used on brown bears, 90% for black bears.

A 50% success rate for firearms.

We reviewed 269 incidents of bear-human conflict.

Why the enormous difference between the two studies? I'm not a scientist nor do I play one on TV. But the data from the attacks in this book paint a completely different picture. Black bear attacks found a 50% failure rate for bear spray. Firearms are 100% effective at stopping or ending a black bear attack.

Of the attacks listed in this book, bear spray when deployed against grizzly bears had a 61.5% success rate and a 38.5% failure rate. Firearms had a 90% success rate and a 10% failure rate at stopping a grizzly bear attack. Also, in two firearms cases, victims were hit by the bullet. One killed Claudia Huber in Canada. The second one, Wilf Lloyd, was hit in the thigh, but he credited his son-in-law for saving his life from the bear. When guns were used sometimes after the victim was attacked but deployed to stop the attack was added as successful. As was bear spray that failed the first time but worked the second time.

Before anyone accuses me of cherry picking the cases, I have stated numerous times this is all the cases I could find. It's not like the government agency provided me with all the cases to review. Nor is there a national database to list all attacks. If the person was carrying bear spray or a firearm and didn't get the chance to use either, they were not counted. Only when shots were fired or when bear spray was used.

Toss this thought into the whole bear spray debate. Bears sprayed once before may learn to close their mouth and eyes as they run through the spray. Is it possible? I don't see why not. Bears can learn and adapt.

The scientists can fight it out but in Stephen Herrero's book, *Bear Attacks: Their Causes and Avoidance*, he admits to his bias and said, *"I will side with the bears every time."* I will admit to my bias—human safety first. It is up to the reader to decide for themselves.

It's interesting that the cases listed in this book closely align with Miller and Tutterrow's study and are almost the complete opposite of the Tom S. Smith, Stephen Herrero study. But what for the life of me I can't understand is how they came up with 50% failure rate with firearms. It doesn't match any of the data collected for this book.

If I was designing a hiking stick, I would make it with a quick detachable bottom with a 16-inch spike. On top, I would put in a small can of bear spray, especially for our Canadian friends where ridiculous gun laws restrict people from carrying firearms in defense of life.

On July 29, 2016, Kim Woodsman in Humpy Creek, Alaska, stopped the attack with a Glock 20 10mm. What an amazing story. A 400-pound sow grizzly charged him. He fired three rounds, killing the bear literally at his feet. He was backing away and tripped. As he was falling, he kept shooting. One bullet hit his foot, taking the top of his toe off. Park Ranger Jason Okuly found Kim's sunglasses at the scene two feet from the bear's head. Three hits in four seconds. One in the left eye, one in the mouth, and one in the chest.

Here is a truly amazing story by Dean Weingarten for Ammoland.

Bella Twin, the .22 Used to Take the 1953 World Record Grizzly, and More

Ammoland Inc. Posted on June 7, 2017, by Dean Weingarten

What .22 Rifle did Bella Twin use to Kill a World Record Grizzly in 1953?

On 10 May 1953, Bella Twin was hunting small game with her partner, Dave Auger, along an oil exploration cutline south of Slave Lake, in Alberta, Canada. She was 63 years old.

They saw a large grizzly bear coming toward them. Wishing to avoid an encounter, they hid off the side of the cut.

But the bear kept coming closer and closer. The bear got so close that Bella Twin thought it less risky to shoot the bear than to not shoot it. It was probably only a few yards away. Some accounts say 30 feet. Perhaps she saw it stop and start to sniff as if it had caught their scent. We may never know.

She shot at the side of the bear's head. Knowing animal anatomy very well (she was an experienced trapper, and had skinned hundreds, perhaps thousands of animals) she knew exactly where to aim to penetrate the skull at its weakest point.

She shot, the bear dropped. It was huge. She went to the bear and fired the rest of the .22 long cartridges that she had, loading the single shot rifle repeatedly, to "pay the insurance" as Peter Hathaway Capstick said. She made sure the bear was dead, and not just stunned. My father taught me the same lesson when I was 13.

Here is a picture of the bear's skull and the .22 caliber holes in the left side.

1953 World Record Grizzly Skull

For those curious about how to place that shot on a live bear, the place to aim is halfway on a line from the center of the eye to the ear hole.

From the front, you would aim directly up the nose. If the bear's mouth is open, aim for the back of the roof of the mouth. Aiming above the nose will likely miss the brain.

Bella Twin with her .22 rifle and record bear.

Chapter 14
Banning Hunting

They're a nuisance in our neighborhoods, they tear up our property, they kill our animals, and now they're attacking us. —Sherri Hutchins as reported by the *Orlando Sentinel* after her daughter was attacked by a bear in Florida.

Bobcat attacking a dog in Anthem, Arizona, July 17, 2017.

I was able to interview Steve Verschoor on the phone. Steve was driving by when he saw the bobcat attacking the dog and man. Everyone else was just standing around watching. Steve stopped to render aid. He told me on the phone the security officer was standing around watching the show. No one was helping the man or the dog. He jumped into action. He grabbed the bobcat, trying to pull it off the dog. The bobcat bit down on his thumb. They danced around in a circle as he tried to get the bobcat off. He was bitten on the hands and arm. The bobcat ran off and hid in a storm drain. It happened at 7:45 in the morning.

Asking Steve why he didn't use some type of weapon like a tire iron, he said, "I was in the wife's car, just running down to pick up the Sunday newspaper. If I had my vehicle, I carry a bat." Excellent job Steve for helping the man and dog out.

The medical staff didn't know how to use rabid serum. This increased Steve's anxiety. The staff called another hospital who helped, and they were able to give him the serum. The cat bit down so hard it fractured Steve's thumb. The dog was quarantined for forty-five days in the owner's home. Steve said the owner thanked him. A deputy sheriff arrived, and the cat charged. The deputy was forced to shoot and kill. The cat tested positive for rabies.

Proof that hunting prevents gator attacks

Officials in Louisiana estimate that the state has about 1.5 million alligators (fifty percent more than Florida), yet Louisiana's gators haven't killed a single human in recorded history, according to Noel Kinler, alligator program manager for the Louisiana Department of Wildlife and Fisheries. In fact, there haven't been any serious injuries from the state's 1.5 million alligators in decades. (Minter, 2007)

To this day, Florida has gators killing people. Why? Simple. Florida has been taken over by the coexisting unicorn Disneyland people. Clearly, their fish and game department should be following Louisiana's proven track record of human safety.

Louisiana takes between 30,000 to 35,000 alligators per year. They have been doing that for years. The gator population is stable. The great part is we get to hear "CHOOT EM" on *Swamp People*.

Florida, on the other hand, gave 6,000 permits in 2015, taking over 3,500 gators. Around ten times less than Louisiana.

BC to end grizzly bear trophy hunting after this season closes on November 30, 2017.

Many animal rights groups hailed this as great news but nothing could be further from the truth. This is a disaster for humans. Bear attacks are going to skyrocket, and there will be more missing hikers, missing hunters, never to be found. This fairy tale utopia dreamland always ends with dead people. Timothy Treadwell is a prime example.

The new ultra-liberal BC government is more concerned with the emotional side, ignoring the human safety factor.

Darryn Epp had this to say on a Facebook post October 28, 2017.

My communication to the current leadership of BC regarding management of grizzly bears:

Thank you for allowing users of the outdoor resource to have a voice in the regulation of such as we move forward into a new era of managing key predators such as grizzly bears.

I have a fourfold perspective on the subject. I am an ardent wildlife photographer; I am an avid wildlife conservationist; I am currently a nonresident to BC (though actively contemplating moving there in the next year); I am a hunter and one that has participated in a successful adventure hunting grizzly bears in BC as a non-resident.

We have come to a precipice in the management of species where public perception weighs heavily on the impact of the decisions of wildlife management. We have never been in a place in time where so many people are influenced by misrepresentations on social media. We have never been at a point such as this where the general populous is so detached from the reality of the life cycle, what live food looks like, and where it comes from.

As hunters it has become our greatest challenge to help the people of our society understand the contradictory nature of hunting; to love the animals we spend so much time admiring yet be able to bring ourselves to kill them for food and continued admiration in our homes with the mementos that they provide as a reminder of that experience. Hunters are a key part of the conservation equation, with the advocacy of the management of species and environment, and providing a tool for game managers to use to attain the goals set forth by today's best science.

We need to be ever mindful of the fact that those in our society who are uninformed about true wildlife management and the hard decisions it sometimes requires are not capable of having the mindset to make wise choices for the best long-term outcome of those species. The government shares a role in the education of the masses in those efforts to maintain a healthy balance in the ecology of our sacred animals and places, of which BC is bountifully rich.

The policies proposed in this new attempt to appease the masses concerning grizzly bear management are appalling from any perspective. To suggest to a true consumptive lover of wildlife that they should waste any portion of such a majestic species such as a grizzly bear is heartbreaking. If it is an attempt alone to thwart the activity of grizzly bear hunting, it is truly a distasteful attempt at such.

The waste of any edible portion of a game animal is wrong and in saying so I believe legislation should move forward to eliminate the waste of grizzly bear meat by making it mandatory to preserve all edible portions. In saying that I also reiterate that NO PART of such a magnificent creature should be left behind including the hide, skull, and paws.

In spite of the fact that the current government has wrongfully used this manipulatively charged topic as a method to achieve political gain, I believe it is time for those in positions of influence to be true leaders in a long-term solution. This solution involves wise conservation choices. Ones that don't always appeal to the general uninformed population, but are in keeping with the forward-thinking policies of the great leaders in conservation that created the North American conservation model developed many years ago when wildlife was in peril.

In conclusion, I believe that it the responsibility of the government of BC to value the input of the front-line managers of the resource. All too often the people that dedicate their lives to the conservation of lands and wildlife remain unheard in these discussions. To the many biologists and conservation officers that are involved in such an intimate way with the resource, it is time for their opinions to matter and for those educated perspectives to be told by the government to the masses.

This is your chance for legacy in conservation BC, make the best ecological decisions, not just the most popular ones. Be true leaders, not followers! regulation of such as we move forward into a new era of managing key predators such as grizzly bears.

I have a four fold perspective on the subject. I am an ardent wildlife photographer; I am an avid wildlife conservationist; I am currently a non resident to BC (though actively contemplating moving there in the next year); I am a hunter and one that has participated in a successful adventure hunting grizzly bears in BC as a non-resident.

We have come to a precipice in the management of species where public perception weighs heavily on the impact of the decisions of wildlife management. We have never been in a place in time where so many people are influenced by misrepresentations on social media. We have never been at a point such as this where the general populous is so detached from the reality of the life cycle, what live food looks like, and where it comes from.

As hunters it has become our greatest challenge to help the people of our society understand the contradictory nature of hunting; to love the animals we spend so much time admiring yet be able to bring ourselves to kill them for food and continued admiration in our homes with the momentos that they provide as a reminder of that experience. Hunters are a key part of the conservation equation, with the advocacy of the management of species and environment, and providing a tool for game managers to use to attain the goals set forth by todays best science.

We need to be ever mindful of the fact that those in our society that are uninformed about true wildlife management and the hard decisions it sometimes requires, are not capable of having the mindset to make wise choices for the best longterm outcome of those species. The government shares a role in the education of the masses in those efforts to maintain a healthy balance in the ecology of our sacred animals and places, of which BC is bountifully rich.

The policies proposed in this new attempt to appease the masses concerning grizzly bear management are appalling from any perspective. To suggest to a true consumptive lover of wildlife that they should waste any portion of such a majestic species such as a grizzly bear is heartbreaking. If it is an attempt alone to thwart the activity of grizzly bear hunting, it is truly a distasteful attempt at such.

The waste of any edible portion of a game animal is wrong and in saying so I believe legislation should move forward to eliminate the waste of grizzly bear meat by making it mandatory to preserve all edible portions. In saying that I also reiterate that NO PART of such a magnificent creature should be left behind including the hide, skull, and paws.

In spite of the fact that the current government has wrongfully used this manipulatively charged topic as a method to achieve political gain, I believe it is time for those in positions of influence to be true leaders in a long term solution. This solution involves wise conservation choices. Ones that don't always appeal to the general uninformed population, but are in keeping with the forward thinking policies of the great leaders in conservation that created the North American conservation model developed many years ago when wildlife was in peril.

In conclusion, I believe that it the responsibility of the government of

BC to value the input of the front line managers of the resource. All too often the people that dedicate their lives to the conservation of lands and wildlife remain unheard in these discussions. To the many biologists and conservation officers that are involved in such an intimate way with the resource, it is time for their opinions to matter and for those educated perspectives to be told by the government to the masses.

This is your chance for legacy in conservation BC, make the best ecological decisions, not just the most popular ones. Be true leaders not followers!

the regulation of such as we move forward into a new era of managing key predators such as grizzly bears.

What is the basis for banning the hunt? British Columbia has an estimated grizzly bear population of 15,000. Hunters are taking 250 to 300 bears per year. An unreported 300 bears per year are killed from poaching, people defending their lives, eighty human-caused mortalities, direct conflict, or car accidents. Six hundred and thirty to six hundred and eighty bears out 15,000 is really no concern whatsoever on hurting the population. Miller (1990) estimated the maximum sustainable harvest of Alaskan grizzly bears at 5.7% based on a model. Based on this model, BC could kill 855 bears a year and never hurt the population. Remember this model is to perpetuate the grizzly bear population forever. Also keep in mind the 300 bears per year unreported as killed is a claim based on an estimation, not based on scientific proof. BC government used the Harris model (1986) that estimated a maximum sustainable harvest mortality at six percent.

But the environmentalist loves their cute little pet names. They claim the grizzly bear is an "umbrella species." What the heck does that mean?

Landscapes adequate to maintain long-term viable populations of this species are ipso facto adequate to maintain a host of other species with similar requirements for large landscapes. (Management Of Grizzly Bears In British Columbia: A Review By An Independent Scientific Panel Final Report, 6 March 2003)

But what is the basis of the claim this species is threatened? How can anyone in their wildest imagination claim hunting a mere 300 grizzly bears from a population of 15,000 is going to hurt them?

What does the new law say? Hunters are still allowed to hunt for meat but will no longer be able to possess the hide or the head or the paws of the grizzly bear. WHAT? So, you can kill a grizzly for food but leave the hide, skull, and paws out in the wild to waste away. Sometimes I'm lost for words. How in the world does anyone ever write a law this ridiculous?

Arizona initiative to ban cougar and bobcat hunting.

Arizona is trying to ban cougar and bobcat hunting. But who is behind this? Arizonans for Wildlife? Cute name but the real group is The Humane Society of the United States supporting groups including the Center for Biological Diversity, the Arizona Animal Welfare League, and the Sierra Club's Grand Canyon chapter.

The initiative is to ban the hunting of wild cats but with some exceptions for people who kill wild cats that "threaten personal safety, property, or livestock." Oh, so once again if you're the victim of a cougar or bobcat attack you will have to prove in court that you were indeed in fear of your life. I hope there is no Humane Society corrupt DAs in Arizona that want to ruin your life.I have a four fold perspective on the subject. I am an ardent wildlife photographer; I am an avid wildlife conservationist; I am currently a non resident to BC (though actively contemplating moving there in the next year); I am a hunter and one that has participated in a successful adventure hunting grizzly bears in BC as a non-resident.

We have come to a precipice in the management of species where public perception weighs heavily on the impact of the decisions of wildlife management. We have never been in a place in time where so many people are influenced by misrepresentations on social media. We have never been at a point such as this where the general populous is so detached from the reality of the life cycle, what live food looks like, and where it comes from.

As hunters it has become our greatest challenge to help the people of our society understand the contradictory nature of hunting; to love the animals we spend so much time admiring yet be able to bring ourselves to kill them for food and continued admiration in our homes with the momentos that they provide as a reminder of that experience. Hunters are a key part of the conservation equation, with the advocacy of the management of species and environment, and providing a tool for game managers to use to attain the goals set forth by todays best science.

We need to be ever mindful of the fact that those in our society that are uninformed about true wildlife management and the hard decisions it sometimes requires, are not capable of having the mindset to make wise choices for the best longterm outcome of those species. The government shares a role in the education of the masses in those efforts to maintain a healthy balance in the ecology of our sacred animals and places, of which BC is bountifully rich.

The policies proposed in this new attempt to appease the masses concerning grizzly bear management are appalling from any perspective. To suggest to a true consumptive lover of wildlife that they should waste any portion of such a majestic species such as a grizzly bear is heartbreaking. If it is an attempt alone to thwart the activity of grizzly bear hunting, it is truly a distasteful attempt at such.

The waste of any edible portion of a game animal is wrong and in saying so I believe legislation should move forward to eliminate the waste of grizzly bear meat by making it mandatory to preserve all edible portions. In saying that I also reiterate that NO PART of such a magnificent creature should be left behind including the hide, skull, and paws.

In spite of the fact that the current government has wrongfully used this manipulatively charged topic as a method to achieve political gain, I believe it is time for those in positions of influence to be true leaders in a long term solution. This solution involves wise conservation choices. Ones that don't always appeal to the general uninformed population, but are in keeping with the forward thinking policies of the great leaders in conservation that created the North American conservation model developed many years ago when wildlife was in peril.

In conclusion, I believe that it the responsibility of the government of BC to value the input of the front line managers of the resource. All too often the people that dedicate their lives to the conservation of lands and wildlife remain unheard in these discussions. To the many biologists and conservation officers that are involved in such an intimate way with the resource, it is time for their opinions to matter and for those educated perspectives to be told by the government to the masses.

This is your chance for legacy in conservation BC, make the best ecological decisions, not just the most popular ones. Be true leaders not followers!

The ESA supports predator-killing as a conservation practice, '...predator control, protection of habitat and food supply, or other conservation practices...' (16 USC § 1531 Sec. 4(b)).

Why this is in ESA is to protect endangered species from being wiped out by predators. Food supply would be both domestic and wildlife such as ungulates that people use for food such as elk, deer, and moose. Scientists would not have put this in there unless they understand large predators need to be controlled. To protect the food supply, you must control predator numbers. At least that is how the law was intended to work. But I do not see the Great Lakes region controlling wolves to protect the deer and moose whatsoever.

What studies have been done to prove hunting saves human life?

Predator populations experiencing high levels of human-caused mortality traveled or bred further from settlements and roads. (Mladenoff et al., 2009)

Reliance on hunters is driven in part by the high costs of having to use government employees to do the job.

Wolf harvest Season date: July 15–March 31
Years: 2004–2009
Objective: 156
Harvest: 147

Resource users, such as hunters, are one of the benefactors of sustainable resource management, but can themselves be used as instruments to reach management objectives. Implementation uncertainty when using recreational hunting to manage carnivores.

Isn't it interesting that Latvia has wolf hunting and their population stays stable. Hunters are useful and keep the numbers in check. With hunting pressure, you don't hear about wolf attacks like in other countries where the wolf is protected.

Carnivores were not killed primarily for consumption, but to prevent them from killing livestock, other wildlife, or people. Behavioral traits may also have been subject to human selection. European brown bears are less aggressive to humans. (Zedrosser, A.,2011)

We've learned that predators that fear mankind avoid them. You can't say out of one side of your mouth that hunting doesn't improve human safety and several chapters later say hunting causes predators to fear mankind are harder to view. That's scientific nonsense (see Herrero).

Predators have always been hunted throughout history for three main reasons: 1) Protection of food supply, i.e., livestock. 2) Wildlife protection from being driven to super low numbers from an overabundance of predators. 3) Human SAFETY. Predators that fear mankind avoid mankind. Come on, there is nothing complicated about this at all.

Is there a clear and present danger when predators are protected?

Officials in Louisiana estimate that the state has about 1.5 million alligators (fifty percent more than Florida), yet Louisiana's gators haven't killed a single human in recorded history. But Florida protected their gators claiming endangered species status. Florida from the 1990s to present has had twenty-two people killed. That is known killed. We have missing people in the swamp, so the real number will never be known. Louisiana proves that correct hunting harvest keeps people safe. The great part is the gators will be around forever.

California's cougar population never attacked a single person for seventy-six years. Why? They were heavily hunted. Protection of the species equals human attacks. Barbara Barsalou Schoener was the first victim of a cougar attack after closing hunting in California. Her two children will never see her again.

India protected wolves and stopped hunting. Wolves from roughly five packs in Hazaribagh, India, attacked 122 children from 1980 to 1986.

Grizzly bears are protected in Montana, Idaho, and Wyoming. Attacks skyrocketed. How many? The list goes on and on and on!

Boulder, Colorado, protected the cougar with the end result of a dead child.

Massachusetts banned trapping. On July 29, 1998, a four-year-old boy was bitten by a coyote while playing in the backyard of his home in Cape Cod, Massachusetts. His mother fought the coyote with her bare hands. She literally had to pry the coyote from him. A police officer responded to her 911 call. He shot and killed the coyote. (I actually was emailing with the mother trying to help her get the law changed after the attack.)

Arizona banned trapping in 1995. Coyotes and bobcats are now attacking people. In the past fifteen years, there have been eighteen documented bites to humans by coyotes in Maricopa County, Arizona. That is only one county in Arizona! Bobcat attacked a German Shepard and two adult men in Anthem, Arizona.

California banned trapping of coyotes. Data from the USDA's Wildlife Services, the California Department of Fish and Wildlife, show forty-eight attacks were verified from 1998 through 2003.

How many men, women, and children are we going to sacrifice to the animals?

When bears are coming right into houses, we have a major problem.

September 6, 2017, Incline Village, Nevada. NDOW officials search for injured bear shot by person inside Incline Village home. News 4, Olivia DeGennaro

An unnamed person woke up in the early morning hours to find a bear inside their house. Defending the home, the person was able to grab a handgun and shoot the bear. The bear ran off wounded.

Tyler Turnipseed is the NDOW Chief Game Warden. He said, "Obviously we have a couple concerns: one being the welfare of the bear.... The humane treatment of the bear, number one, and of course the public safety concern.

Their number ONE priority is concern for the bear's welfare? Human safety is number TWO? If that bear was in my house, there would be an answer. It's called a 12 gauge until the bear was dead. The NUMBER ONE priority is human safety.

Are you seeing a pattern here?

Another very interesting devolvement is happening around the world. Protection and worship of large predators. *The Guardian* had a very interesting article on November 22, 2017, titled "How the brown bear became public enemy number one in rural Romania."

"*Further into the hills, in dozens of remote villages that sit sealed off from the world by thick forest, people have begun to take the situation into their own hands, trading recipes for homemade poisons designed to kill a bear.*"

Why are they poisoning the bears? Because of all the attacks on people. "*Last October, the Romanian government made a surprise decision to ban the hunting of bears and other large carnivores altogether. In the 12 months since the hunting ban, the number of attacks on people, crops, and livestock in the region has more than doubled, with 263 so far this year.*"

The article is clearly biased, claiming hunting doesn't save people, ignoring their own evidence that after the hunting ban, the human-bear conflicts doubled in a single year.

Another interesting article from *The Telegraph* September 16, 2017, "Armed and masked men declare war on France's bears." A group of men made a video stating why they are hunting bears.

"*By introducing Slovenian bears and establishing a nursery allowing them to multiply, the French state is implementing land management policies that are gradually restricting access by men and women of the mountains and their freedom to work.*"

The people forced to live with large predators are getting fed up. There is a backlash building in this country that could be very bad for the predators. Too many people reach the breaking point and the poison is going to come out. This is very easy to avoid by allowing regulated hunting.

The New York Times did a very well-balanced article, "A Hunting Ban Saps a Village's Livelihood." Norimitsu Onishi September 12, 2015

Since Botswana banned trophy hunting two years ago, remote communities like Sankuyo have been at the mercy of growing numbers of wild animals that are hurting livelihoods and driving terrified villagers into their homes at dusk.

The plan was to follow the animal rights favorite fairy tale—switch to photographic tourism. What happened? No one showed up to take pictures. Once again proving that eco-tourism never replaces hunting dollars. The local people suffer.

Zambia had a hunting ban for two years; the same thing happened. A local councilor was killed by a lion during the ban. Protecting large predators equals human death.

Chapter 15
US Court System

Altogether, research indicated that some 2.5 million bribes are paid each year within the U.S. Justice System, according to Pew Research, Yale Law School, and other sources. — How Corrupt Is America's Judicial System? Seeker, August 28, 2015

Bears will be bears
By John S. Adams, July 2005

U.S. District Court Judge Donald Molloy dismissed a lawsuit last Thursday dealing with the grizzly bear mauling death of Great Falls hunter Timothy Hilston.

The case stems from an Oct. 30, 2001, incident in which Hilston went hunting in the Blackfoot Clearwater Wildlife Management Area about 45 miles east of Missoula. Hilston was successful in downing an elk and was in the process of field dressing the animal when he was attacked and killed by a grizzly bear.

One of the most biased judges in America has clearly ruled that human safety means nothing and grizzly bears should be protected to kill American citizens.

Grizzly bears are becoming a major problem in the Northwest, not only killing and maiming Americans but huge livestock numbers. Citizens are being dragged to court and spending tens of thousands of dollars explaining why they protected their life from a fake endangered species, while all the drama queen screamers have a fit over grizzly hunting season. It's based on the irrational fear that the animals will be wiped out. No scientific evidence supports it. But corrupt judges are playing scientist and making a ruling on ridiculous nonsense.

Federal judge hears arguments about Yellowstone grizzly bears ' threatened status. March 10, 2011, Nigel Duara, Associated Press

May 2010 U.S. District Judge Donald Molloy ruled on removing grizzly bears from the threatened species list to allow hunting. In his ruling, Molloy said the government relied too heavily on population monitoring and failed to spell out what steps would be taken if grizzly numbers started to fall.

Honnold said after the hearing that the Greater Yellowstone Coalition is similarly concerned that the government won 't keep tabs effectively on the grizzly population if it were delisted.

What scientific facts support his ruling? None.

We are talking about a hunting season of 5.6% of the population. That means 94.4% of the population will survive. We are talking about harvesting forty bears out of 717. My God, that is called a sustainable harvest. That can go on and on for thousands of years. It's clearly no threat to the grizzly bear population whatsoever.

Widow of man killed by grizzly bear near Yellowstone sues US Government

By Mead Gruver, Associated Press, Oct 26, 2011

Botanist Erwin Frank Evert, 70, of Illinois, was hiking a trail about 7 miles east of Yellowstone in June 2010 when he was attacked by an adult grizzly that had been snared, tranquilized, collared and released hours earlier by government scientists.

His wife, Yolanda Evert, claimed in a suit filed Tuesday that the researchers had failed to warn cabin owners in the Shoshone National Forest outside Cody of nearby bear-trapping activity and that they did not follow established protocols for posting warning signs.

She is seeking $5 million in damages.

This was later dismissed by Judge Donald Molly.

Feds Immune in Deadly Mountain Goat Attack

7/28/2015 11:22:00 AM, June Williams

SEATTLE (CN) - The National Park Service is not responsible for a mountain-goat attack that killed a hiker in Olympic National Park, the Ninth Circuit ruled.

A divided three-judge panel on Monday found the Park Service had no duty to destroy the animal despite numerous complaints about its aggressive behavior.

Again, this is a case of neglect. The goat was reported numerous times to the park official as dangerous, but they did nothing. Once again, animals are more important than human safety.

The goat was well-known to park staff and visitors and frequently harassed hikers, according to a federal complaint filed by Chadd after the attack.

"Susan Chadd and the friend went on ahead and suddenly heard a scream. They rushed back to where Boardman and the goat were and saw Boardman lying on the ground and the goat standing over him. Apparently, Klahhane Billy had lowered his head, charged Robert Boardman and gored him through one thigh," Chadd's complaint said.

Boardman bled to death after the goat severed the man's femoral artery. Park rangers finally did their job and shot and killed the goat.

Chadd sued the park service for breaching the reasonable duty of care by failing to destroy the goat in the years leading up to the attack.

US District Judge Robert Bryan dismissed the case finding the government had sovereign immunity from Chadd's suit.

The Ninth Circuit agreed, finding the park service had discretion in dealing with the goat and is exempt from prosecution. Poor discretion is an excuse?

"Letting an identified aggressive 370-pound goat threaten park visitors and rangers for years until it killed one amounted to a failure to implement the formally established park policy for managing dangerous animals," the dissenting judge continued. "Written park policy provided a series of steps for dealing with animals dangerous to park visitors, from frightening the animal away to removing or killing it. The park had used the earlier steps, including repeatedly shooting the goat with nonlethal loads such as beanbags, but they did not work. Yet the

superintendent left the animal free to terrorize tourists for another summer season instead of following the next step of the written policy, removing or killing it. "

Chris Detrick, Salt Lake Tribune File #_2CD6841
Utah courts: Wildlife Resources Division will pay Sam Ives' family but won't have to make policy changes.

The Ives family sued the state and DWR in 2008, claiming the state was liable for the boy 's death because officials failed to warn the public that a dangerous bear was in the area and had attacked other campers.

Sam's death could have been prevented if the officials would have acted and removed the problem bear. But as normal with the new policy of animals are always in the right, the bear was allowed to live.

Straight out of a horror film, the family was sleeping in a tent. The parents woke up hearing their son scream. Racing outside they looked but saw nothing. Returning to the tent, they thought a person had abducted Sam because the cut in the tent was so exact. Sam, their 11-year-old son, was missing.

Running down the trail they found a discarded sock next to the boy's pants. The next time the mother saw her son was on the medical table at the morgue.

Two state judges tossed it out in 2009 and 2011. The Utah Supreme Court overturned one dismissal in 2013 because the state had a duty to protect the young boy due to DWR officials knowing about the problem bear.

The family won a settlement of $1.9 million but failed to require the state to enact new safety policy related to problem animals.

Farm and Dairy, Pennsylvania, man receives maximum penalty for killing bear
By Other News -September 19, 2002

HARRISBURG, Pa. – A Mifflin County man was sentenced recently to pay nearly $6,000 in fines and replacement costs for killing a large black bear in April that he claimed was killed in self-defense.

David Vogt, 45, of Lewistown, Mifflin County, was sentenced on Sept. 6 by

District Justice Jackie Leister to pay a mandatory $800 fine for illegally killing a black bear and $5,000 replacement costs after Pennsylvania Game Commission Wildlife Conservation Officers and a biologist proved he did not kill a bear in self-defense.

Really, how did they prove it?

Auburn Man Facing Charges After Killing Bear In His Backyard
April 7, 2013

When did it become a promising idea to treat senior citizens with no respect? Auburn, Massachusetts

Richard Ahlstrand told WBZ-TV he was stocking his bird feeder Friday night when a bear about seven feet tall and 300-to-400 pounds started chasing him.

That's when he turned his shotgun on the bear.

"I didn't have time to aim through the sights, but I aimed in the direction of the head on this thing and I pulled the trigger before it got to me. It just dropped," he said.

Ahlstrand said he was carrying this shotgun for protection Friday night because he thought he saw the bear in his yard on Thursday.

"If that ever jumped on me, I wouldn't even be here right now, I don't think. I know it was going to seriously maul me," he said.

What did the authorities do? Charged him with illegally killing a bear, illegally baiting a bear, illegal possession of a firearm, and failing to secure a weapon. Say what?

Police don't believe the bear was a threat to people. This is where it turns into the surreal. A senior citizen feeding birds and enjoying watching the birds is not baiting a vermin bear. When did it become illegal to protect yourself from a vicious bear attacking you?

Wrongful death lawsuit.
The parents of 35-year-old Mark Reynolds killed last year by a cougar in Whiting Ranch Wilderness Park have filed a wrongful-death lawsuit against Orange County, California, alleging that officials should have known the park was dangerous.

Mark Reynolds was mauled by a mountain lion while he crouched to fix his bicycle resulting in his death on Jan. 8, 2004.

Donna and Joseph Reynolds of St. Joseph, Mo., said in a suit filed March 16 in Orange County Superior Court that the county should have known the park was in "dangerous condition" because mountain lions were present.

A county spokeswoman declined to comment on the pending litigation. Attorneys for the family were not available for comment.

A similar suit was filed in 1986 by the parents of Laura Small, who as a youngster was attacked and permanently disfigured when a cougar pounced on her as she looked for tadpoles in a river in Ronald W. Caspers Regional Park near San Juan Capistrano. The county agreed to settle that suit for $1.5 million in 1993.

Wallace Weatherholt, who lost hand to alligator, arrested for feeding the alligator

Global Post, July 29, 2012

It's bad enough that Wallace Weatherholt, a Florida airboat captain, had his left hand bitten off by a 9-foot alligator in June. Now he's being charged with unlawfully feeding that alligator, the Associated Press reported.

You would think losing a hand was punishment enough. In Florida, feeding alligators is a second-degree misdemeanor, punishable by up to 60 days in jail and a $500 fine. Of course, the fish and game department can't give the guy a break.

Our court system is set up to be abused. Two documentaries really help show the level of corruption in our judges in America. The first is "The Patent Scam" available on Amazon. The corruption runs deeper than you'd ever think. A multi-billion-dollar industry you've never heard of. This is the world patent trolls thrive in: created for them by the US Patent system. It's worth your time to watch how the court system supports these billion-dollar rip offs.

Second is "Divorce Corp," which shows how the lawyers donated to judges to get them on board. More money flows through the family courts, and into the hands of courthouse insiders, than in all other court systems in America combined—over $50 billion a year and growing. Through extensive research and interviews with the nation 's top divorce lawyers, mediators, judges, politicians, litigants, and journalists.

But our court system relies on experts, peer review scientists like the ones referenced in this book. You see, we as humans have been taught to rely on experts. The vast majority of people will accept an expert's word as Gospel straight from God. It's called expert bias. Forgetting that experts are humans with their own bias and they do make mistakes. "A dingo took my baby" case is a great example. The mother was convicted in part by expert testimony that claimed the dingo didn't tear the child's clothing. The mother spent three years in prison over that mistake.

But what is peer review science?

Journal of the Royal Society of Medicine. Peer review: a flawed process at the heart of science and journals. Richard Smith 2006

Peer review is at the heart of the processes of not just medical journals but of all of science. It is the method by which grants are allocated, papers published, academics promoted, and Nobel prizes won. So we have little evidence on the effectiveness of peer review, but we have considerable evidence on its defects. In addition to being poor at detecting gross defects and almost useless for detecting fraud it is slow, expensive, profligate of academic time, highly subjective, something of a lottery, prone to bias, and easily abused.

CONCLUSION

So, peer review is a flawed process, full of easily identified defects with little evidence that it works. Nevertheless, it is likely to remain central to science and journals because there is no obvious alternative, and scientists and editors have a continuing belief in peer review. How odd that science should be rooted in belief.

From what I can tell, a peer-reviewed paper is submitted to a journal for publication. The editor now must decide if this paper is worthy of publication. If he is having a difficult day or his own bias interferes, that paper never sees the light of day.

Let us look at the USFWS story behind alligators.

Capital Research Center. The Great Gator Hoax February 8, 2013

The alligator never merited the ESA's protection for two reasons: its population was large and healthy at the time of the act's passage—around 734,000 and rising.

The ESA harmed alligator conservation because it halted trade and stymied research efforts. "The only thing the Endangered Species Act did was to slow up research," says Ted Joanen, because it "took management away from states" and was "a hindrance." Joanen and McNease assert that "probably the most detrimental effect of the endangered species program at our state level has been the loss of landowner, land manager, and public respect for the program."

USFWS has been taken over by the Borg thinking that hates commercial trade in animal products. Even though scientific research has proven putting a value on animals actually protects them better. The environmental groups and their inside FWS cronies couldn't care less. This is all about human control not saving wildlife.

Because of the powerful environmental groups and USFWS, the following people might be alive today. From 1973 until 1987 in Florida.

July 1987
George Cummings III, 29, was killed while snorkeling in the Wakulla River.

May 1985
Paul Mirabito, 27, harassed small alligators in a canal in West Palm Beach and vanished. His body was found two days later with severe injuries to the neck and puncture wounds on the arm. The medical examiner said the cause of death was drowning.

August 1984
Robert Crespo, 11, was killed while swimming in a canal in St. Lucie County.

September 1978
Phillip Rastrelli, 14, was killed while swimming across the Hidden River Canal off Bessie Creek in Martin County.

September 1977
George Leonard, 52, died three days after an alligator attacked him while swimming in the Peace River Canal in Charlotte County.

August 1973
Sharon Holmes, 16, was killed by an 11-foot, 3-inch alligator while swimming at dusk in a lake at Oscar Scherer State Park in Sarasota County.

Louisiana has zero attacks. Florida still has attacks because they will not go with the true experts on alligator Louisiana Fish and Game alligator management plan. Shouldn't the people responsible for the fake listing of the alligator be put in prison for wrongful death?

Grizzly bears should have been delisted in 1990. Who is responsible for all these deaths? Clearly, the government USFWS and their environmental cronies are involved. Why are they not being brought up on charges?

Brad Treat, 38, male, June 29, 2016
Lance Crosby, 63, male, August 7, 2015
John Wallace, 59, male, August 24, 2011
Brian Matayoshi, 57, male, July 6, 2011
Kevin Kammer, 48, male, July 28, 2010
Erwin Frank Evert, 70, male, June 17, 2010
Craig Dahl, 26, male, May 17, 1998

How many Americans do we have to sacrifice to this Gaia worship? How many predators is enough? When we have bears and cougars entering our homes because they no longer fear mankind, we have a major problem. Until we as a society stand up to the drama queen screamers and say, "Not one more human will die," this problem will only get worse.

Chapter 16

Government Corruption, Cover-ups, and Refusal to Release Documents

I believe that transparency is the solution to our problem on corruption.
—Grace Poe

I was naive going into this, believing through FOIA requests, I would able to find out what is going on. The Freedom of Information Act (**FOIA**) is the law that gives the right to access information from the federal government. It is the law that is often described as keeping citizens in the know about their government.

I called United States Fish and Wildlife Service, wanting a few simple questions answered. I was told on the phone to submit a request on their website. I filed the request and was then told to submit a FOIA to obtain this information. Here is what happened.

Dear Mr. Hemming:

The United States Fish and Wildlife Service, Freedom of Information Act (FOIA) office received your FOIA request, dated February 13, 2017, and assigned it control number FWS-2017-00431.

Please cite this number in any future communications with our office regarding your request.

You have requested the following information:

"...I would like the following information.

"Under the Endangered Species Act. How much money does Montana, Idaho, and Wyoming collect each year for grizzly bears?

"If the grizzly bear is delisted how much money will the state lose?

"How many grizzly bear attacks have happened in the three states mentioned above?

"What happens to the grizzly bear biologist if the bears are delisted? Will anyone lose their job?

"According to Helen Chenoweth in 1990 the grizzly bear was fully recovered but that the grizzly bear biologist changed the recovery number.

"How many times has the recovery goal numbers changed?

"Why did the USFWS tell the public we would have grizzly bear hunting in the lower 48 by the year 2000 and to this day no hunting season has been set?

"When does public safety come first or do grizzly bears have more rights than American citizens?"

You have asked for expedited processing of your FOIA request. The Department's FOIA regulations state that a bureau will provide expedited processing if a requester demonstrates a compelling need for the records by explaining in detail how the request meets one or both of the criteria below and certifying the explanation is true and correct to the best of the requester's knowledge and belief. The two criteria are as follows:

1. Failure to expedite the request could reasonably be expected to pose an imminent threat to the life or physical safety of an individual; or

2. There is an urgency to inform the public about an actual or alleged government activity and the request is made by a person primarily engaged in disseminating information. (The requested information must be the type of information which has particular value that will be lost if not disseminated quickly; this ordinarily refers to a breaking news story of general public interest. Information of historical interest only or information sought for litigation or commercial activities would not qualify, nor would a news media deadline unrelated to breaking news.)

Because your request does not contain enough evidence to support either of these criteria, your request for expedited processing, therefore, has been denied.

You have asked us to waive the fees for processing your request. Our FOIA regulations state that bureaus will waive, or partially waive, fees if disclosure of all or part of the information is:

(1) In the public interest because it is likely to contribute significantly to public understanding of government operations or activities, and

(2) Not primarily in your commercial interest.

See 43 C.F.R. § 2.45(a). Our FOIA regulations also provide four specific criteria that are used to determine whether these two requirements are met. See 43 C.F.R. § 2.48(a). Your request does not contain enough evidence to demonstrate you meet each of these criteria.

In light of this fee waiver denial, you may wish to modify your request to reduce your fees. For example, you may wish to consider reducing the locations or time period in which you are seeking records.

Our regulations require that your request must explicitly state that you will pay all fees associated with processing the request, that you will pay fees up to a specified amount, and/or that you are seeking a fee waiver. Your request does not fulfill this requirement because you have not agreed to pay fees up to a certain amount; therefore, we are unable to process your request at this time. If you wish to pursue your request, please provide your willingness to pay fees.

The FOIA requires that requests describe the records sought with sufficient detail to allow an agency employee familiar with the subject area of the request to locate the records with a reasonable amount of effort. Your request does not adequately describe the records sought, therefore, we are unable to process it at this time. If you wish to pursue your request, rather than questions, please provide the FWS with descriptions of the specific records you are seeking.

According to our regulations, if we do not receive your written response clarifying these points within 20 workdays from the date of this letter, we will presume that you are no longer interested in pursuing your request, we will not be able to comply with your request, and we will close our file on it. See 43 C.F.R. § 2.6(c)

Carrie Hyde-Michaels, FWS FOIA Officer is responsible for this denial.

Larry Mellinger, Solicitor, in the Office of the Solicitor was consulted.

You may appeal this response to the Department's FOIA/Privacy Act Appeals Officer. If you choose to appeal, the FOIA/Privacy Act Appeals Officer must receive your FOIA appeal as soon as possible after this letter. Appeals arriving or delivered after 5 p.m. Eastern Time, Monday through Friday, will be deemed received on the next workday. Your appeal must be made in writing. You may submit your appeal and accompanying materials to the FOIA/Privacy Act Appeals Officer by mail, courier service, fax, or email. All communications concerning your appeal should be clearly marked with the words: "FREEDOM OF INFORMATION APPEAL." You must include an explanation of why you believe the FWS's response is in error. You must also include with your appeal copies of all correspondence between you and FWS concerning your FOIA request, including your original FOIA request and FWS 's response. Failure to include with your appeal all correspondence between you and FWS will result in the Department 's rejection of your appeal unless the FOIA/Privacy Act Appeals Officer determines (in the FOIA/Privacy Act Appeals Officer's sole discretion) that good cause exists to accept the defective appeal.

Please include your name and daytime telephone number (or the name and telephone number of an appropriate contact), email address and fax number (if available) in case the FOIA/Privacy Act Appeals Officer needs additional information or clarification of your appeal.

DOI FOIA/Privacy Act Appeals Office Contact Information
Department of the Interior Office of the Solicitor 1849 C Street, N.W.
MS-6556 MIB
Washington, DC 20240
Attn: FOIA/Privacy Act Appeals Office
Telephone: (202) 208-5339 Fax: (202) 208-6677
Email: FOIA.Appeals@sol.doi.gov

The 2007 FOIA amendments created the Office of Government Information Services (OGIS) Public safety is not an urgent public need to know. I was stunned, after all, the public is being killed by grizzly bears and the public is being attacked by grizzly bears. This information should be available to we the people. My appeal was denied.

The National Park Service did provide some documents then jerked me around for months on other documents. After we came to an agreement to send files already converted to PDFs to save them time in the spirit of cooperation. After waiting for months, this is what happened.

Mr. Hemming,

I apologize for the delay in getting back to you with the data you requested. Unfortunately, we received over 25 requests for expedited processing from members of the media in the week after the inauguration and under our regulations, I was required to process those requests before the ones in my regular processing track. I am attaching a copy of the data we located during a search of our IMARS system. This completes our response to your request.

I trust that this information fully satisfies your request. Please do not hesitate to contact me, as the NPS FOIA Liaison and the person responsible for processing your request, if you have any questions regarding your request.

In addition, as part of the 2007 OPEN Government Act FOIA amendments, the Office of Government Information Services (OGIS) was created to offer mediation services to resolve disputes between FOIA requesters and federal agencies. You may contact OGIS in any of the following ways:

Office of Government Information Services (OGIS)
National Archives and Records Administration
Room 2510
8601 Adelphi Road
College Park, MD 20740-6001

Why did they send a file that listed six attack titles with no files?
Because we have determined that your request is being made in

furtherance of commercial interests relating to the sale of a book you will be publishing on animal attacks, we have therefore classified you as a commercial use requester for the purposes of calculating fees. Accordingly, we are required to charge you for time spent searching for and reviewing potentially responsive records, as well as copy charges. The fees for extracting the data on the spreadsheet we provided did not exceed the $50 threshold for charging fees, so we could provide that information without assessing any fees.

Under our regulations we have classified you as a commercial requester we must, therefore, assess search, review, and copy charges that exceed $50. In accordance with 43 CFR 2.49(b), because you did not either agree to pay all fees associated with this request or specify an amount you are willing to pay we are providing you with an estimate of the costs to process your request for copies of case incident files and images. Currently, the estimated costs to process your request come to $255, which was calculated as follows:

$63 = 1.5 hours Search time @ $42/hr (Professional Rate)
$9.00 = 60 pages @ $0.15/page
$183 = 3 hours Review time @ $61/hr (Managerial Rate)
$255 = Total Estimated processing costs

Because the estimated fees exceed $250 and we do not show any history of your having paid fees in the past, we are required under 43 CFR 2.50 to collect payment for the full amount before we can begin processing your request. If you are still interested in obtaining these records, please make your check payable to the National Park Service and mail it, along with a copy of this letter to my attention at the address below. You also have the right to modify your request in order to reduce the estimated fees, for example limiting your request to the four incidents where the visitors sustained injuries.

In accordance with 43 CFR 2.43(e) as a commercial requester, we are required to charge you review fees even if we do not ultimately disclose all or parts of the records. As I advised you earlier, the information you are requesting is maintained in a Privacy Act System of Records. As a third-party requester, we will be required to redact personally identifiable information (PII) that relates to individuals other than yourself. Accordingly, after reviewing the materials, we may determine that we have to withhold copies of graphic images of the visitor 's injuries while we release general photos of the scene.

In accordance with 43 CFR 2.51 if we do not hear from you in writing within 20 workdays, either through receipt of a payment for the estimated fees or a modification in the scope of your request that reduces the estimated fees to less than $250 and included your written assurance of payment, we will presume you are no longer interested in this matter. If that occurs we will close the file on your request.

Sincerely,
Ms. Charis Wilson, Ph.D., CRM
NPS FOIA Officer
12795 W. Alameda Parkway
PO Box 25287
Denver, CO 80225-0287
303-969-2959

When did our government become anti-American and say commercial interest is bad? But the mainstream press is provided with all information when requested. Did anyone tell them that all mainstream news is a commercial for-profit business? This is a PDF file; there is nothing to copy. It can be sent in an email. They already found the files but refused to email them to me. Ridiculous.

The worst of them all is the United States Forest Service. Whoever oversees FOIA is a national disgrace. Repeated requests were ignored. What was requested? Information on bodies found. Killed by animals. So, we have wild animals attacking citizens and the USFS is like, who cares if people are dying? We are just going to ignore all requests for information.

I wrote all the providences in Canada requesting information on attacks; only one provided any information.

Dear Mr. Hemming,

This is what I have for you.

Q: Does the Ministry of Environment keep track of bear encounters/attacks in the province?

- Any issues or concerns with bears are managed by Ministry of Environment conservation officers.
- Information is tracked at a regional level, but is not centrally collected or tabulated by the Ministry of Environment.
- The Ministry of Parks, Culture, and Sport collects their own data for bear-related safety incidents at provincial parks but has only had one reported incident in the last five years (detailed below).

Q: Does the province break it down between predatory and defensive attacks?

- Each case is looked at separately and a determination is made based on the facts of the incident.

Q: How many people attacked since 1995 to present day?

- We do not have that information available.
- The following are some anecdotal reports of bear incidents in Saskatchewan from 2014-16.

September 16, 2016 – La Ronge (Unconfirmed)

- A 44-year-old man was attacked by a bear in a remote area near La Ronge.
- Injuries were claw marks on his arm and a sore back.
- Used a wine bottle to fend off/kill the bear.
- Conservation officers (COs) were not contacted. No sign of the bear or bottle were found at the scene.

- The individual was taken to Saskatoon where he was treated and released.

August 24, 2016 – Cumberland House **(Unconfirmed)**

- During the early morning hours, a man claimed he was charged and attacked on a trail south of Cumberland House. The individual called conservation officers about the incident and indicated that he had some abrasions.
- COs went to Cumberland and set a trap in the area. They also talked to the RCMP and local councilors to see if there were any bear issues in the area.
- The individual did not seek any medical attention and would not provide the RCMP or COs any additional information or to take any pictures of alleged injuries.

April 21, 2016 - Paradise Hill, northeast of Lloydminster **(Defensive in nature)**

- A woman, who was out walking her dog in a wooded area near Frenchman Butte, was attacked by a black bear. She was able to fight off the bear and reach safety.
- The attack may have been triggered when the individual's dog came in contact with the bear and ran back to the woman for protection. The bear then turned its attention to the woman. She was treated at a hospital in Lloydminster and released.
- The Ministry of Environment issued a public warning in light of the incident.

July 4, 2014 - Jade Lake, Narrow Hills Provincial Park **(Possibly habituated – poor bear safety/food storage measures)**

- Two campers from Prince Albert (1 male and 1 female) were tenting at the day use site. The female camper was woken up by a sharp stinging pain in her left foot.

- The campers then heard their stuff being rummaged through the outside of the tent and found a black bear going through their stuff. They began yelling at the bear, and the bear eventually took off into the woods with one of their coolers.
- The campers ran down to the lake and got on their raft until it was safe to return to the site. When they returned to the site, they observed the bear ripping up the tent and camping gear.
- They drove to Lower Fishing Lake Lodge to get help and conservation officers responded to the scene.
- The injuries to the female were minor and there were no visible puncture wounds. The bite did not break the skin.
- Later that morning, the bear was observed in the bush near the site and was destroyed by COs.

<u>September 16, 2016 – La Ronge</u> **(Unconfirmed)**

Used a wine bottle to fend off/kill the bear. Wow, I would love to interview that person. Did he really kill the bear with a wine bottle?

Ministry of Environment

Regina, Canada

Canada provided more help than my own government. US Forest Service ignored and refused to answer all FOIA requests. US Fish and Wildlife Service refused to help answer any of my questions. They are supposed to work for we the people. How ridiculous is the thinking that your appeal goes through the same department? The appeals are a joke.

I filed and paid Montana Fish and Game for FOIA for their main areas with animal attacks. They mailed me a thumb drive and here is an example of what they sent me.

Grizzly Bear Mortality Report
Date Reported: 10/12/00
Date of Mortality: 10/12/00
Reported by: Kevin Frey - MTFWP
Cause of Mortality: self-defense (hunting guide- _ & client), client injured (leg)
Location of Mortality: Middle & North Fork Bull Creek Ridge - Slough Creek
Drainage, AB-BT Wilderness, Park, MT
UTM:
Bear ID:
Age of Bear:
Sex of Bear:
Investigated by:
Disposition of Bear:
564.1 Ex 4997.8 N (T8S, RI2E, sec 14)
unknown adult
9+ years (estimate)
Female with 3 yearling cubs (large, possibly 2 yr olds)
Mark A Anderson-MTFWP Enforcement, Doug Goessman-USFWS _
interviewed about incident by K Frey - MTFWP
head and feet at MTFWP research laboratory, Bozeman, MT

MORTALITY SCENARIO: Hunting guide_ and a male client (Ohio) were walking along a scattered timber (whitebark) hillside when the guide heard a branch crunching, he then noticed a grizzly bear at approximately 30 feet away. It was snowing quite heavily at the time and conditions were quiet. He stopped and told the client "bear", the client moved next to the guide. The bear (large cub) became aware of the hunters and began to bawl and move around. The sow bear came running through the timber, charging the hunters. The guide (who has been in numerous bluff stalking situations) hollered and waved his arms at the charging sow bear, who seemed to be veering off her charge to the right of the guide when a second and third cub appeared and began running around and bawling. The sow bear then turned in a running circle and ran past the guide and grabbed the client by the shin Lower knee of the leg, knocking him downslope. As the sow bear hit the client, he fired a shot at the bear. The client and sow bear then tumbled downslope. The sow bear then got up and began to charge back to the client and guide, at which time the guide shot the bear in the chest with a .44 magnum pistol, killing the sow grizzly bear. Field examination of the female bear carcass was unable to conclude if the client had hit the bear, due to both shots being fired at the chest area and causing extensive tissue damage. An investigation by MTFWP and the USFWS deemed the incident as legal self-defense.

One thing that is very misleading to the public is the subject of cubs. The mother generally drives them off on the second year when she comes into heat again. These are not the cute cuddly type of cubs but fairly large bears that can be 150 pounds or more. I paid for professional reports and was charged top dollar for these reports.

Where is the picture of the dead bear? Where is the necropsy report on the bear? Where are the field notes from the investigator? Where are the written statements from the victims of the attack? Was the bear hit by one or two bullets? What was the extent of the injuries to the client?

The vast majority of the reports I received were very incomplete. I contacted a state representative and asked for the full reports. Montana Fish, Wildlife, and Parks said they were working to put these together and would send me the full reports. Still waiting.

Chapter 17
Safety

The safety of the people shall be the highest law. —Marcus Tullius Cicero

After reviewing all these cases, there are safety concerns to think about.

Children are targets. Predators normally kill the newborns of prey species. With the over protection of predators, mankind has changed from being the top predator to be feared and avoided to a new prey species. How many missing children are the predators taking? I can't help but remember "A dingo ate my baby" is a phrase attributed to Lindy Chamberlain-Creighton and also to Meryl Streep's depiction of Chamberlain in the movie *A Cry in the Dark* (1988). If you never saw the movie, it's very well done showing how society can be massive taught a lie about wildlife and believe it. The correct phrase is "A dingo took my baby."

Now think what would happen here in America today if God forbid a wolf took a child out of a tent in the dark. The mother sees the wolf and reports it. The animal rights groups would go all out to ruin the family life. The press would hound the parents and search all their history for anything they can find to use against them. The fish and game department would help to cover up. They never heard of wolves baby snatching. Even though in old historical records of America, you can find actual cases of baby snatching by wolves.

Think of the cases here in America and how quick people are to blame the parents. You should teach your children to always yell and fight. Scream for help.

Teach your wife how to handle any guns you have. That includes how to load them, shoot, and clear a jam.

The Amber Alert Child Location & GPS tracker comes with a lithium battery that runs up to 40 hours on a single charge. Measuring just 2 ¾ inches, the idea is put it in a child's pocket. It offers a real-time GPS tracking SOS button and two-way communication.

I would think a wrist watch style with GPS locator would be the best, but after checking and reading reviews on some models, I do not have one to recommend at this time. Do your own research and pick the one you feel is best. It could be lifesaving.

I read an interesting theory from a scientist that said urban people should be considered high risk. *Indeed, many people living in cities should also be included within the category of groups at risk because of the increasing number of them enjoying outdoor activities in areas inhabited by large carnivores. (1)* Children from the city are at even higher risk because they are exposed to talking animals on cartoons that lead them to believe animals are nice and friendly.

Keep a loaded gun, loaded as in one in the chamber safety on ready to fire. But yet I read cases where people are not sure if there is one in the chamber. Look, you never know when you're going to be in a struggle for your life against a large predator ten times stronger than you are. It might never happen to you. But if it does, you are in a battle for your life; have your weapon ready. Same with ammunition. People don't want to spend the extra money on quality ammunition. When you're in the hospital facing up to a million dollars in medical bills because you wanted to be cheap and save ten dollars, you might feel a little foolish.

Bear spray versus gun is a personal decision only you can make. My stance is carry a gun IF you are properly trained. Or carry both. My life is more important than any animal. Remember, it's legal to carry guns in national parks!

My interview with UDAP Industries, INC. in Butte, Montana, was a very interesting conversation. The unique part of the company is why they got started. Mark Matheny was attacked by a grizzly bear in 1992. His hunting friend had bought some pepper spray designed to be used for a human to stop a person from attacking you. The bear was sprayed several times before the attack was over. After healing, Mark started selling pepper spray for a company.

"*Within months I had ideas for improving the product: a much hotter pepper concentrate for more effectiveness, a 'fluffier' formulation that would hang in the air longer, a carrying holster with a tied-on trigger safety wedge that wouldn't be as easily lost as the customary loose one, and even a glow-in-the-dark safety clip so a spray canister could be quickly located at night in a tent. I didn't invent the wheel, I just improve it.*"

The company resisted his ideas, so he opened his own company.

The Safety Orange Bear Spray with Griz Guard Holster is designed to be clipped on whatever you're wearing. When seconds count you need to get this out of the holster right now and that is what they are designed for. At $49.95, it's well worth the money, especially for women or children. Like anything else in life, you need to practice drawing and firing it. The great part of this design is you can shoot it right from the holster. They also sell Magnum Bear Spray Inert for training only.

Think about guns. How fast are you at drawing and firing in a high-stress life and death struggle? The same applies to pepper spray. Practice and training will take over if you have practiced ahead of time. Look at the inert can as buying practice ammo for your gun. Of course, it's not nearly as fun as shooting your gun but it's the same idea. Practice ammo for your bear spray.

What about all those innocent people sleeping at night in a tent, what can they do? UDAP again came up with a heck of an idea. The Bear Shock Electric Fence covers a 27ft. x 27ft. sq. area, is ultra-light at 3.7 lbs., and runs on two D-cell batteries good for five weeks. It sells for $269.99.

Like old Billy Mays' commercials, "But wait there is more!" They also sell outfitter-sized electric fences and food storage fences. I did not receive any payment or products from this company. Recommendation is based on proven track record.

Hunters tracking a wounded bear and being attacked were not listed in this book but only three cases were found. The theme of this book is sudden attacks.

Our friend Dean Weingarten from www.Ammoland.com wrote a great article: "Father Uses .44 Magnum to Shoot Grizzly Bear off Son"

The quick-thinking father saw his 30-something-year-old son being attacked by a grizzly bear. Firing one warning shot in the ground, for fear of hitting his son, he used his .44 magnum and the second shot was in the bear's hip. He was using hollow points. Buffalo bore hard cast bullets I believe would have caused more damage. The bear dropped the son and spun around to attack the father. He fired his next shot intending for the chest and it hit the bear in the neck. The bear was still coming at him. He fired his last shot in the gun when the bear was two feet away. *The bullet went alongside the bear's head, into its neck, penetrating the chest cavity.* It worked; the bear ran off.

I received nothing from Buffalo Bore company either. The recommendation is based on a proven track record. When a tiny 9mm stopped a charging, huge Alaskan brown bear, that speaks for itself.

Get some lead in them. I don't know how many times people could have helped if they would just put some lead in the attacking critter. Hunters get in a tight mindset of it has to be in the boiler house heart-lungs area. Change your thinking to break em down. Hips are a great target. But remember, strange things happen to bullets. They still could hit the person you're trying to save. For example, a friend of mine when I was twelve years old was on a ranch and they were going to put a big old bull down. The bull was in a corral and my friend was watching on the fence line; the bull was facing my friend. With a .22 long rifle, the bullet hit the side of the head through the skull to the nasal cavity and came out the front of the nose, hitting my friend in the head. A freak accident. He was permanently brain damaged. Only you can decide if the risk is worth it. If I'm being attacked and someone shoots the animal in the hip, I would cheer that person on.

Understand basic first aid. It would be a good idea to review the basics of it before you go in the woods. I cannot stress enough to never depend on one person for their knowledge because Murphy's Law means that is the person who will be attacked. A first-aid kit is one that can handle large wounds and might be a good idea to carry. QuikClot Trauma Pak would be a great item to carry with you in your daypack. Not only for animal attacks but for accidents when you're in the woods.

Carry extra ammo. This sounds like one of those no-brainers everyone should know but that's not always the case. I knew one guy that only put three rounds in his rifle while deer hunting and left the rest of the box in the truck. When asked why, he smiled and said, "I don't miss; three is all I have ever needed." If your gun holds five rounds, put all five in and carry extra with you.

A fully charged cell phone is another great item to have. Tell people where you're going and when you plan to come back. Know how to use a compass. With our modern tech society, we get caught off guard when it fails. That fancy GPS is a great tool. But what happens when it breaks, or you lose it? What then?

When you get out of your vehicle, pull your compass and take a reading. A compass is worthless if you don't know which way to head. Take a flashlight even if you plan to be back before dark, plus a fire starter like Trioxane Heating Fuel Bars and a BIC lighter or two. They weigh nothing. One lesson I learned the hard way was if you put a rubber band double around a BIC lighter under the red button, you will keep the fuel longer. I was backpacking and tossed the lighter in my pack. It shifted in my pack. The red button was pressed, and all the gas was released by the end of the day. Luckily for me, I had a flint and steel as a backup or that first night would have been a long cold one. A couple bottles of water and some type of snacks are also a good idea. How much after that is up to personal preference.

There are several different wildlife conflict encounters. You can have the sudden attack where you never even knew the animals were there. The ambush style attack is very hard to defend against. Most times you have some type of warning. If the animal is charging, use your gun or bear spray.

1. Never ever run. This triggers the predator instinct that you're prey to be eaten.
2. If you're unarmed, stand tall, wave your arms, and yell in a firm voice. If you're armed with pepper spray or a gun, the moment you first see the animal is when you remove it from the hostler or shoulder and get ready to fight.

3. If all you have is a pocket knife, pull it out, open it, and get ready to fight. If you can hurt the animal enough, he will leave.

4. On grizzlies, you can get in a fetal position using your hands to protect your neck if it's a defensive attack. All other predators, go down fighting.

5. The nose is a weak spot. Punching them on the nose has worked for driving animals off as a last resort.

6. For wolf and coyote attacks, climb a tree if you can.

7. Any animal closer than thirty yards, you're in the danger zone. People need to understand this. It's not normal for large predators to get that close to humans unless it's a surprise encounter.

In the book, *Fighting for Your Life, Man-Eater Bears*, Tom Hron (2009) talks about what he feels is the perfect bear rifle. Remington 7400 semi-auto in 30-06. Change out the magazine for ten rounds. One in the chamber means eleven rounds of 200-grain bullets. Why did he like it? Short, reliable, light, noisy as hell, everything he wanted in a rifle. Today it's the Remington 750. Remington bullet, 220 grain, is an excellent choice.

Did you ever wonder why the Native American hunting parties west of the Mississippi River were ten to fifteen braves? West of the Mississippi was grizzly country. Over thousands of years, the Native Americans worked out a survival strategy. In a grizzly's world, if you get hurt, other grizzlies will kill and eat you. Bears think in those terms. A hunting party with ten or more people is too big of a risk. But less than ten braves, it could mean game on. It's too bad the Native American's didn't have a written history. That would have been fascinating reading of how and why they did things. One of the best well-researched books on Native Americans I have ever read was John Alan Ross's *The Spokan Indians*. Yes, that is the correct spelling on the book.

The grizzly and black bear were both hunted during hibernation. On the black bear, they used different methods to get the animal out of the den including smoking them out and killing them with bow and arrows. On grizzlies, they used bow and arrow and heavy maple-wood thrusting spears. Enraged grizzly bears coming out of hibernation were a force to be respected. They had a special ritual to go through before the hunt.

Chapter 18
Solutions

Qui tacet consentit. Silence gives consent. —Thomas More

How do we put this all together so the average person understands it? Animal attacks are going to increase. For overall general public safety, we need to increase hunting tags or in the case of grizzly bears, cougars, and wolves, in some states we need to remove protection and open a hunting season. Regulated hunting has never caused any animal to be listed as an endangered species. For some reason, the public and scientists have a hard time understanding that simple concept. It seems to be either wipe them out or let them live, totally ignoring 100 years of science that there is a third option called regulated hunting.

We as hunters for too long have been told by our so-called leaders to shut up and not engage the animal rights movement. If you don't engage and go on the defensive, you can't win the game. Seriously, think about this for a minute. Would you want to play a football game where you're only on defense the whole game? Of course not; you can never win that way.

Hunters need to start educating the public on the truth behind the save the animal groups like PETA, Sierra Club, HSUS, Center for the Biological Diversity, etc., and show the public what they are really all about. A great website called www.PETAkillsanimals.com is a powerful tool to show the public that PETA doesn't care about helping animals as they slaughter pets by the thousands each year.

Yes, people have been tricked into believing they truly love and care about animals. Sorry, the truth is that PETA hates animals and their goal is human control. You can't tell me a group that has a gross annual budget of

$42 million can't afford to feed 1,000 dogs and cats until they find a good home. You see, PETA's goal is to end all pet ownership. Ingrid Newkirk, the cult leader for PETA, said, *"The animals... got the gift of euthanasia, and to them, it was the best gift they've ever had. How dare you pretend to help animals and turn your back on those who want an exit from an uncaring world!"*

A quick web search will find plenty of information that PETA is a death cult. The websiteNathanJWinograd dotcom actually has that as a title to his well-written article "The (Death) Cult of PETA."

"I would go to work early, before anyone got there, and I would just kill the animals myself," she once told the New Yorker *about her first job at an animal shelter. "I must have killed a thousand of them, sometimes dozens every day." Newkirk not only began her career in "animal rights" killing animals at a shelter, a shelter with regressive policies at the time, she went into work early to perform the job: "a thousand of them, sometimes dozens per day."*

I would say that PETA President Ingrid Newkirk has most likely killed more animals than the average hunter.

A really great website for in-depth research into the animal rights movement is Protect the Harvest.

PETA is not the only one; the Humane Society is run by Wayne Pacelle. Another pet-hating lunatic who said, "If I had my personal view, perhaps that might take hold. In fact, I don't want to see another dog or cat born." – Wayne Pacelle quoted in Bloodties: Nature, Culture, and the Hunt, by Ted Kerasote, 1993, p. 266.

Protect the Harvest webpage on HSUS Exposed is a great tool for educating the public on where their donation money is going. It's not going to feed and shelter animals, that is for sure.

Hunters need to collect the information on these groups with the quotes and links and use it to educate the public on the truth. You won't change the mind of hardened cult members in these groups, but the public is seeing and learning the truth.

Equal Access to Justice Act (EAJA)

But the real scam that most people have no understanding of is the Equal Access to Justice Act (EAJA). Now we get down to the nitty-gritty. Have you ever wondered why these groups are suing the federal government for saving the gay triple toed spotted frog? Or thousands of other animals, plants, trees, and anything else they can dream up? Because they care so much about mother earth, right? My donation money is going to save the animals. Well if you believe that I have the Brooklyn Bridge for sale.

The real reason is these groups have full-time welfare lawyers. You see, when they sue the government, the attorney fees can be collected from the taxpayers. The real kicker is that it's not based on the national average for lawyers' fees; it's whatever the judge agrees to. They can ask for $750 an hour from the government. You read that right. Now our senior citizen can't get a cost of living raise on Social Security but these welfare lawyers can and do collect multi-millions of dollars from the taxpayers.

You thought the Sierra Club and Center for Biological Diversity really cared about the animals, right? They care all right because they see millions of dollars screwing over "we the people." If you really want to understand this, a great book is, *Inside the Equal Access to Justice Act* by Lowell E. Baier. The top two organizations that collect the most from "we the people" are Sierra Club and Center for Biological Diversity.

How much are we talking? Hundreds of millions each year. The NRDC is another big welfare lawyers' organization that loves charging we the people top dollar for their services.

To understand the EAJA intent, Congress was trying to help the little guy out against government overreach. The idea was small business owners, veterans, and the average citizen could not afford to go to federal court to protect their rights. What is the old saying, **The road to hell is paved with good intentions!** The lawyers' fees would be covered by the government. Representative Kastenmeir snuck in an 11th-hour amendment providing a free pass for nonprofit organizations to use the EAJA. This opened the floodgates for environmental lawsuits.

Today, Harvard University has environmental law classes that not only teach how to sue the government, but how to get filthy rich doing it off the taxpayers. Have to make sure the Ivy League stays rich, now don't they.

I barely scratch the surface on this issue. What the reader needs to understand is the stranglehold these groups have on land use policy. The government agencies are simply overwhelmed defending all these lawsuits. Think about that for a moment. Not only are we the taxpayer paying all the legal costs to sue the government, but all the legal costs of defending against them. A double-edged sword that is cutting quickly and deeply.

The solution on the EAJA is really simple.

1. Demand Congress end all nonprofits using the EAJA.
2. Demand that law is changed so nonprofits are only allowed to sue the government no more than twice a year.
3. Change the law so piggybacking is illegal. Piggybacking is when one nonprofit sues the government, say for grizzly bear delisting, and other groups join the lawsuit.
4. EAJA must be set to pay lawyer fees based on the national average.

So why is this in an animal attack book? Because for the safety of your family, your children, and your grandchildren, if we don't educate the public about what is really going on, the animal attacks and death tolls are going to skyrocket.

It's time the NRA stands up. They should be picking ten states a year to fund a massive agenda to get all states hunting, fishing, and trapping as their constitutional right. Ballot initiatives should also be made illegal.

This stops the anti's in their tracks from putting in ballot initiatives to ban certain types of hunting and trapping. And don't think for one second you fishermen are safe. PETA has already announced they want to end all fishing too.

It's time the big outdoor companies step up to the plate and help fight this battle. Remington, Ruger, Winchester, Federal, and all the other gun and ammo manufacturers need to start donating big time to fight the anti-human save the animal groups. There is no reason in the world that the Humane

Society can outspend hunters by the millions. We as hunters need to pressure these companies to help defend our rights.

Sportsmen's Alliance National Headquarters
801 Kingsmill Parkway
Columbus, OH 43229
Phone – (614) 888-4868
Fax – (614) 888-0326
Email – info@sportsmensalliance.org
Web site- www.sportsmensalliance.org/

Without a doubt, the leader in protecting your hunter's rights is Sportsmen's Alliance. They are in all fifty states and courts to protect hunters' rights.

I interviewed Brian Lynn from Sportsmen's Alliance. Here is a portion of that interview.

We as hunters for too long have been only playing defense against the huge million-dollar animal rights movement. What is the solution to this problem?

The problem is each year the animal rights movement targets a new state. Last year we fought in the court and helped the state fight. It cost $1-2 million per fight. This year the fight is in Arizona with a ballot initiative to ban cougar hunting. All these anti groups can spend $3-4 million. They are not trying for all-out ban on hunting but a tiny bit each year. A death by a thousand cuts.

The number one thing we must do is EDUCATE THE DEER HUNTERS on the need for predator control. Hunters must stand together. Stop the infighting. States need to build a war chest because they are coming for you next.

The media is animal rights friendly. Eighty percent of the public support hunting but methods are easy emotional targets, fragment by species.

Washington State banned hound hunting but when they have a problem animal, who do they call? The houndsman. Now instead of hunters paying into the system, the state must now pay people to kill the same number of cats.

How do we educate the public on the human safety issue of why we need predator hunting?

We must explain what carrying capacity of the land means. There are only so many resources to support the animals. How does nature cure overpopulation? Starvation, disease, human conflict.

What kind of statistics on wildlife conflict do you have? How far back do your statistics go?

No, we are not tracking animal attacks. Washington State is not tracking cougar kills since the law changed.

We talked for an hour. He was a down to earth straight-talking real American. Fighting for all our rights. If you haven't joined yet, get on board. The other side is coming for you next. Stand up for your rights before it's too late.

Looking at the pattern of increased attacks is startling. The only decrease in attacks has been cougars. That could be directly related to game Departments killing more problem animals. Finding the records of how many are being killed is like pulling teeth. But as we saw in California, the animals are still being killed and the numbers are just about the same as what hunters were doing for free. Actually, the hunters were paying the state to hunt. Lost income from the hunters' dollars buying licenses leads to the taxpayers being stuck with the bill.

The scientists appear to be clearly biased in their studies. Human safety is barely a concern or a scapegoat to blame the humans for being attacked. This is the type of thinking we must stop. Grizzly bears are at record high population. How many is enough?

Black bears are at a record high population of one million. Cougar population is at record highs in the Western US. Wolves in North America are at a 100-year high population. Coyotes might be the highest population they have ever been in North America. Grizzly bears are at the highest population ever recorded.

When are we going to put a stop to this nonsense? How many people must die? How many people must be maimed for life? Why are we as a society allowing this to go on?

There are two main problems. The first is clear bias on scientists to hug predators. Everyone has biases; that is human nature. We all are resistant to change even when facts and evidence prove us wrong. It's a belief system not founded in facts or reason but emotions.

Second, groupthink may be at work. Groupthink from not only scientists and their peers but also transferred to the public. This creates a peer pressure and expert bias. Well so and so is the expert. There is also an emotional investment of an authority figure who put forth a misguided theory. The public is bombarded with feel-good nonsense about large predators. To change this, we must inform the public of the facts and expose the fear-mongering nonsense. We are not killing the planet if grizzly bears are actually 6,800 above the historical records. It's up to the scientists to clean up their act. Human safety should be the number one priority. Put the bias aside; we don't need a record high predator population. With regulated hunting, the predators will be there for generations to come but human safety will greatly improve.

Are we creating man-killers? The more we protect and allow aggressive animals to attack humans with no punishment, the more we create super predators.

I think the real question is, when are we going to save the humans?

References

Alaska Fish and Game Overview of Relationships Between Bears, Wolves, and Moose in Alaska

American Man-Killers 1997
By Don Zaidle

Bacteriology of a Bear Bite Wound to a Human: Case Report 2004
By Dennis Kunimoto

Beware of predatory male American black bears: Attack rates are rising with human population growth 2011
By Stephen Herrero

Bear Attacks: Their Causes and Avoidance 2002
By Stephen Herrero

The Beast in the Garden: The True Story of a Predator 's Deadly Return to Suburban America 2005
By David Baron

Board of Review Report: The death of Mr. Brad Treat due to grizzly bear attack June 29, 2016, on the Flathead National Forest.

Brown bear conservation and the ghost of persecution past. Biological Conservation 144, 2163–2170. 2011
By Zedrosser, Steyaert, Gossow, & Swenson.

A Case History of Wolf-Human Encounters in Alaska and Canada
By Mark McNay

Change in occupied wolf habitat in the Northern Great Lakes Region. In Recovery of Gray Wolves in the Great Lakes Region of the United States: An Endangered Species Success Story (eds A. P. Wydeven, T. R.Van Deelen, and E. J. Heske), pp. 119–138. Springer, New York. 2009

Characteristics of nonsport mortalities to brown and black bears and human injuries from bears in Alaska 1999
By Sterling Miller and V. Leigh Tutterrow

Conserving Cougars in a Rural Landscape: Habitat Requirements and Local Tolerance in West-Central Alberta. Master Thesis 2011
By Aliah Adams Knopff

The Cost of Being Green Before Green was Cool 2013
By TJ Elsbury

Cougar Attacks: Encounters of the Worst Kind 2004
By Kathy Etling

Cougar Attacks on Children: Injury Patterns and Treatment 1998
By Kevin M. Kadesky

Cougar attack: Case report of a fatality. Journal of Wilderness Medicine 3,387-396 1992
By Lily Conrad MD, PhD

Cougar Attacks Family on Horses - Outdoor life
The myths and realities of cougar attacks in the great outdoors 2007
By Don Zaidle

Coyote attacks on humans, 1970–2015: Implications for reducing the risks 2017

Coyote Attacks on Humans in the U.S. and Canada 2009
By Lynscy A. White

Current Conservation Special: Wildlife-Human Conflict Vol 4 Issue 4 201

Dead Men Walking: Search and Rescue in US National Parks 2009
By Travis W. Heggie

Does Sex Matter? Temporal and Spatial Patterns of Cougar-Human Conflict in British Columbia 2013
By Kristine J. Teichman

Efficacy of firearms for bear deterrence in Alaska 2012
By Tom S. Smith, Stephen Herrero The Wildlife Society.

Factors governing risk of cougar attacks on humans 2011
By David Mattson

Factors associated with human killing tigers in Chitwan National Park, Nepal
Bhim Gurung 2008

Fair Chase: Death by wolves and misleading advocacy. The Kenton Carnegie Tragedy.
By Dr. Val Geist

Fighting for Your Life Man-eater Bears 2009
By Tom Hron

Forensic Evidence: Human Fatality along the Mary Mountain Trail of Yellowstone National Park on August 25, 2011 (59-year-old John Wallace fatal attack).

Forensic Taphonomy The Postmortem Fate of Human Remains1997
By William D. Haglund Marcella H. Sorg

How Will We Survive? The destruction of Congo basin Tribes in the name of conservation 2017
By Baka Cameroon

Human behavior can trigger large carnivore attacks in developed countries. Sci. Rep. 6, 20552; 2016.
By Vincenzo Penteriani

Human-Carnivore Conflict and Perspectives on Carnivore Management 2003
By Adrian Treves

Human Encounters in Alaska and Canada 2002
By Mark McNay

Human injuries inflicted by bears in Alberta: 1960-98
Stephen Herrero

Human Injuries Inflicted By Bears In British Columbia: 1960-97
By Stephen Herrero

Illinois resident attitudes toward recolonizing large carnivores. Journal of Wildlife Management. 2014 Vol 78 (930-943)
By Julia B. Smith

Implementation uncertainty when using recreational hunting to manage carnivores. Journal of Applied Ecology 49, 824–832. 2012
By Bischof, Nilsen, Brøseth, Mannil, Ozolins, Linnell

Inside the Equal Access to Justice Act 2016
By Lowell E. Baier

Investigation Team Report. Attack by grizzly bear in Soda Butte campground in Gallatin National Forest on July 28, 2010

Is a vegetarian diet really more environmentally friendly than eating meat? CNN February 6, 2017
By Wayne Martindale

Man-eaters of Kumaon 1944
By Jim Corbett

Mountain Lions Attacks are still rare, but just in case... Backwoods Home magazine, March/April 1998
By Gene Sheley

Mountain lion found, killed; Officials believe animal attacked boy in Cupertino. Sept. 14, 2014, Mercury News
NPS Report-Fatality of Mr. Brian Matayoshi from a bear attack on the Wapiti Lake Trail in Yellowstone National Park on July 6, 2011

NPS Report-Fatality of Mr. Adam Thomas Steward Bear Attack in Cub Creek on the Bridger Teton National Forest Sep 4, 2014

NPS Report-Fatality of Erwin Evert from bear attack Kitty Creek on the Shoshone National Forest June 17, 2010.

Off the Wall Death in Yosemite 2007
By Michael Ghiglieri Charles Farabee, Jr

Peer review: a flawed process at the heart of science and journals. Journal of the Royal Society of Medicine. 2006
By Richard Smith

The Politically Incorrect Guide To Hunting 2007
By Frank Miniter

Prey Specialization by Individual Cougars in Multiprey Systems
By Kyle II. Knopff

Public Officials as Fiduciaries. The values behind government ethics laws. Markkula Center for Applied Ethics May 31, 2016

Public Trust Principles and Trust Administration Functions in the North American Model of Wildlife Conservation: Contributions of Human Dimensions Research
By John F. Organ, US Fish and Wildlife

The Spokan Indians 2011
By John Allen Ross

Why Does the Regulated Harvest of Black Bears Affect the Rate of Human-Bear Conflicts in New Jersey? 2017
By Jarod D. Raithel, Melissa J. Reynolds-Hogland, Patrick C. Carr and Lise M. Aubry

Wolves: Behaviour, Ecology, and Conservation. 2003
By David Mech

Index

ɔott, Kristy L., 142, 170

olph, Bernice, 132

Istrand, Richard, 217, 276

ck, Virginia, 176

xander, Gabriel, 136, 155

aire, Noah, 83

perse, Jason, 138, 146

undson, Michael E., 235

derson, Phil, 59, 137, 156

na, 78

sdell, Richard, 187

thony, Tammy, 83

oyo, Darron, 47

enault, Ryan, 74

dero, Jaryd, 34

ɔugar, Joe, 138, 159

a, Peter, 138, 146

ley, Ingrid, 172, 173

er, R. O. and R. M. Timm, 213, 15

er, R. O., 213, 216

tlett, 12, 55

duza, Christopher, 133

liss, Charlie, 179

ille, Hayley, 45

r Hunting Magazine, 14

Bear, Anton, 64

Begg, 10

Beier, LaVern, 77

Bell, Robert, 64

Belter, Mykaela, 37

Berghorn, Jacqueline, 140

Berkeley, Stanley, 230

Berner, Candice, 176, 186

Berube, Summer and Tom, 212

Biggs, Robert, 41

Black bears, 7, 15, 18, 19, 20, 25, 27, 55, 57, 99, 100, 97, 129, 130, 146, 144, 253, 307, 309

Blackmore, Jake, 3, 67, 68

Blasioli, Anthony, 140, 164

Boardman, Robert, 273

Boccia, Dan, 97

Bombay, Camille, 137, 154

Boyd, Gary, 89

Braconnier, Brian, 80

Bradley, Glenda Ann, 134

Braun, Andrew, 46

Brekken, Joshua, 72

Brenner, Kalen, 93

Britton, Dustin, 42

Brown, Gerald, 137, 157

Brownlow, Dale, 13

Brush, Greg, 53

Bryant, Alan, 136, 150

Bryant, Anne, 233

Buckallew, David, 243
Burdett, Arthur, 161
Burseth, Rosalie Tsannie, 197, 199, 203, 205
Busch, Steve, 55
Butt, Kelsi, 35
Bwalya, 10
Byers, Steve, 94
Bysterveld, Peter, 48

C

Caldwell, Alyssa, 36
Camarós, Dr. Edgard, 24
Cannamore, Al 95
Capstick, Peter Hathaway, 257
Carnegie, Kenton Joel, 189, 194
Carrying capacity, 2, 130, 224, 304
Carter, Merlyn, 132
Catalan Institute, 24
Cates, Ken, 62
Catlin, George, 53
Cerda, Harold, 165
Chadd, Susan, 273
Chaik Bay, 77
Chand, Khem, 181
Chelminiak, John, 126, 140, 161
Chenoweth, Helen, 8, 285
Childress, Jeromy Ivan, 238
Chitwan National Park, Nepal Bhim Gurung, 27, 310
Clark, Elliot, 72
CNN, 5, 160, 192, 313
Coder, Mary Jane, 57
Coexisting, 3, 19, 25, 259
Colburn, Tracey, 138
Conrad, Lily MD, Ph.D, 21

Constable Noey, 199, 201, 203, 206, 207, 209
Cookey, Laurie, 136, 153
Cooper, Patrick, 130
Corbett, Jim, 29, 313
Corle, Cary, 93
Courter, Michael, 154
Courtney, Christine, 64
Cox, Jason, 100
Cox, Leigh Ann, 51
Crayne, Kelly, 203, 205
Crespo, Robert, 281
Crosby, Lance, 57, 283
Cross, Rick, 58, 237
Cummings III, George, 281

D

Dahl, Craig, 64, 240, 283
Daigle-Berg, Colette, 93
Dale, Kelly, 137, 153
Daniel, 10, 91, 130, 191
Davis, Petra, 87
Davis, Ron, 136
DeBolt, Brian, 11
Deedy, Alexander, 13
DeGennaro, Olivia, 269
DeGrave, Rafael, 59
Deliberate Indifference, 5, 6
Denali National Park, 24, 58, 83
Dennis, Robert, 197, 205
Derr, Mark, 240
Desjarlais, Fred, 191
DeWitt, Garrett, 134
Dickinson, Chad, 103
Doctor Val Geist, 191
Doherty, Kaylum, 39

yle, Chris, 35
be, Isabelle, 62
nagan, Justin, 93
nbar, Ian, 134
nbar, Todd, 57
sel, Cynthia 127
odahl, Josh, 77

gebroten, Duane, 173
el, Mark, 196, 197, 199, 205, 207
bury, TJ, 242, 309
o, Darryn, 259
er, Bob, 59
inosa, Maya, 42
noff, George, 62
ns, Adrienne, 233
rhart, Chris, 140

r, Carrie-Lynn, 142
abee Jr, Charles, C220
kas, Keith, 80
z, Clivia, 85
e, Scott, 59
k, K, 27
ning, Maria, 101
A, 15, 144, 220, 284, 285, 282,
84, 285, 286, 288, 292
ncois, Jean, 60
nk Evert, Erwin, 272, 283
nk Jr, John, 39
drick, James, 73
ele, Deborah, 101
he, Carola 134, 176

Frost, Frances, 34
Fumerton, Shane, 64

G

Galavi, Monali, 209, 242, 278
Galder, Van, 194, 205
Gates of the Mountains, 13
Gaudet, Mario, 203, 205
Gereghty, Rob, 180
Gerre Ninneman, Gerre, 137, 158
Ghiglieri, Michael, 220, 313
Gnoske, 10
Google, 3, 5, 6, 230
Gottsegen, Sam, 83
Graham, Noah, 181
Grangaard, Lance, 183
Greeve, Nick, 142, 167
Griffin, Charlie, 135, 148
Groves, Susanne 61
Gullufsen, Kevin, 72

H

Halfkenny, George,173
Halfkenny, Mark, 173
Hall, Carly, 136
Hamm, Jim, 45
Hanson, Catherine, 134, 146
Harlicker, Doug, 137, 156
Harris, 100, 263
Harry, Kyle, 134
Hazaribagh, 10, 267
Hechtel, John, 127
Hedges, Aaron Joseph, 237
Hedingham, Frank, 172, 173
Hemstock, Ronn, 3, 74, 76

Hensley, Nicole, 239
Hepp, Dawn, 183
Herbert, Jeff, 85
Herrero, 19, 21, 55, 253, 255, 267, 307, 310, 312
Hill, Jeremy, 3, 218
Hilsabeck, Rita, 53
Hilston, Timothy, 62, 272
Hjelle, Anne, 49, 51
Hollan, Mac, 182
Hollingsworth, Lana, 132
Holmes, Sharon, 283
Houghton, Kyle, 215
Hron, Tom, 297, 310
Huber, Claudia, 57, 255
Huff, Darren, 51
Huffman, Kathy, 60
Huffman, Rich, 60
Hug a predator, 8, 18
Hughes, Ryan, 44
Huston, Joe, 95
Hutchins, Sherri, 258
Hyde-Michaels, Carrie, 282

I

Impey, Simon, 42
India, 10, 29, 192, 193, 267
Ippoliti, Alex, 73
Ives, Samuel Evan, 132

J

Jackson, Karina, 51
Jakubauskas, Raymond, 134, 176
Jemison, N.K., 27
Jessica, Miller, 138

Joanen and McNease, 281
Joanen, Ted, 281
Johnson, Craig, 218
Johnson, Erin, 130
Johnson, Jim, 91
Jones, Ken, 46
Judge Donald Molloy, 272
Judge Robert Bryan, 273
Justa, Michael, 78

K

Kamlesh, Rita, 181
Kammer, Kevin, 59, 102, 283
Kant, Emanuel, 216
Karanth, 144
Kelley, Tev, 67
Kenna, Iris M., 34
Kerzman, Chris, 51
Kinler, Noel, 259
Kitchen, Raymond, 134
Klinghammer, Dr. Erich, 213
Kluting, Don, 78
Kochoorek, Robin, 132
Konopasek, Michael, 76
Kopenstonsky, Kyra, 37
Kress, Christopehr, 63
Krichbaum, Steven, 137, 152
Kruuk, 10
Kunimoto, Dennis, 102, 307

L

Lambert, 64
Lancaster, Kellen, 42
Lancaster, Scott, 34
Langevin, 192

zier, Sebastien, 134

ille, Dan, 36

oie, Cecile, 132

ch, Larrane, 47

der, Herald, 163

lond, Marc, 213

nard, George,283

pold, Starker, 23

in, Kevin, 225, 234

ebarger, Eddie, 51

iger, Matthias, 81

inger, Gary, 138

yd, Wilf, 80, 255

ie, Arthur, 60

well, Meredith Marie, 231

s Cortes, Audelio, 64

sey, 102

cdonald, Kirsten, 81

c-Innes, Scott, 89

estras, Adelia, 134

lenfant, Maurice, 132

n-Eaters of Kumaon, 29

nwati, 192

rkel, Gabrielle, 78

rois, Gerald, 140

rtin, Victor, 83

rtinez, Victoria, 55

ssey, Don, 58

tayoshi, Brian and Marilyn, 86

tayoshi, Brian, 58, 283, 313

theny, Mark, 293

tterson, 10

Carthy, Shannon, 74

Clelland, Colin, 134

McConnell, Patti, 134, 172, 173

McCoy, Johnny, 93

McDougal, 10

McKay, Sarah, 48

McKoen, Jerry Lee, 237

McNay, Mark, 189, 192, 209, 212, 309, 312

Mech, Dr., 177

Medred, Craig, 74, 78

Mellinger, Larry, 284

Mersereau, Dennis, 23

Metzler Jr, David, 42

Miedema, Mark, 34

Milden, Judy, 134, 144

Miller, 100, 134, 253, 255, 263, 309

Miller, Sterling D., 253

Milnar, Paul, 95

Miner, Tom, 66, 70, 77

Mirabito, Paul, 281

Mish, Nick, 138

Mitchell, Taylor, 124

Moe, Gene, 95

Moerlein, Mike, 89

Moore, James, 68

Moore, Nathaniel, 47

Morehouse, Andrea T., 25

Morgan, Leah, 188

Morris, Brian, 173

Moyer, Angela, 138

Moyer, Richard, 138, 160

Munn, Mary, 142, 166

Munson, Donna, 132

Murphree, Patti, 88

Murphy, Matthew, 142

N

Nawojski, Robert, 33
Nellessen, Matthew, 180
Nelson, Mickey, 13
Nelson, Rick, 134
New Jersey Division of Fish and
    Wildlife, 25
Newkirk, Ingrid, 300
Nielsen, Bree, 36
Nissman, Jeff, 142, 167
Noey, Alfonse, 196, 197, 205
Nostdal, Jon, 53
Novotny, Ken, 57

O

O'Connor, Ward Folland, 191
O'Neill, Ian, 153
Oliver, Judy, 89
Organ, 27, 314
Orr, Todd, 77, 252
Orwell, George,6, 20
Osborne, Karen, 133, 143
Otter, Johan, 89
Outside Magazine, 23

P

Page, David, 91
Pala, Evan, 140
Park, Jair, 222
Parker, David, 53
Parker, Shannon, 49
Parolin, CIndy, 34, 62, 63, 64
Patel, Darsh, 130
Patterson, Brent, 209
Pattison, Roy, 251

Patton, Keelan, 142, 167
Patty Miller, 82, 235
Pennington, Matt, 91
Penteriani, 25, 27, 312
Percy, Trevor, 64
Perry, Jacqueline, 132
Peterhans, 10
Peterson, Andy, 57
Petranyi, John, 64
Petrasek, Elora, 132
Petronino, Christopher, 134
Pinero-Cebrian, Andrea, 39
Plona, M., 91
Poljacik, John, 87
Predator pit, 2
Prime, Angie, 39
Puerta, Tomas, 58

Q

Queen, Chris, 66

R

Raithel, Jarod, 25, 146, 314
Rajpurohit, 10
Rasmussen, Ned, 62
Rastrelli, Phillip, 282
Reeb, Colton, 44
Rees, Devon, 87
Reggie Riebe, 77
Reynolds, Donna and Joseph, 278
Reynolds, Mark Jeffrey, 33, 49, 51
Reynolds, Mark, 276, 278
Reynolds, Sallie, 242
Rhindress, Billy, 173
Rice, Grant C., 238